Process Compendium
2004 – 2010

Published in an edition of
500 to accompany the exhibition
Process Compendium 2004–2010

10 September to 3 November 2010
Gallery [DAM]Berlin
Tucholskystraße 37
10117 Berlin
+49 (0)30 280 98 135

http://dam-berlin.de
berlin@dam.org

All works appear courtesy of the
artist and Gallery [DAM]Berlin.

Designed by REAS Studio

Edited by Shannon Hunt

Printed and bound in the United
States by Typecraft, Inc., Pasadena

TheSansMono typeface designed
by Luc(as) de Groot

Front Cover: *Process 13 (A)*, 2010
Back Cover: *Process 13 (B)*, 2010

Photography credits:
p. 4, © Steven Brooke Studios
p. 116, © Robert Downs

REAS Studio
Los Angeles, California
http://reas.com

Library of Congress Control Number:
2010910761

ISBN: 978-1-4507-2713-6

Process Compendium
2004 – 2010

C.E.B. REAS

REAS Studio, Los Angeles

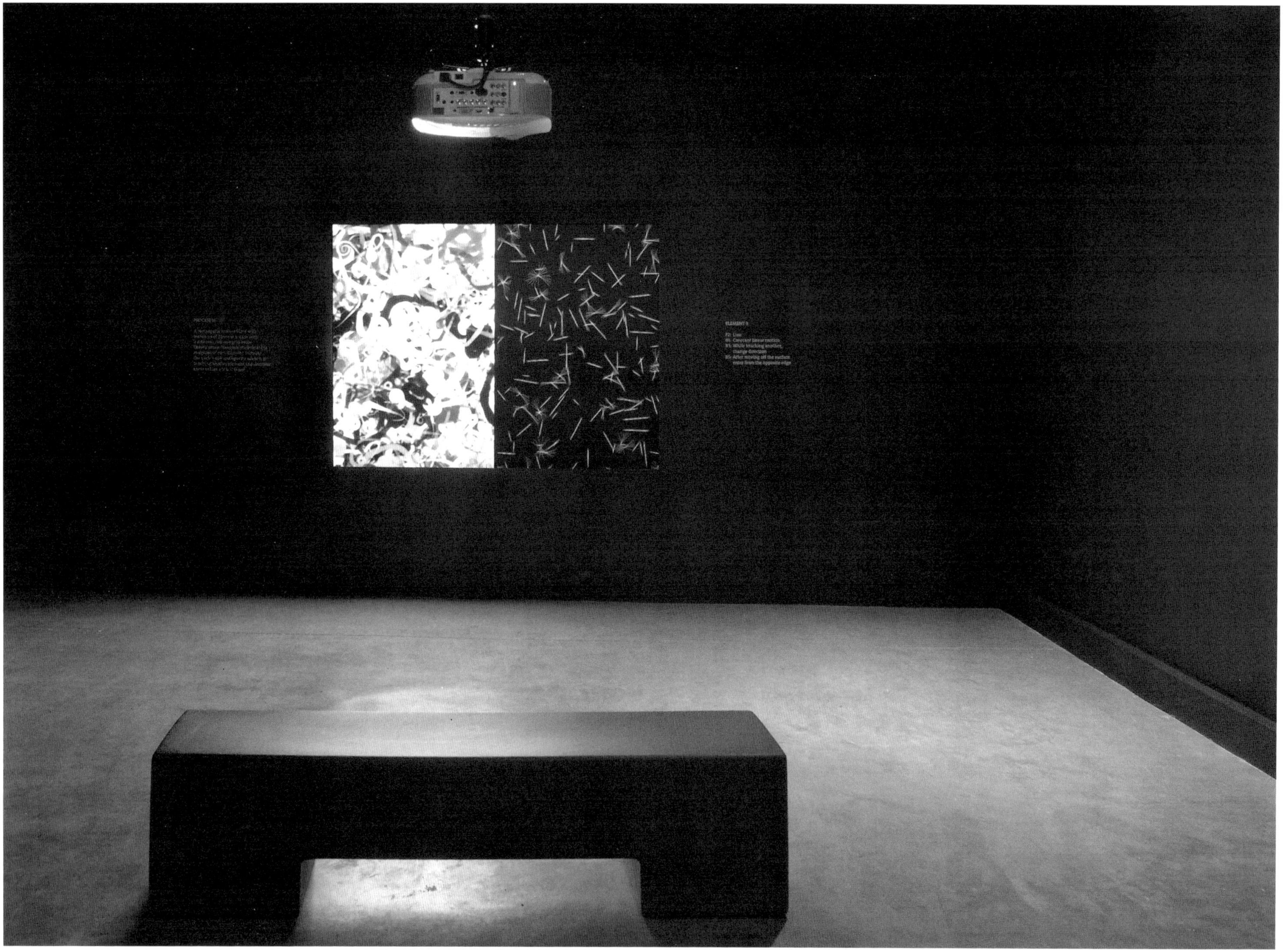

Contents

Process 16 at the Abstract Cinema exhibition, Museum of Contemporary Art, North Miami, FL

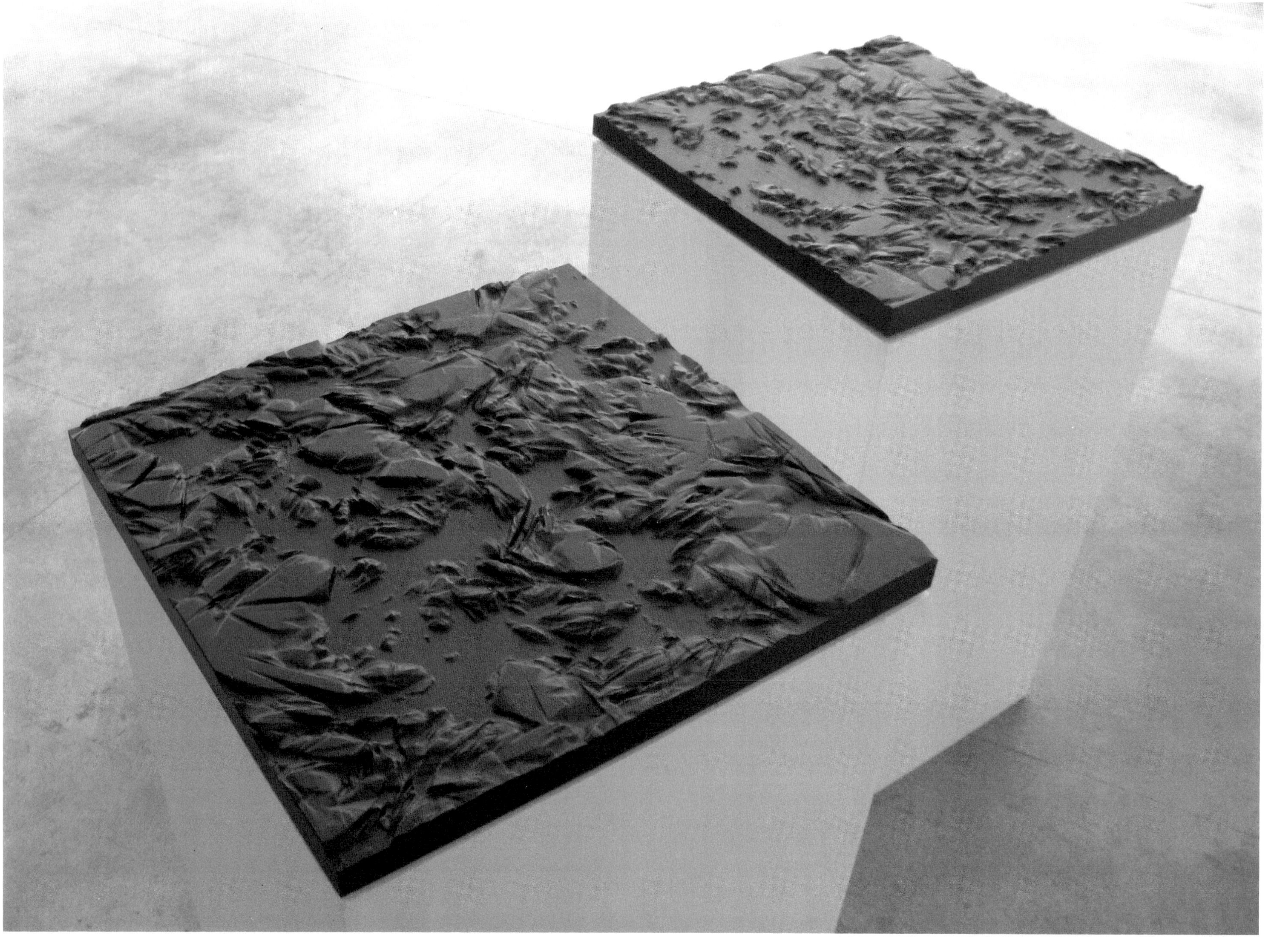

Introduction

An Element is a simple machine that is comprised of a Form and one or more Behaviors. A Process defines an environment for Elements and determines how the relationships between the Elements are visualized. For instance, Element 1 takes the form of a circle and one of its behaviors moves it along a straight line at a constant speed. Process 4 fills a surface with Element 1 and draws a line between elements while they overlap. Each Process is a short text that defines a space to explore through multiple interpretations.

A Process interpretation in software is a kinetic drawing machine with a beginning but no defined end. It proceeds one step at a time, and at each discrete step, every Element modifies itself according to its behaviors. The corresponding visual forms emerge as the Elements change; each adjustment adds to the previously drawn shapes.

During the last seven years, I have continuously refined the system of Forms, Behaviors, Elements, and Processes. The phenomenon of emergence is the core of the exploration and each artwork builds on previous works and informs the next. The system is idiosyncratic and pseudo-scientific, containing references ranging from the history of mathematics to the generation of artificial life.

The *Process Compendium 2004-2010* consists of two editions of fifteen prints that document *Process 4* to *Process 18*.* In each case, two static images have been selected from an infinite number of potential variations. This book documents these prints, alternate software interpretations, and the emergence of the forms through a series of time-lapse images.

Process 18 (Object 1, 2) at the Process / Form exhibition, bitforms gallery, New York, NY

* The first three *Process* works are named *Structure 1, 2,* and *3*. This is explained briefly on page 115.

Element 1–5

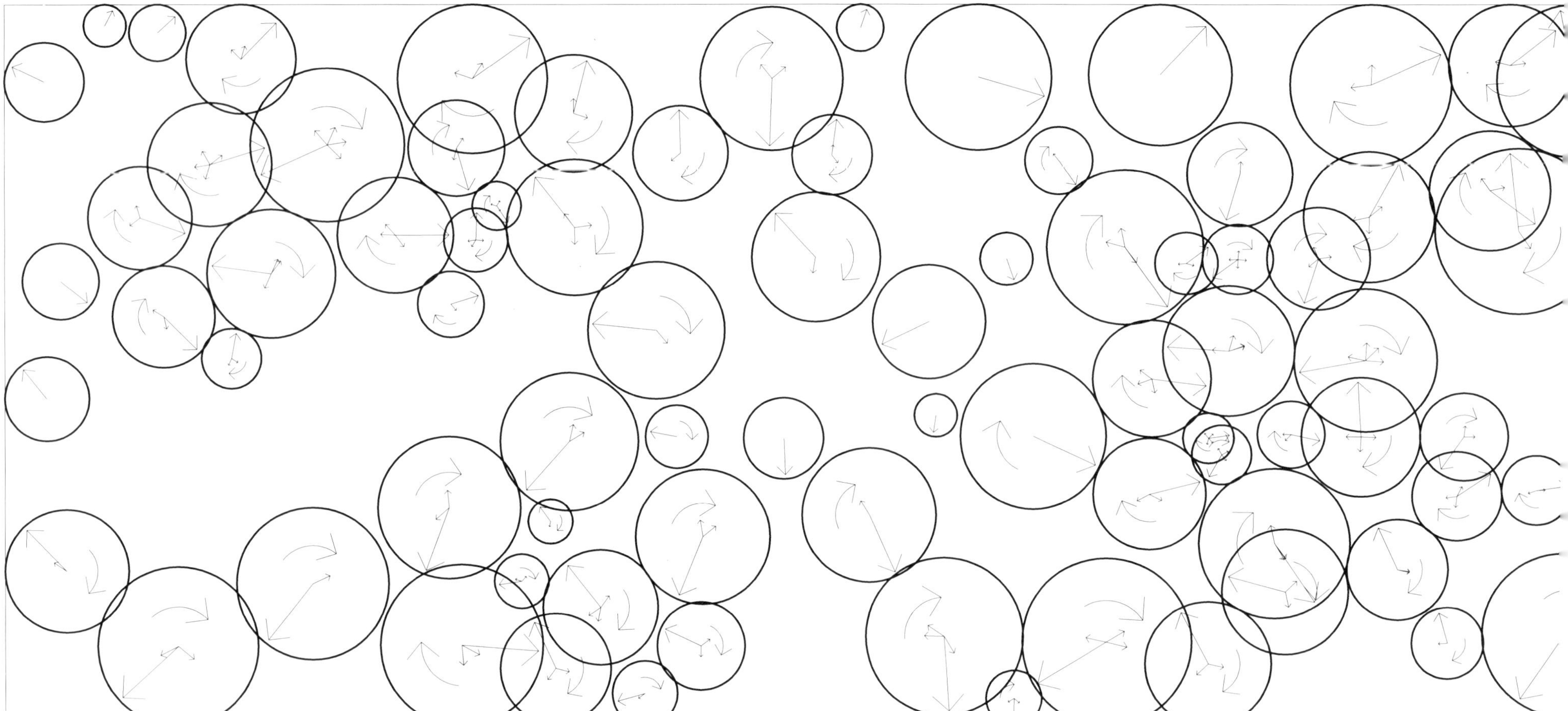

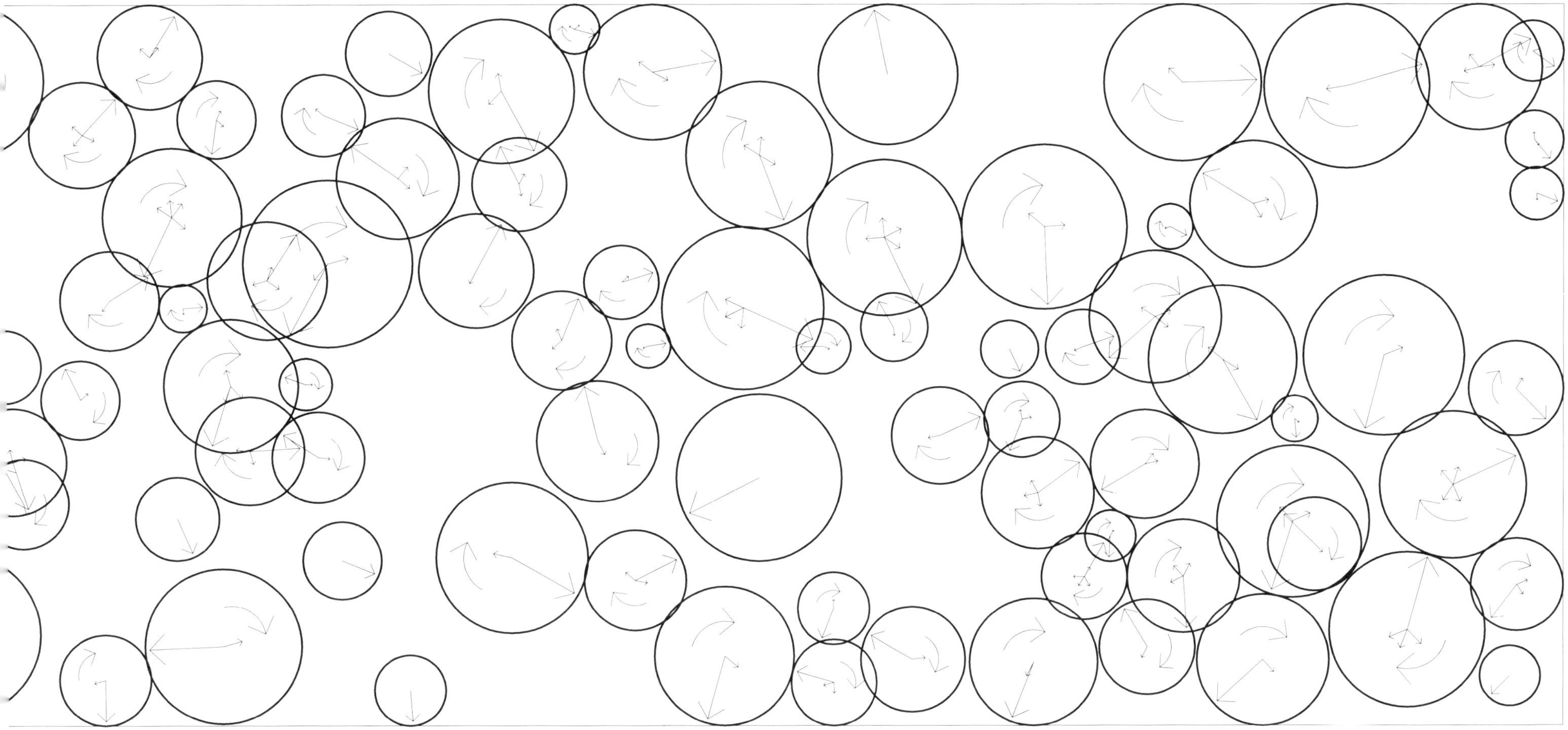

Element 1

Form 1: Circle
Behavior 1: Move in a straight line
Behavior 2: Constrain to surface
Behavior 3: Change direction while touching another Element
Behavior 4: Move away from an overlapping Element

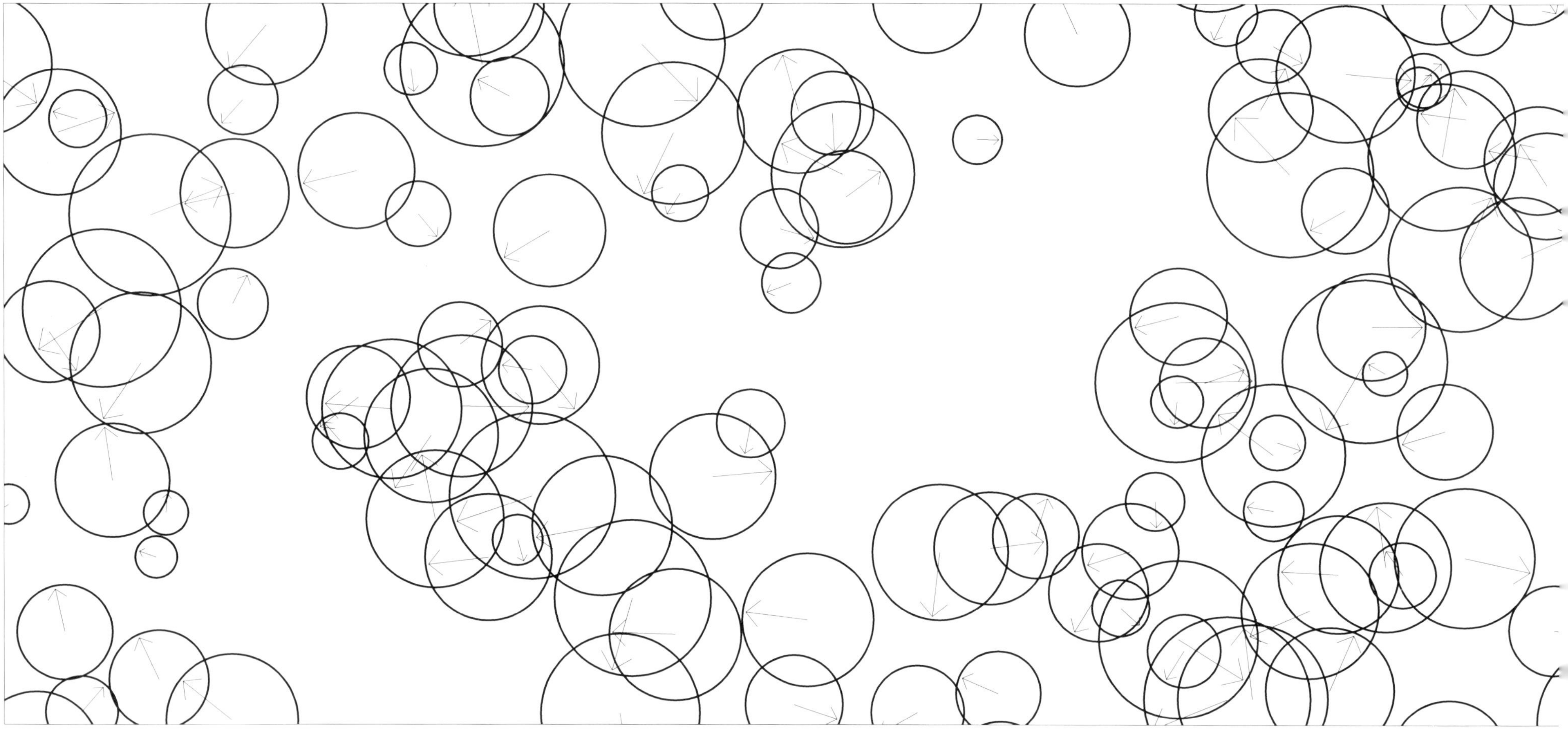

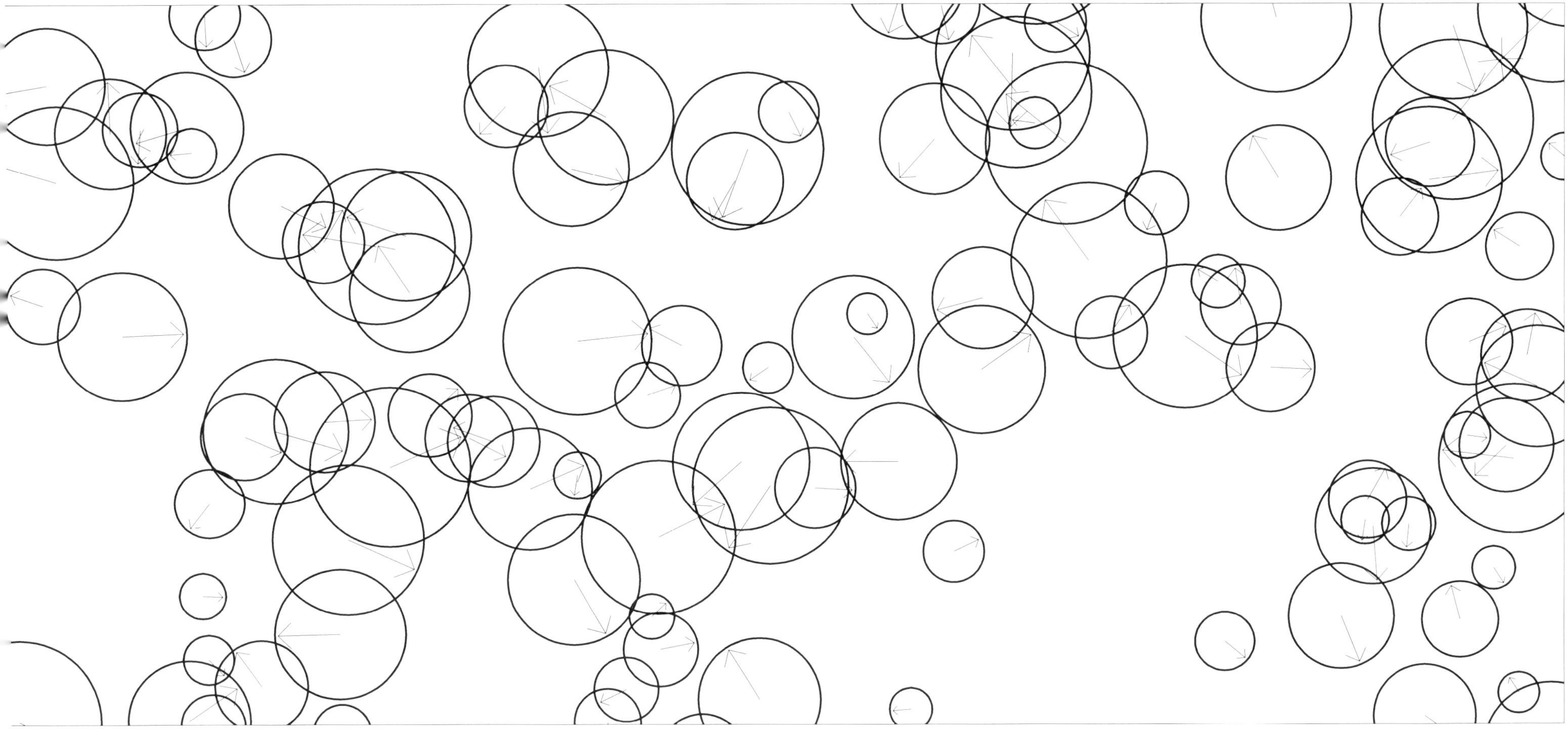

Element 2

Form 1: Circle
Behavior 1: Move in a straight line
Behavior 5: Enter from the opposite edge after moving off the surface

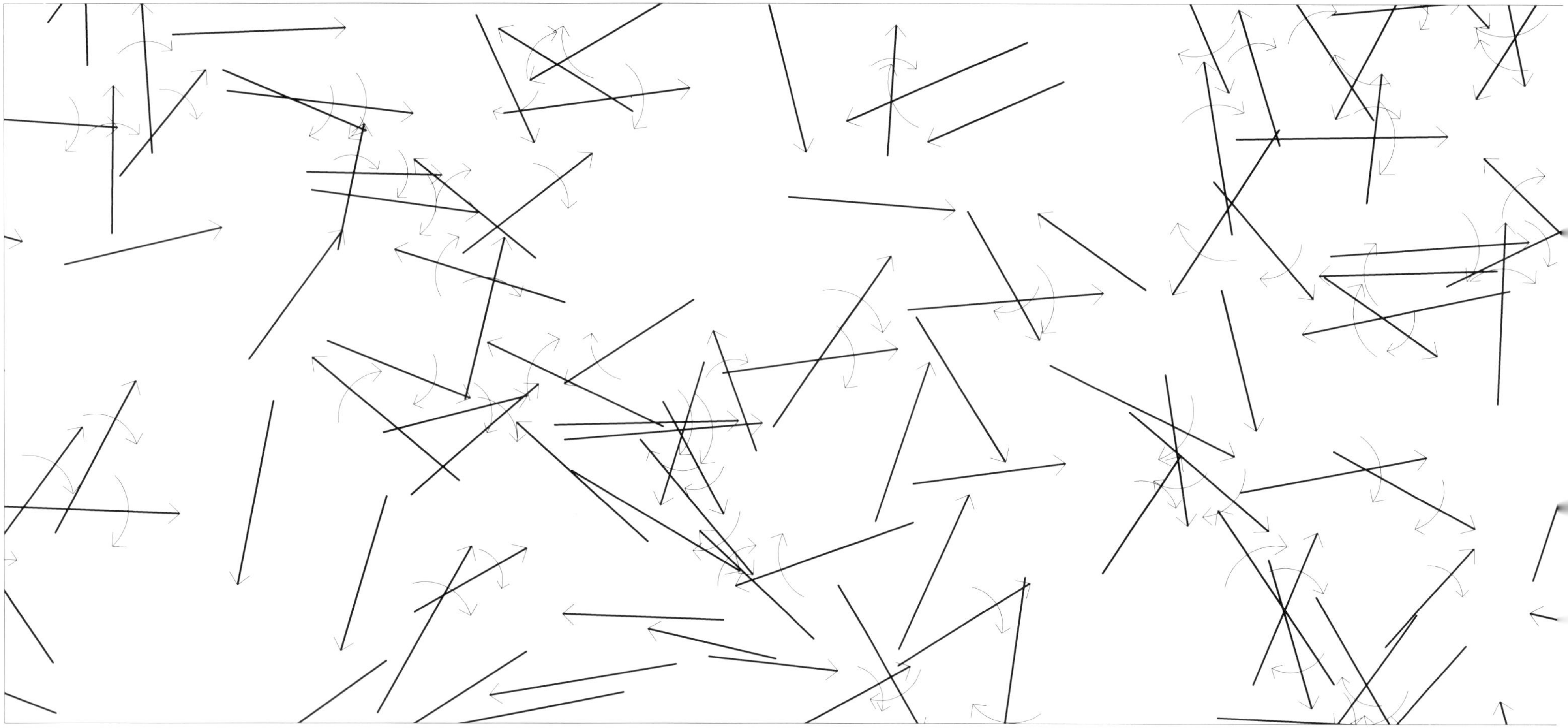

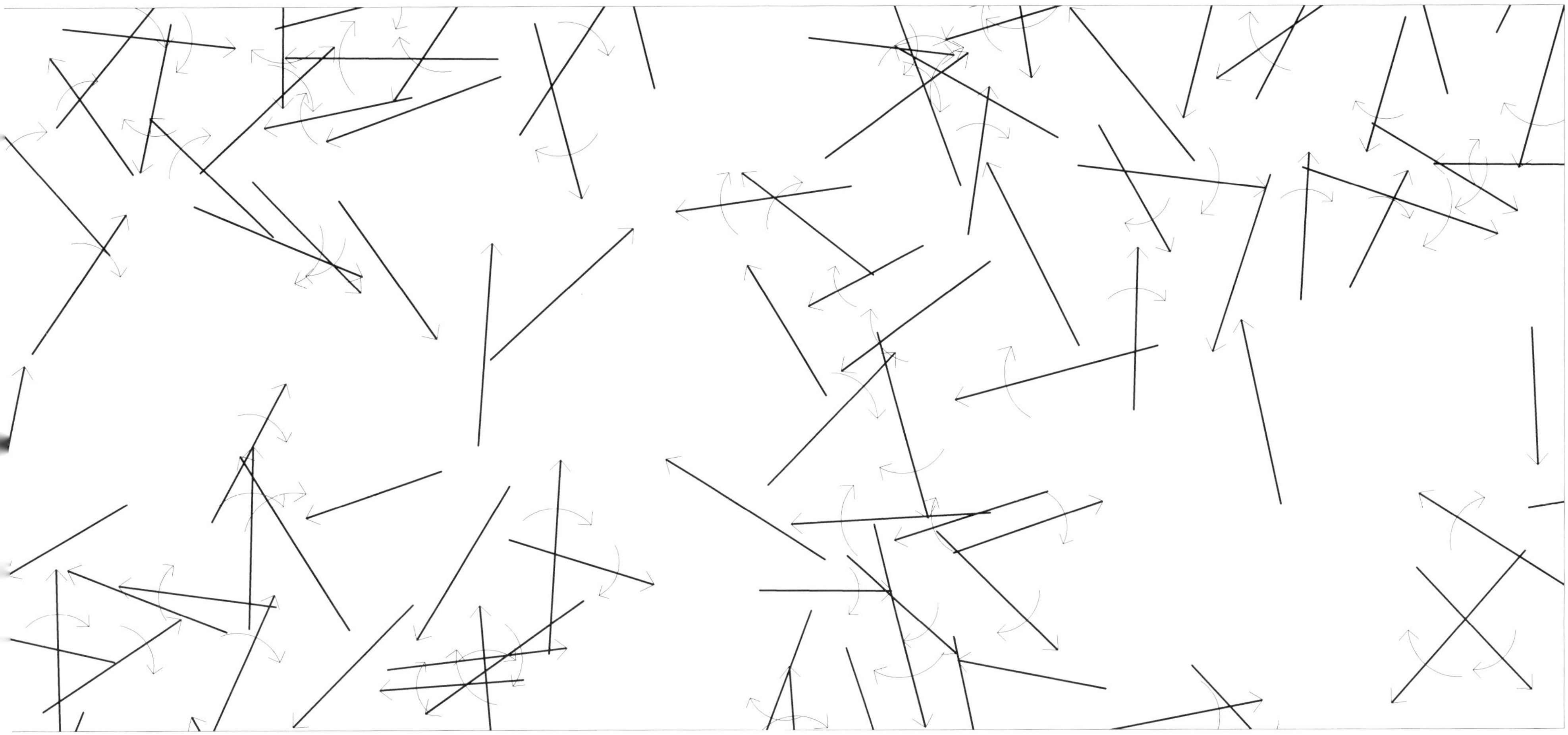

Element 3

Form 2: Line
Behavior 1: Move in a straight line
Behavior 3: Change direction while touching another Element
Behavior 5: Enter from the opposite edge after moving off the surface

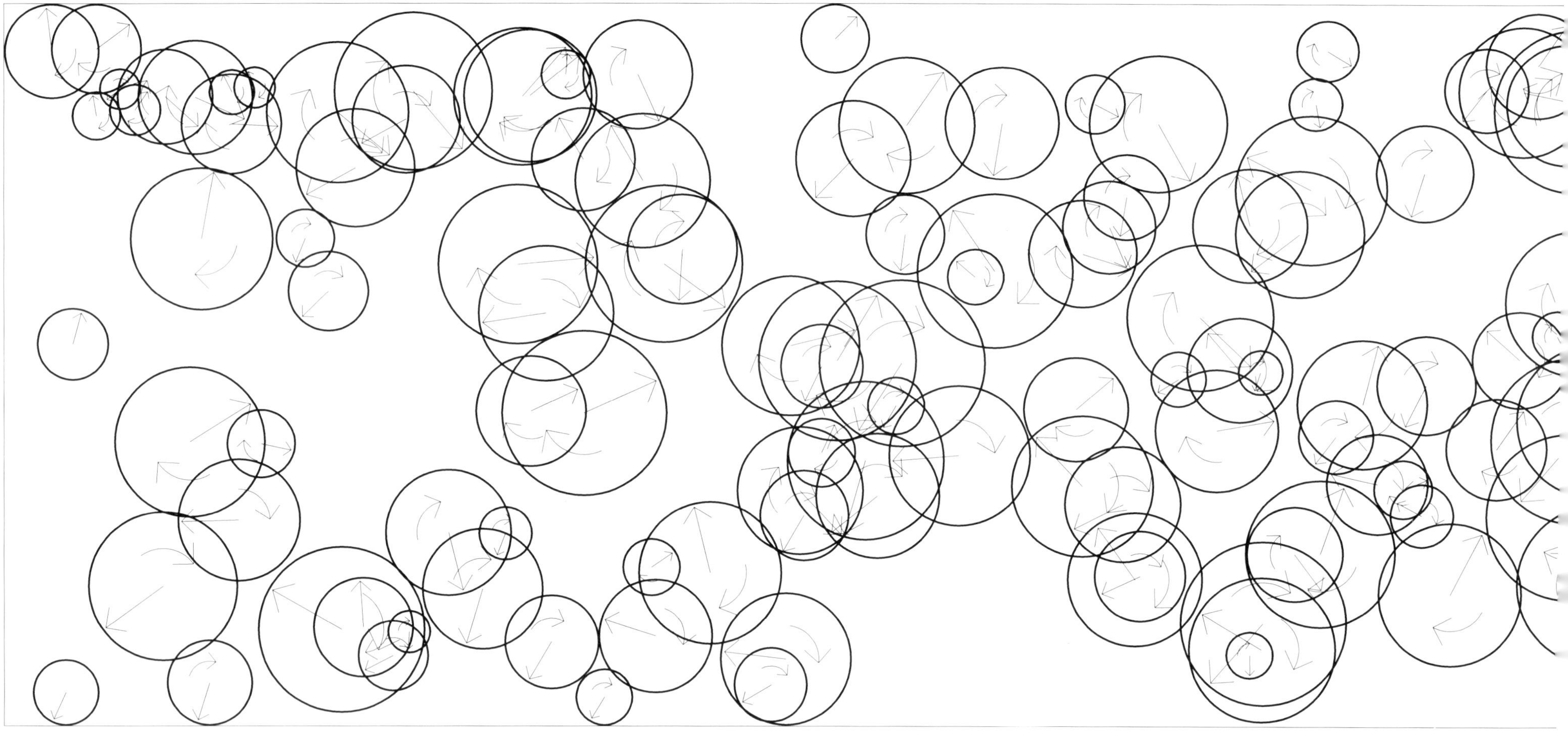

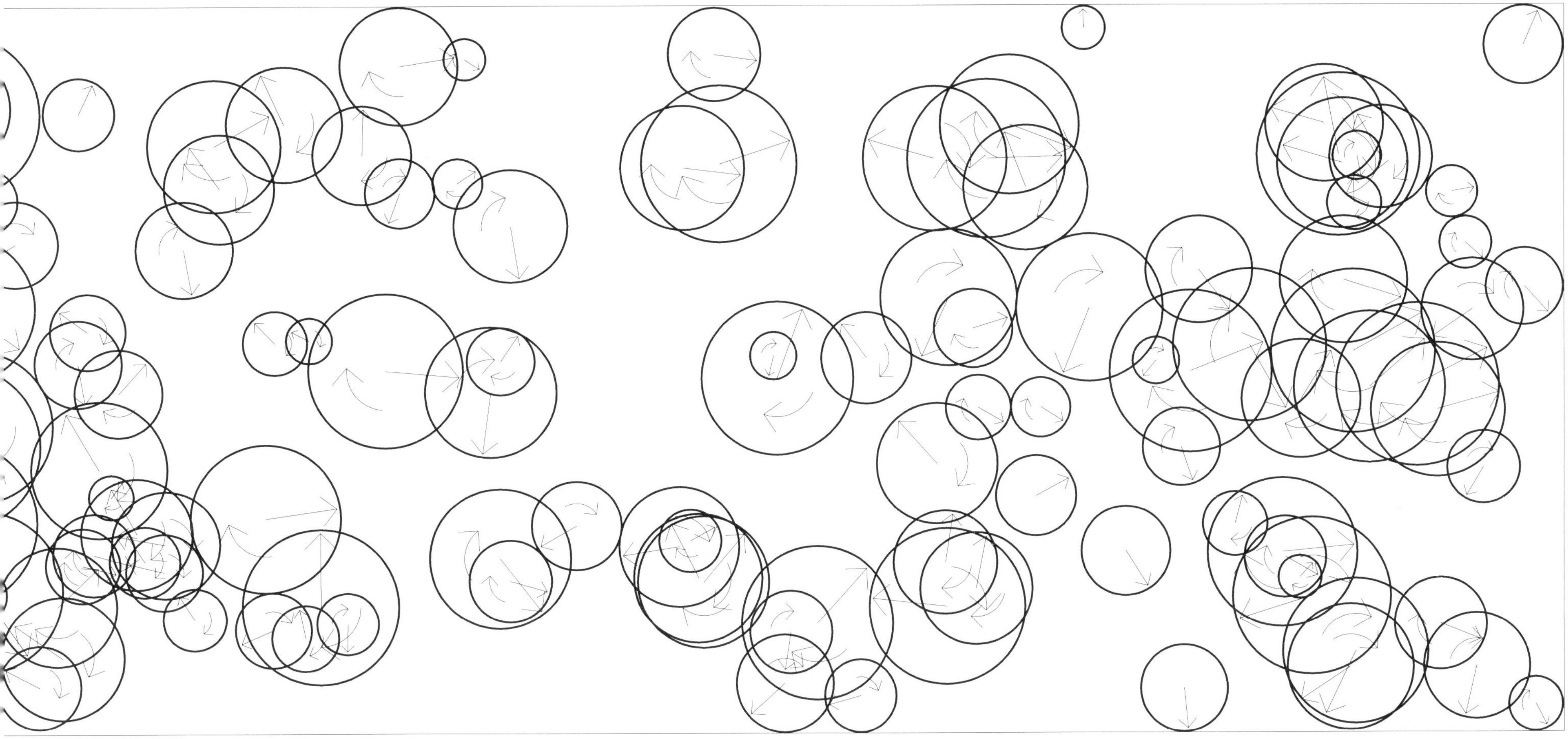

Element 4

Form 1: Circle
Behavior 1: Move in a straight line
Behavior 2: Constrain to surface
Behavior 3: Change direction while touching another Element

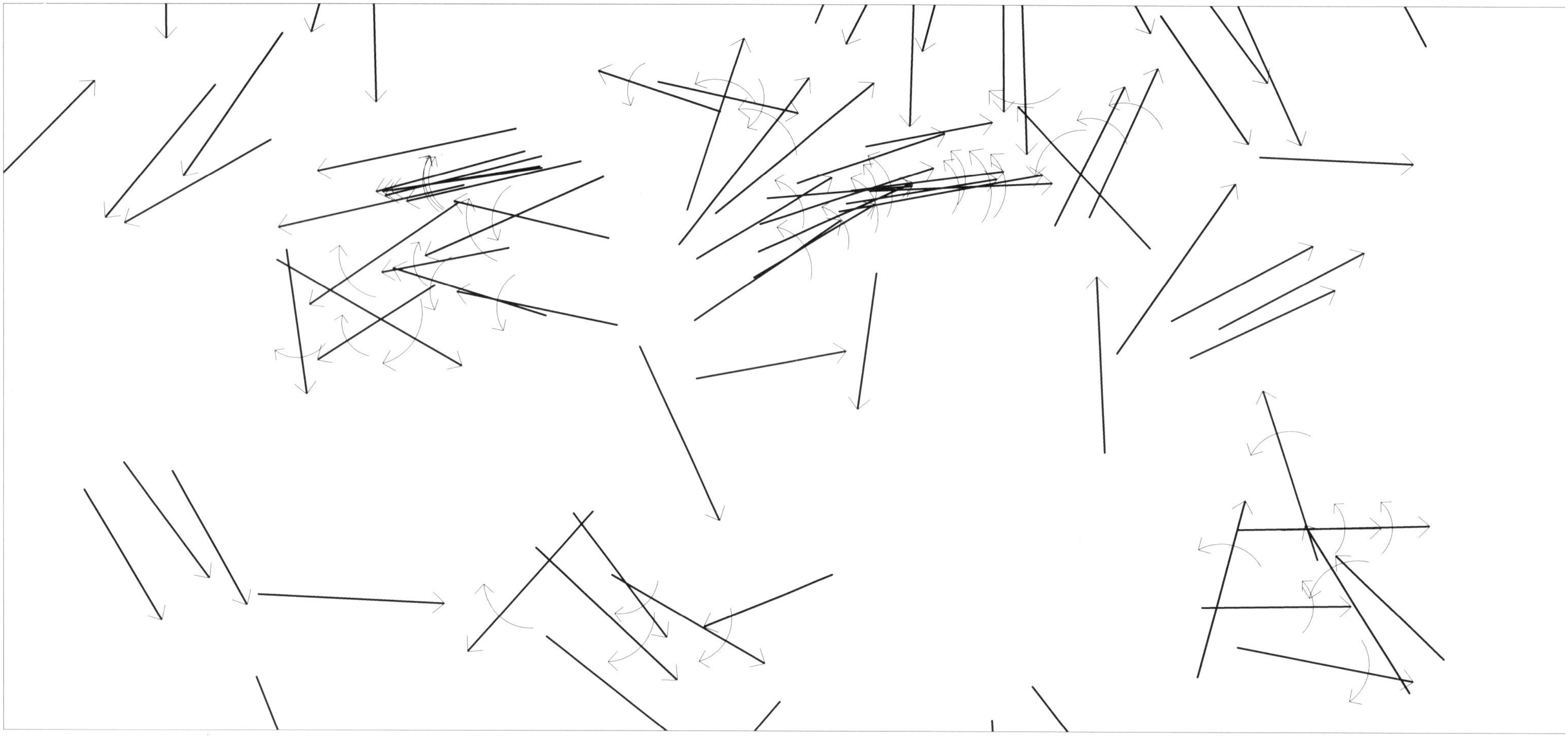

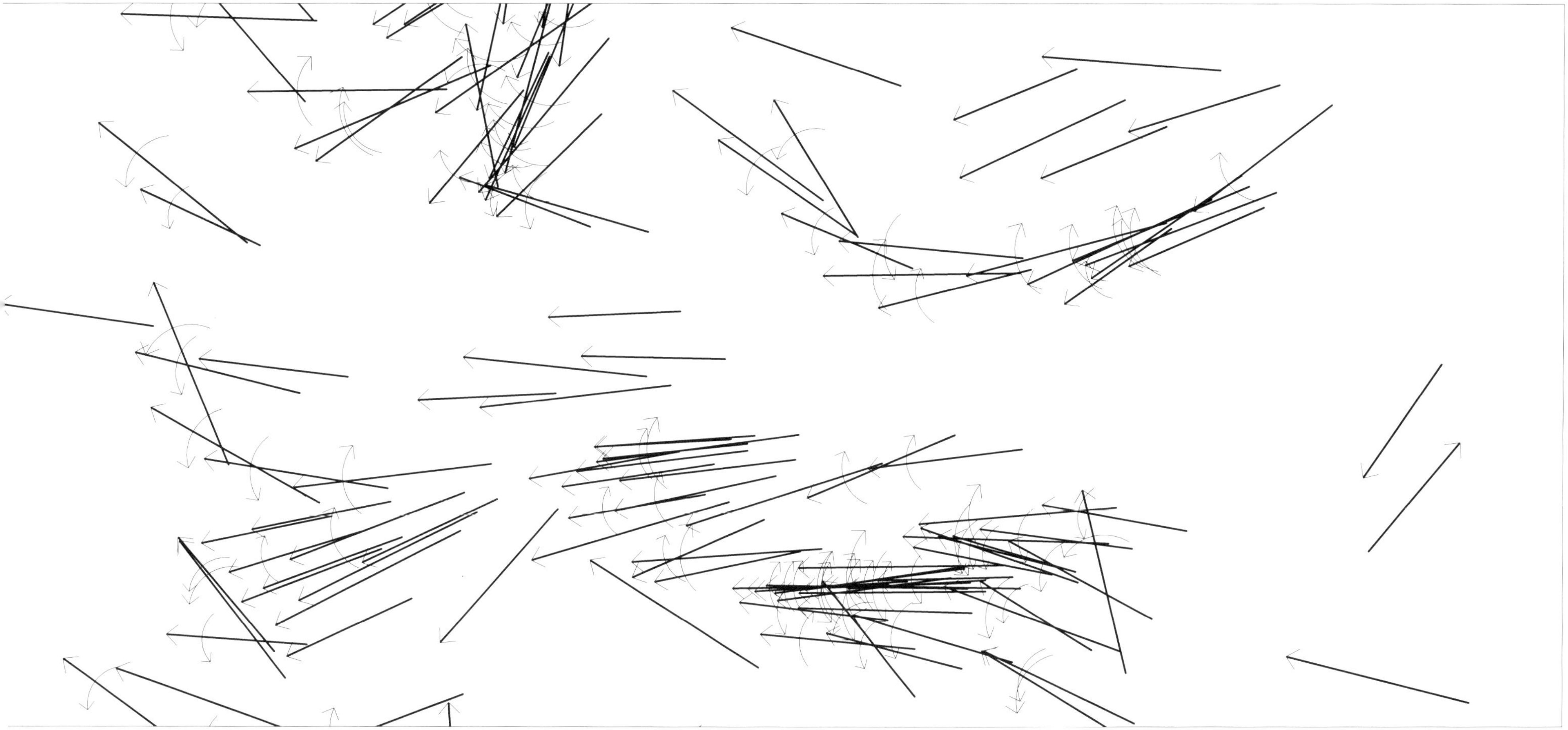

Element 5

Form 2: Line
Behavior 1: Move in a straight line
Behavior 5: Enter from the opposite edge after moving off the surface
Behavior 6: Orient toward the direction of an Element that is touching
Behavior 7: Deviate from the current direction

Process 4–18

Process 4

A rectangular surface filled with varying sizes of Element 1. Draw a line from the centers of Elements that are touching. Set the value of the shortest possible line to black and the longest to white, with varying grays representing values in between.

Process 4, 2005
Text, unique custom software, computer, documentation prints
Dimensions variable

Process 4 (A), 2010
C print
Edition of 8 + 2 AP
50cm x 50cm

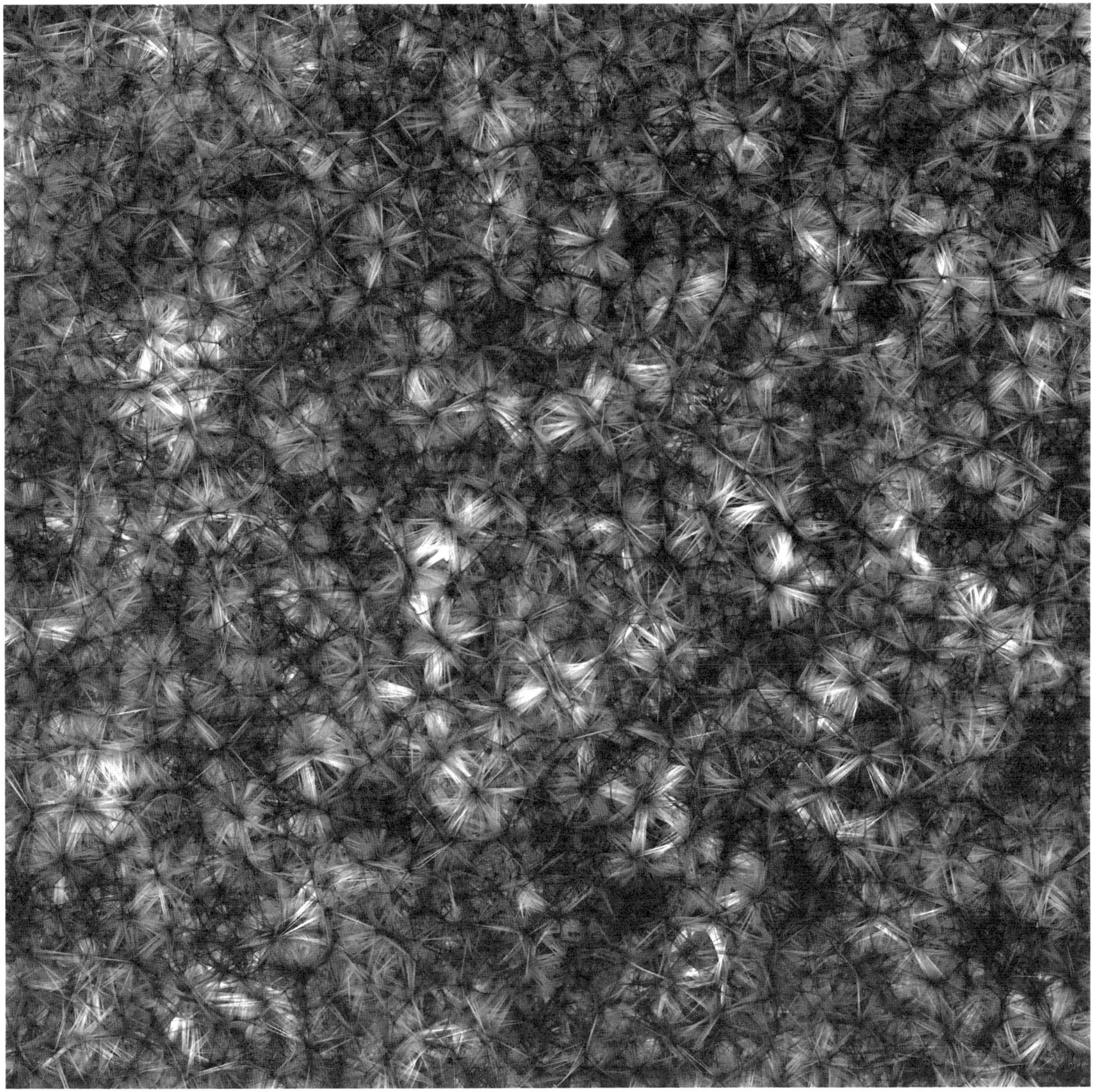

Process 4 (B), 2010
C print
Edition of 8 + 2 AP
50cm x 50cm

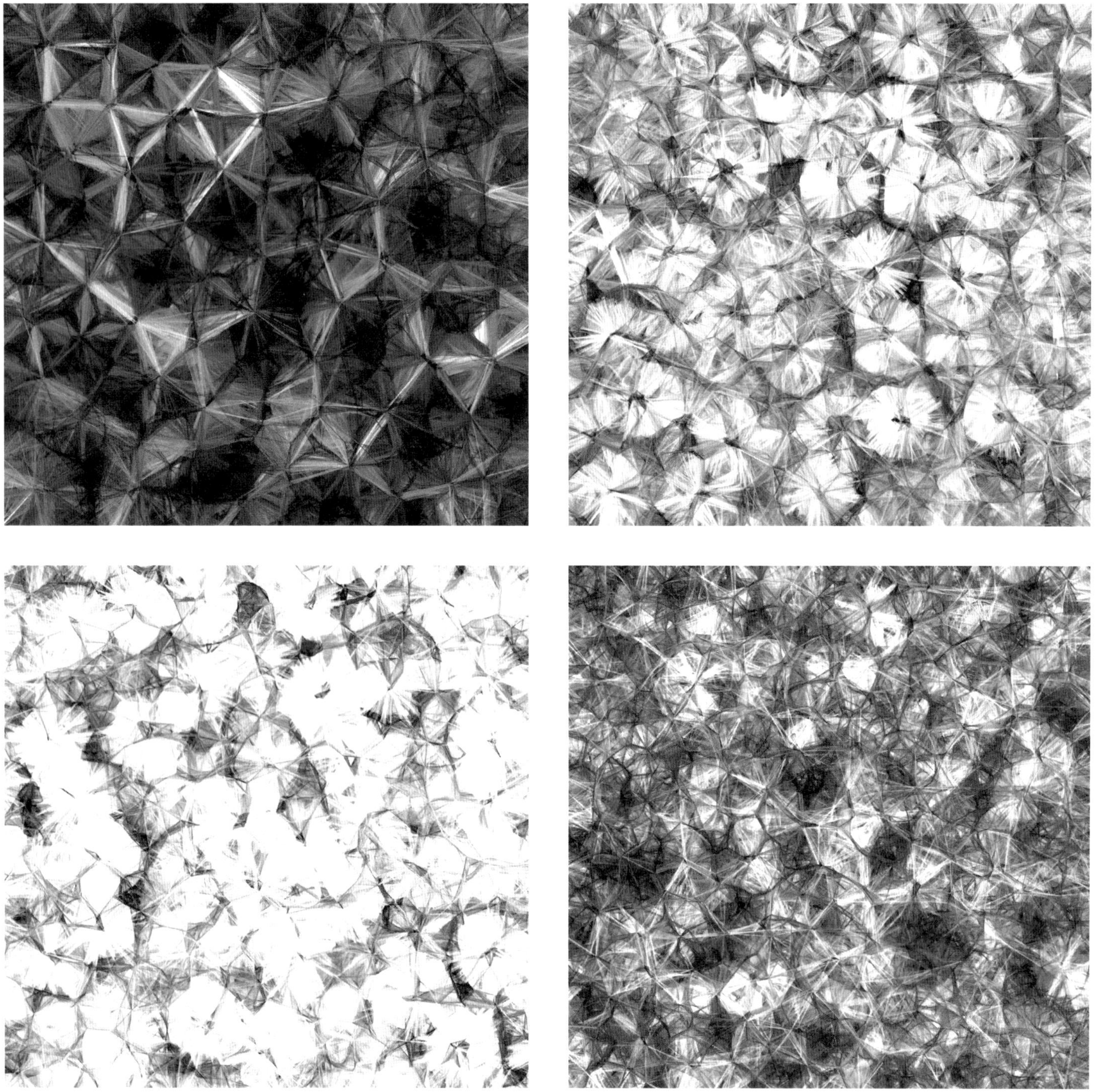

Images captured from different software interpretations of *Process 4*

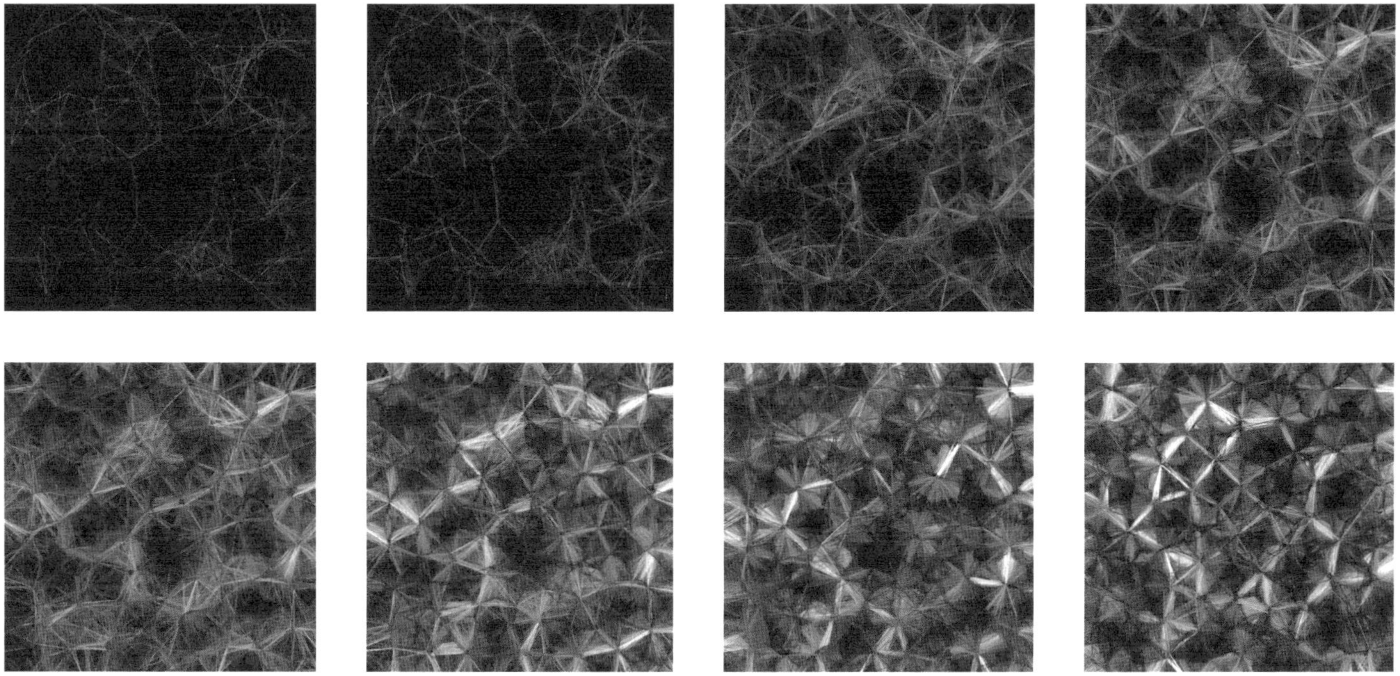

Image sequence from a software interpretation of *Process 4*

Process 5

A rectangular surface filled with varying sizes of Element 1. Draw the perimeter of each Element as a black line and the center as a white dot. Draw a gray line from the centers of Elements that are touching.

Process 5, 2005
Text, unique custom software, computer, documentation prints
Dimensions variable

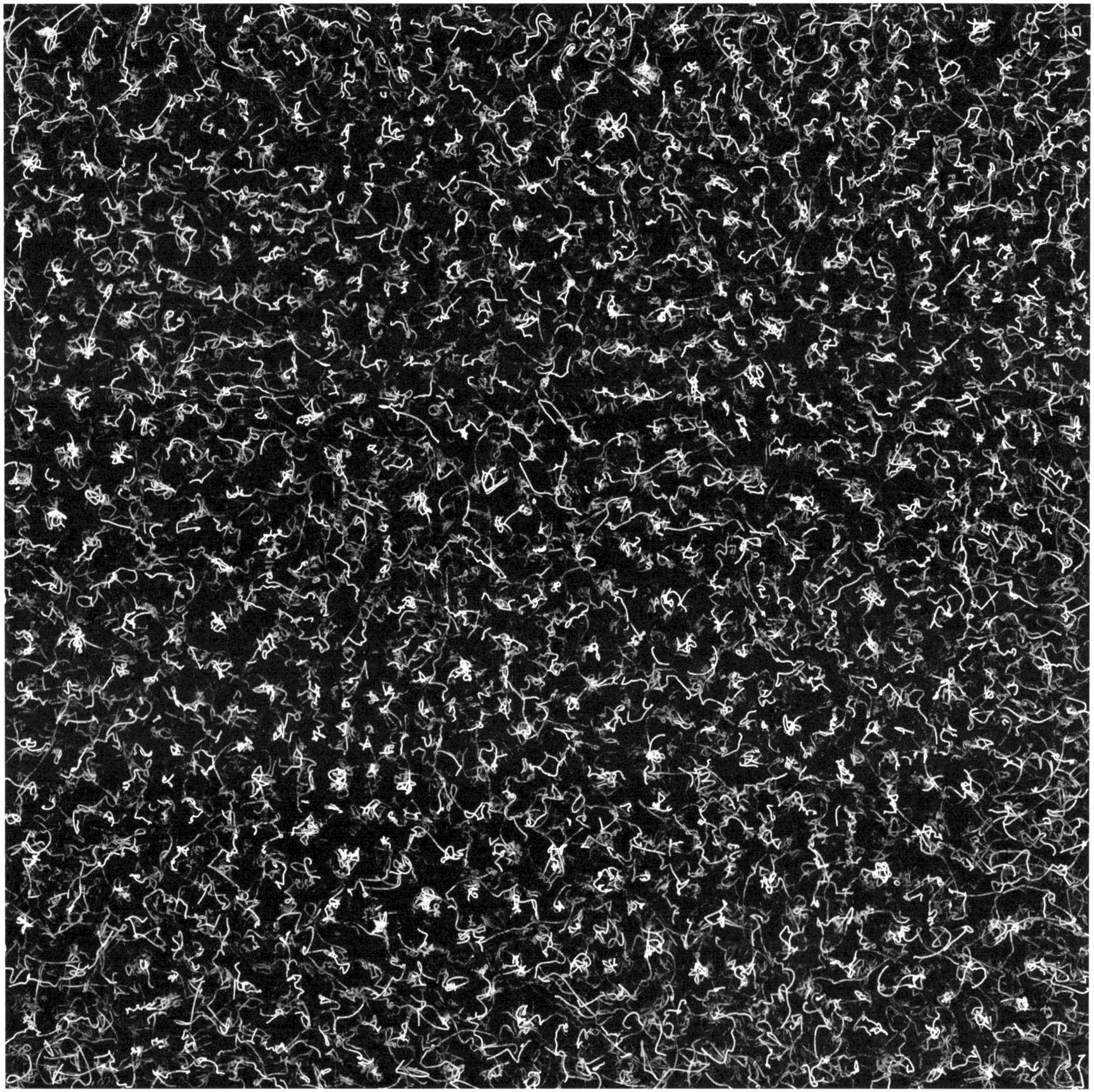

Process 5 (A), 2010
C print
Edition of 8 + 2 AP
50cm x 50cm

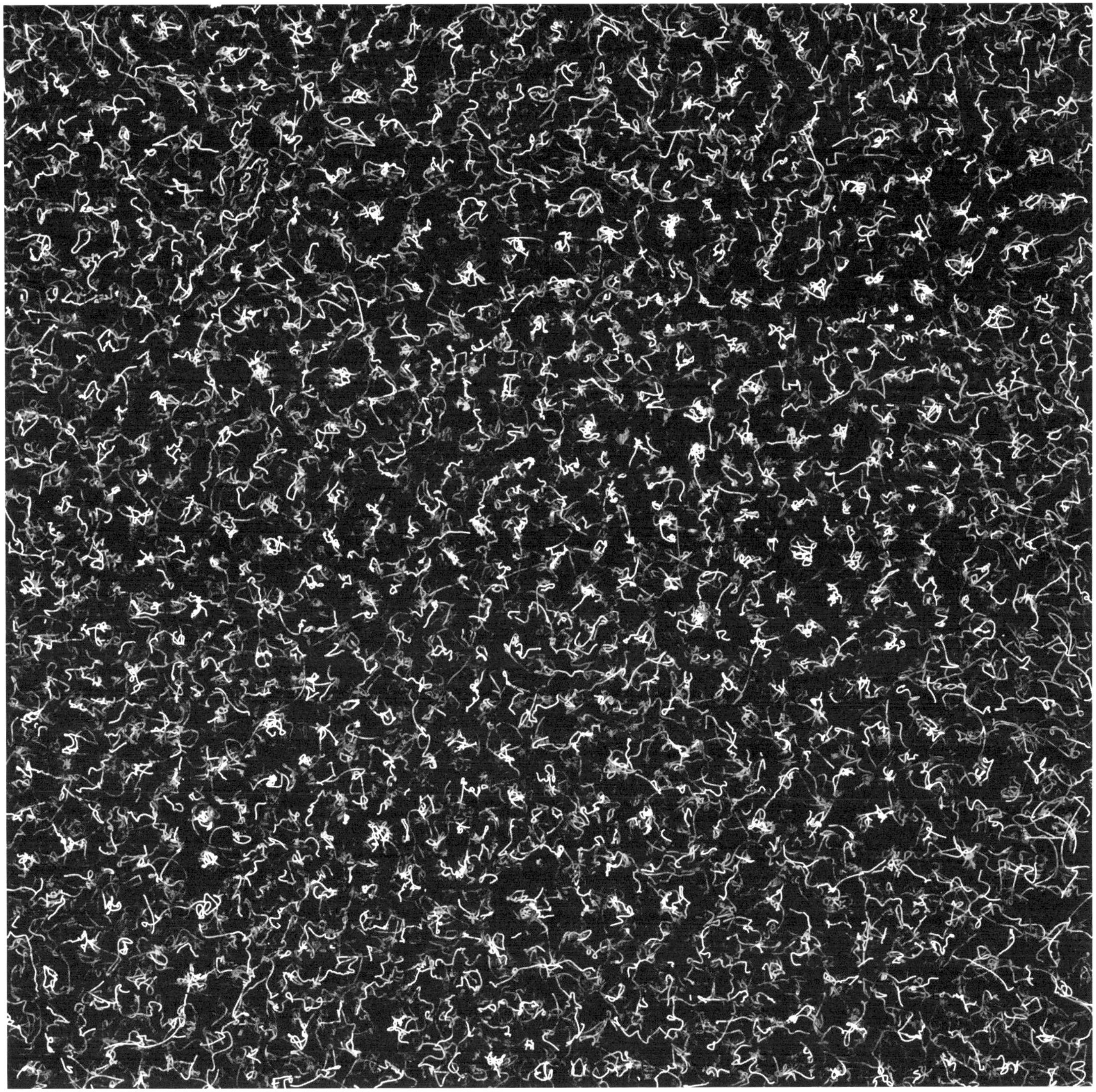

Process 5 (B), 2010
C print
Edition of 8 + 2 AP
50cm × 50cm

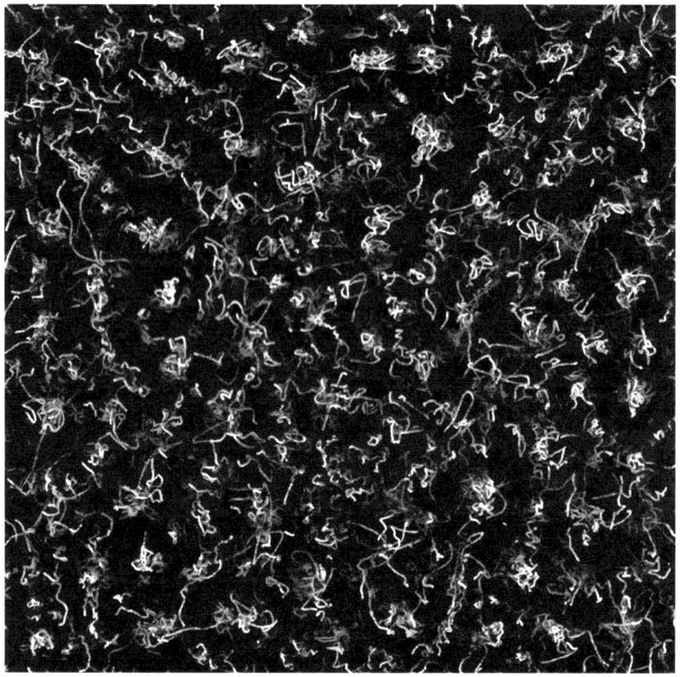

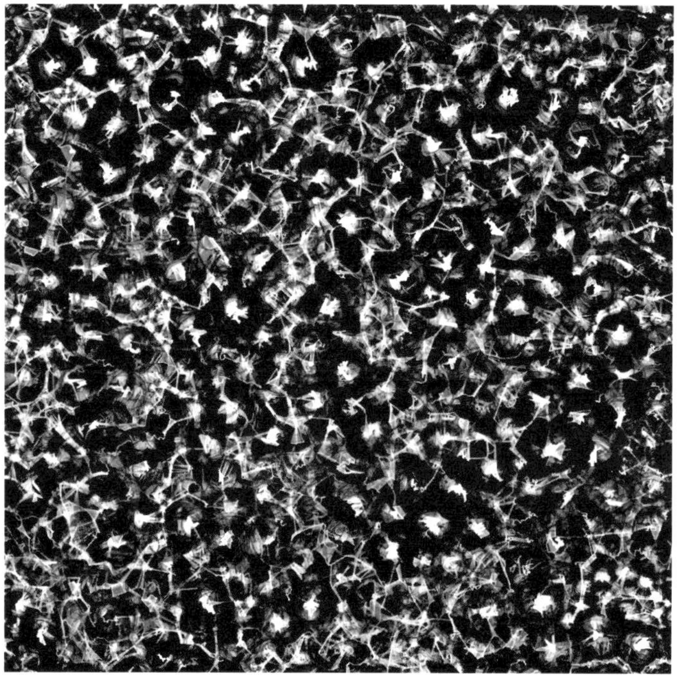

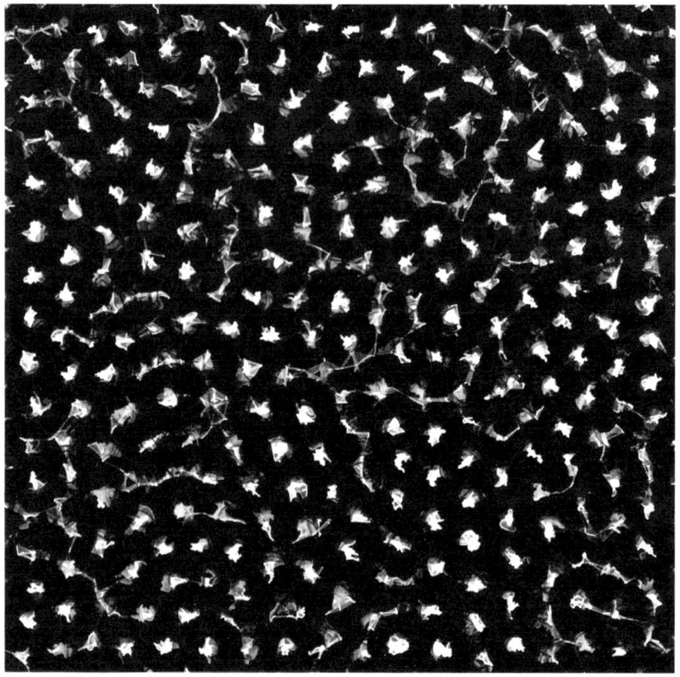

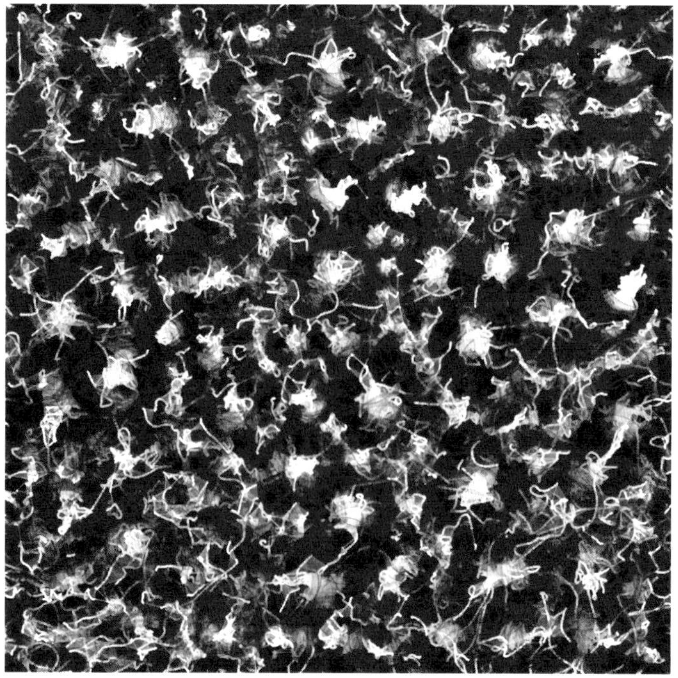

Images captured from different software interpretations of *Process 5*

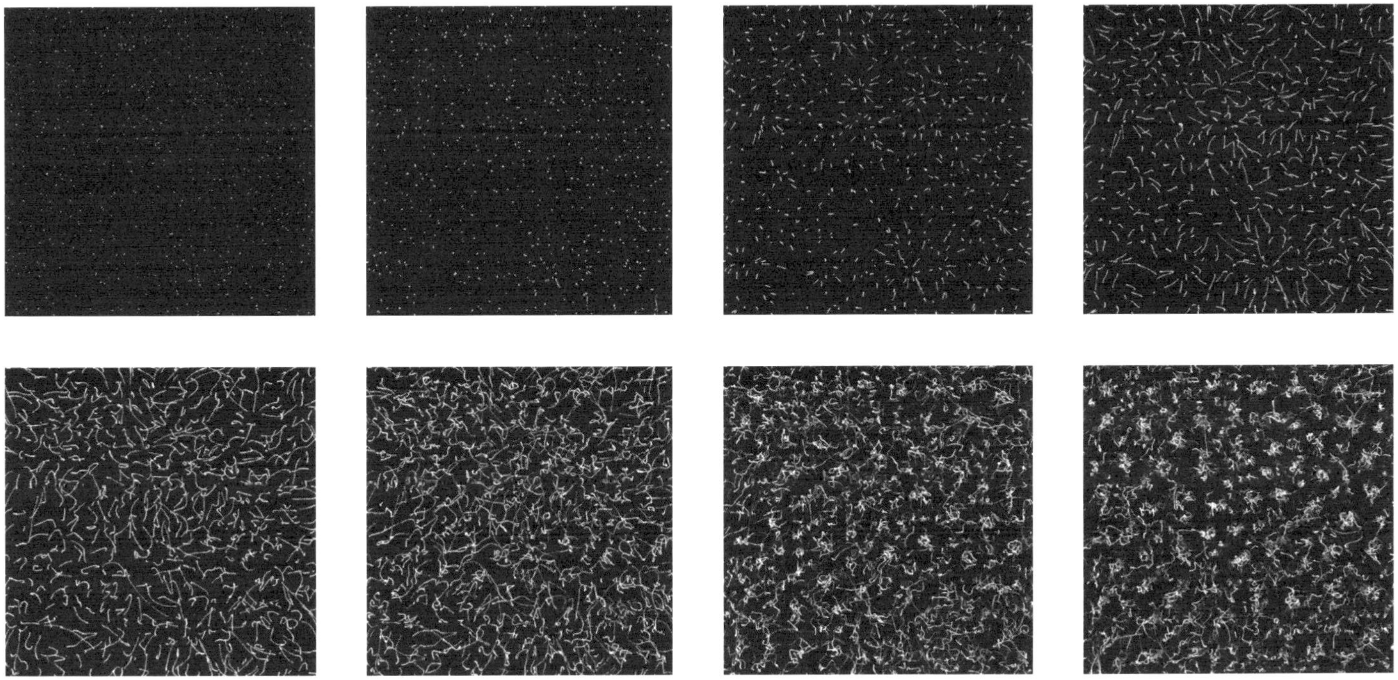

Image sequence
from a software
interpretation
of *Process 5*

Process 6

Position three large circles on a rectangular surface. Set the center of each circle as the origin for a large group of Element 1. When an Element moves beyond the edge of its circle, return to the origin. Draw a line from the centers of Elements that are touching. Set the value of the shortest possible line to black and the longest to white, with varying grays representing values in between.

Process 6, 2005
Text, unique custom software, computer, documentation prints
Dimensions variable

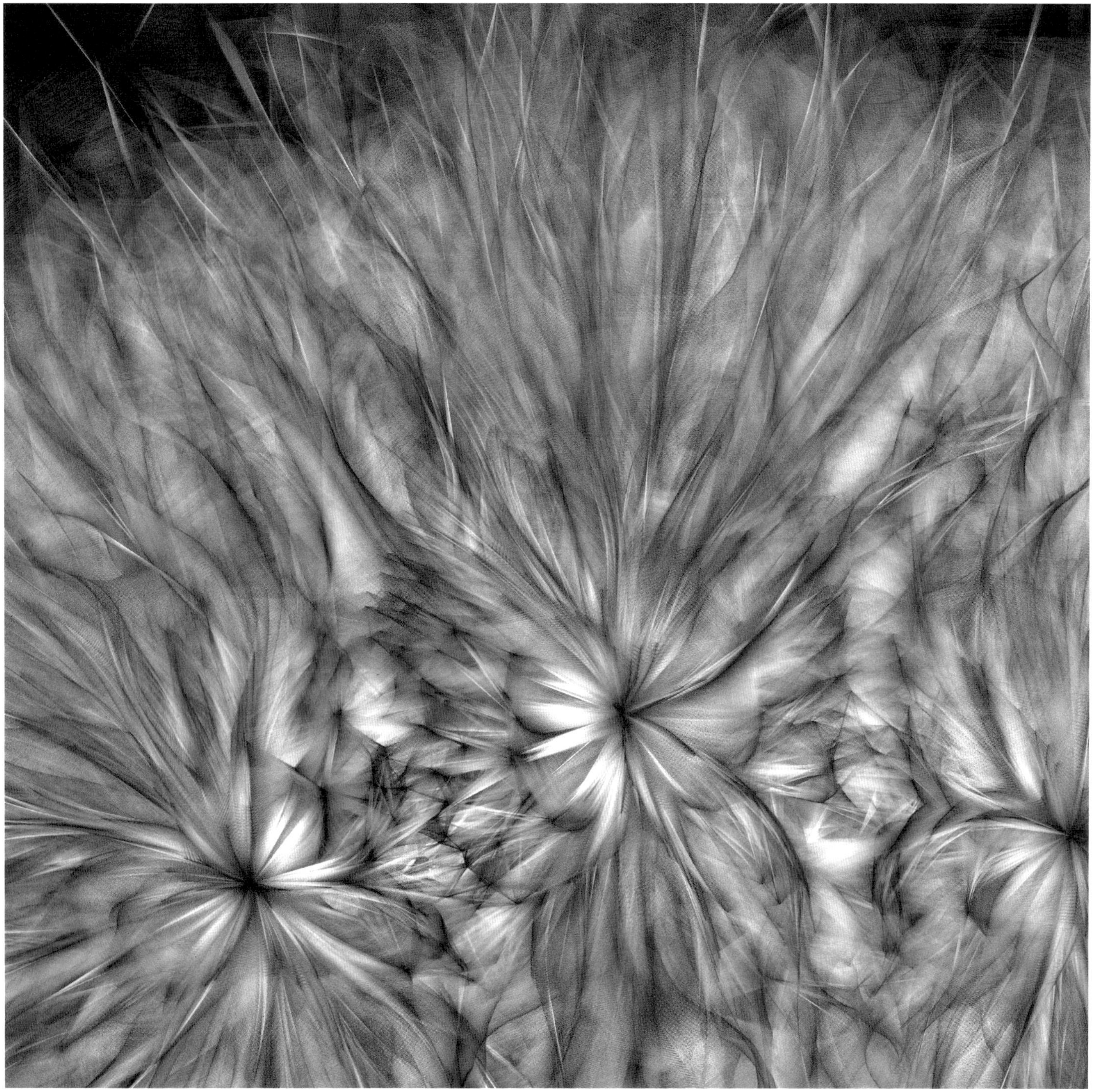

Process 6 (A), 2010
C print
Edition of 8 + 2 AP
50cm x 50cm

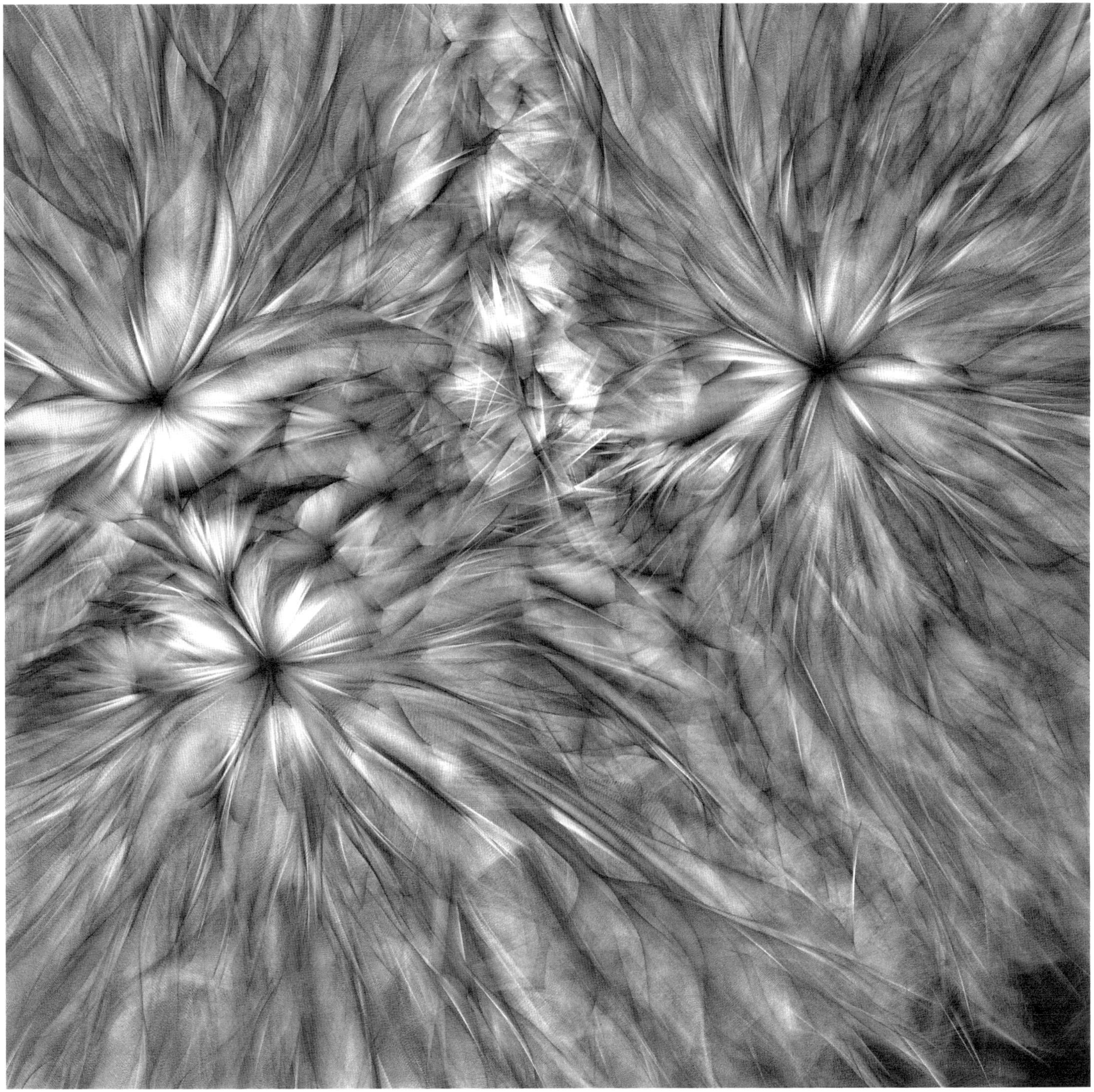

Process 6 (B), 2010
C print
Edition of 8 + 2 AP
50cm x 50cm

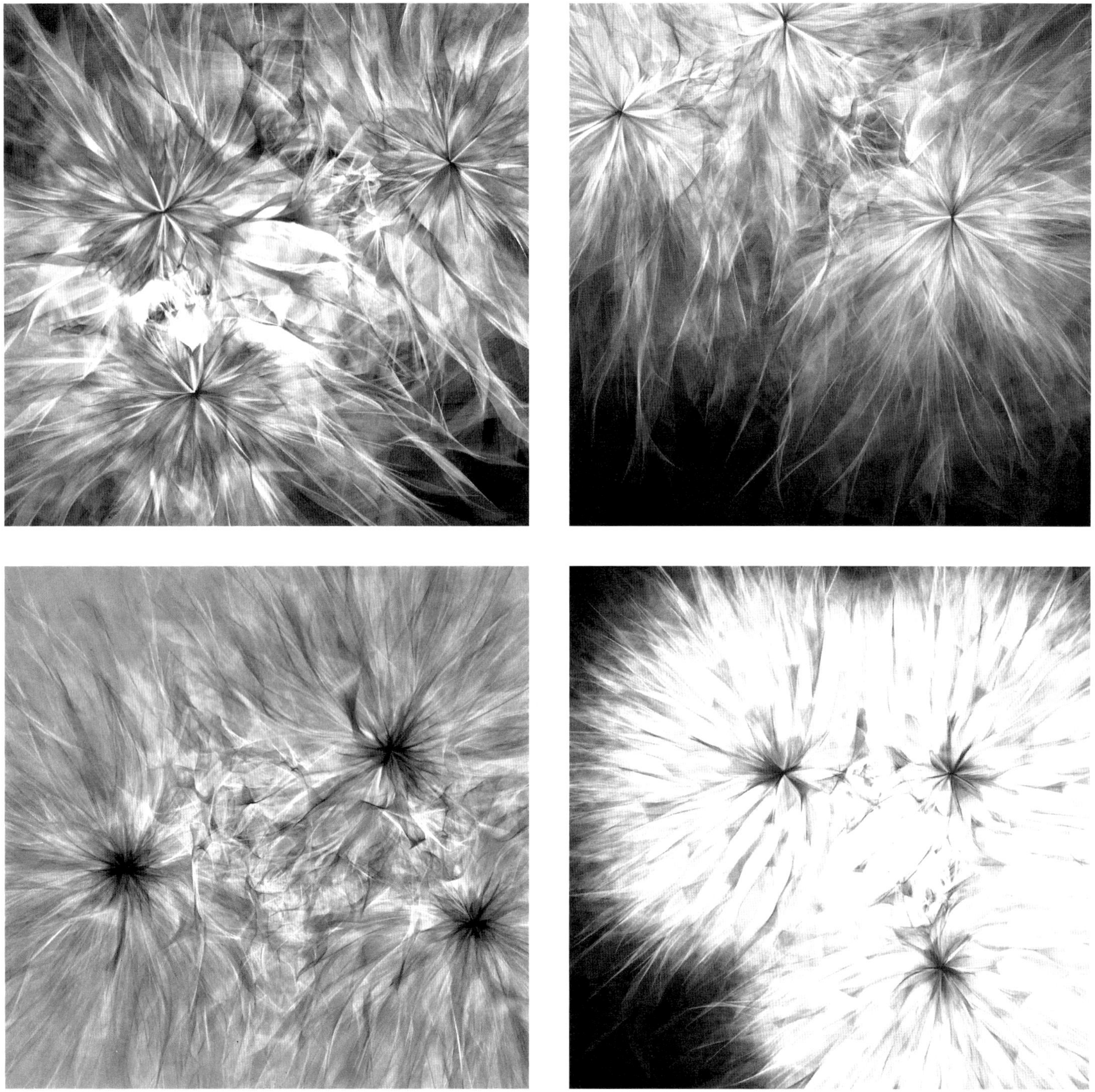

Images captured from different software interpretations of *Process 6*

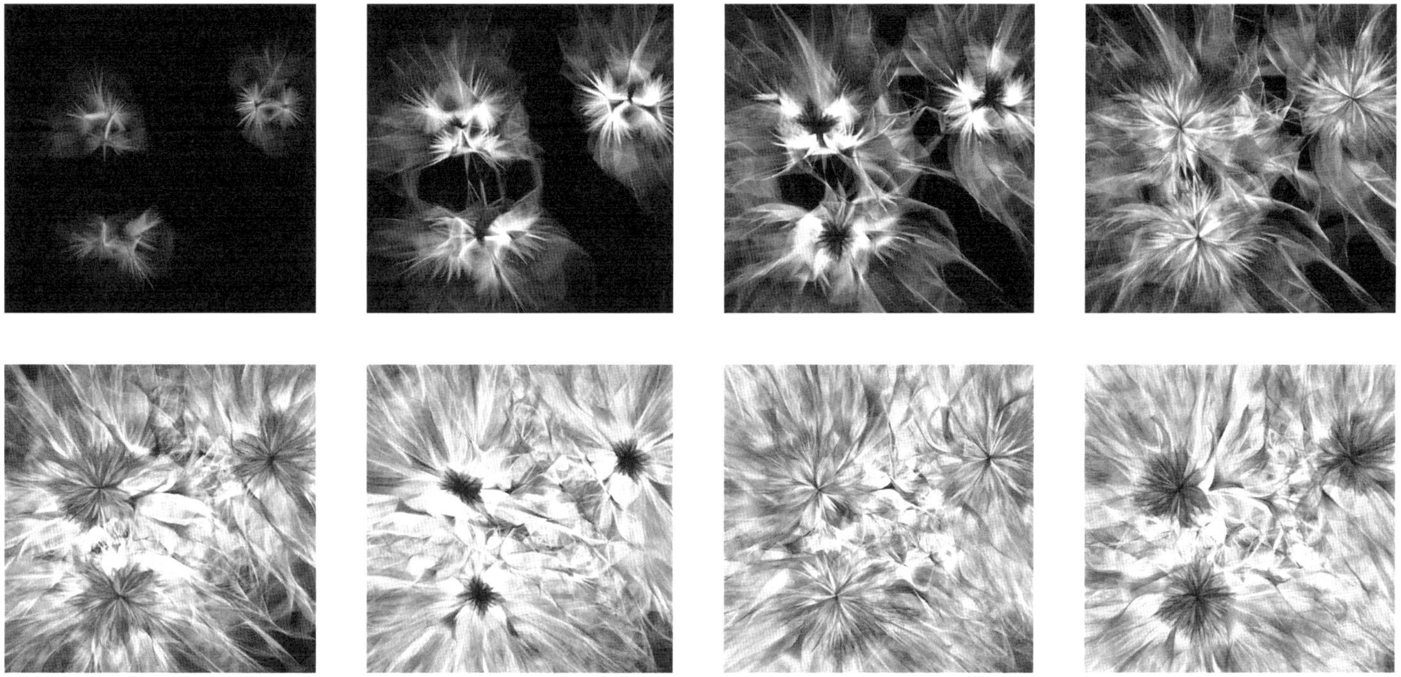

Image sequence
from a software
interpretation
of *Process 6*

Process 7

A rectangular surface filled with varying sizes of Element 1. Draw a line from the centers of Elements that are touching. Set the value of the shortest possible line to white and the longest to black, with varying grays representing values in between. Draw the perimeter of each Element as a black line and the center as a white dot.

Process 7, 2005
Text, unique custom software, computer, documentation prints
Dimensions variable

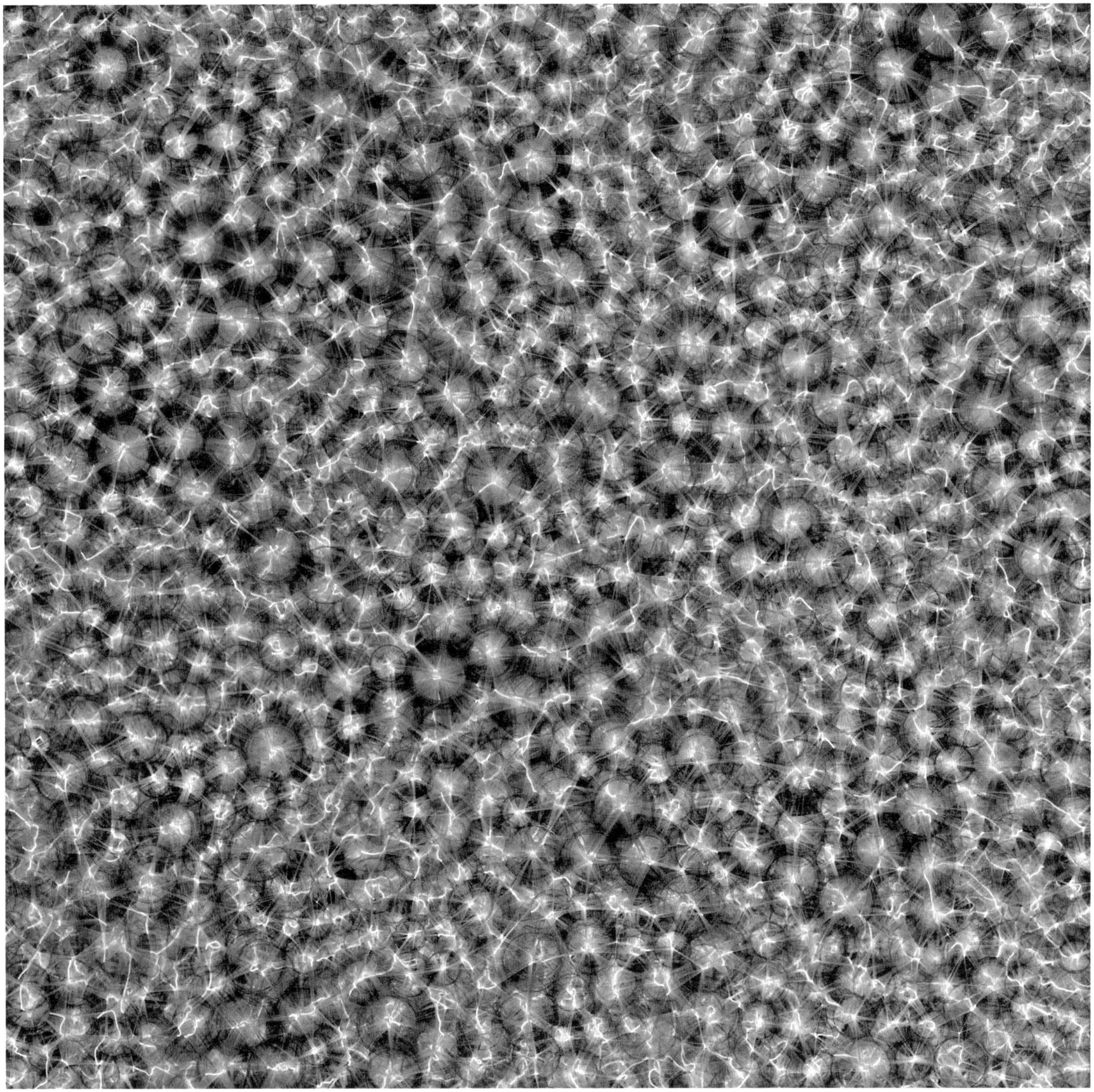

Process 7 (A), 2010
C print
Edition of 8 + 2 AP
50cm x 50cm

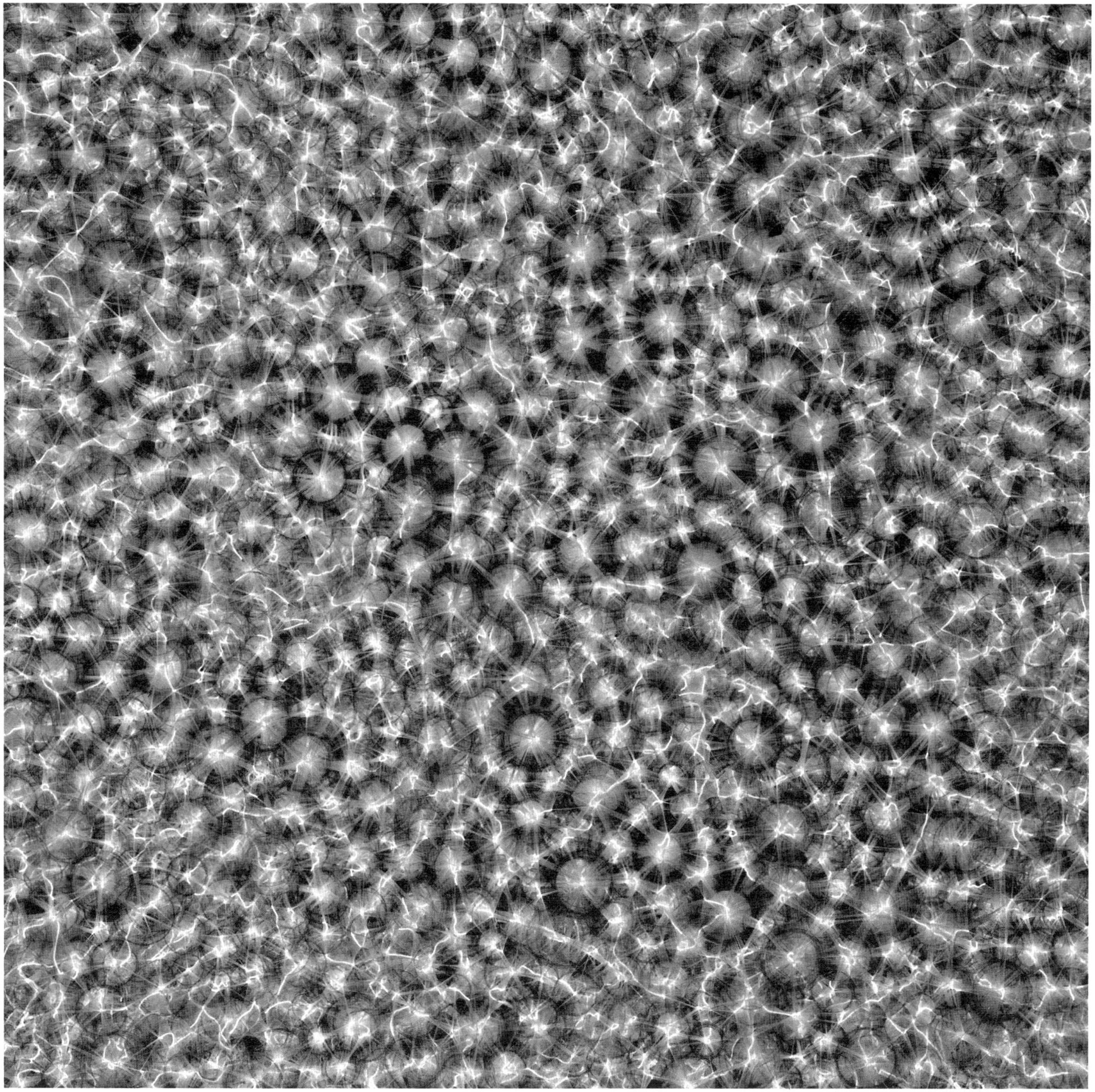

Process 7 (B), 2010
C print
Edition of 8 + 2 AP
50cm x 50cm

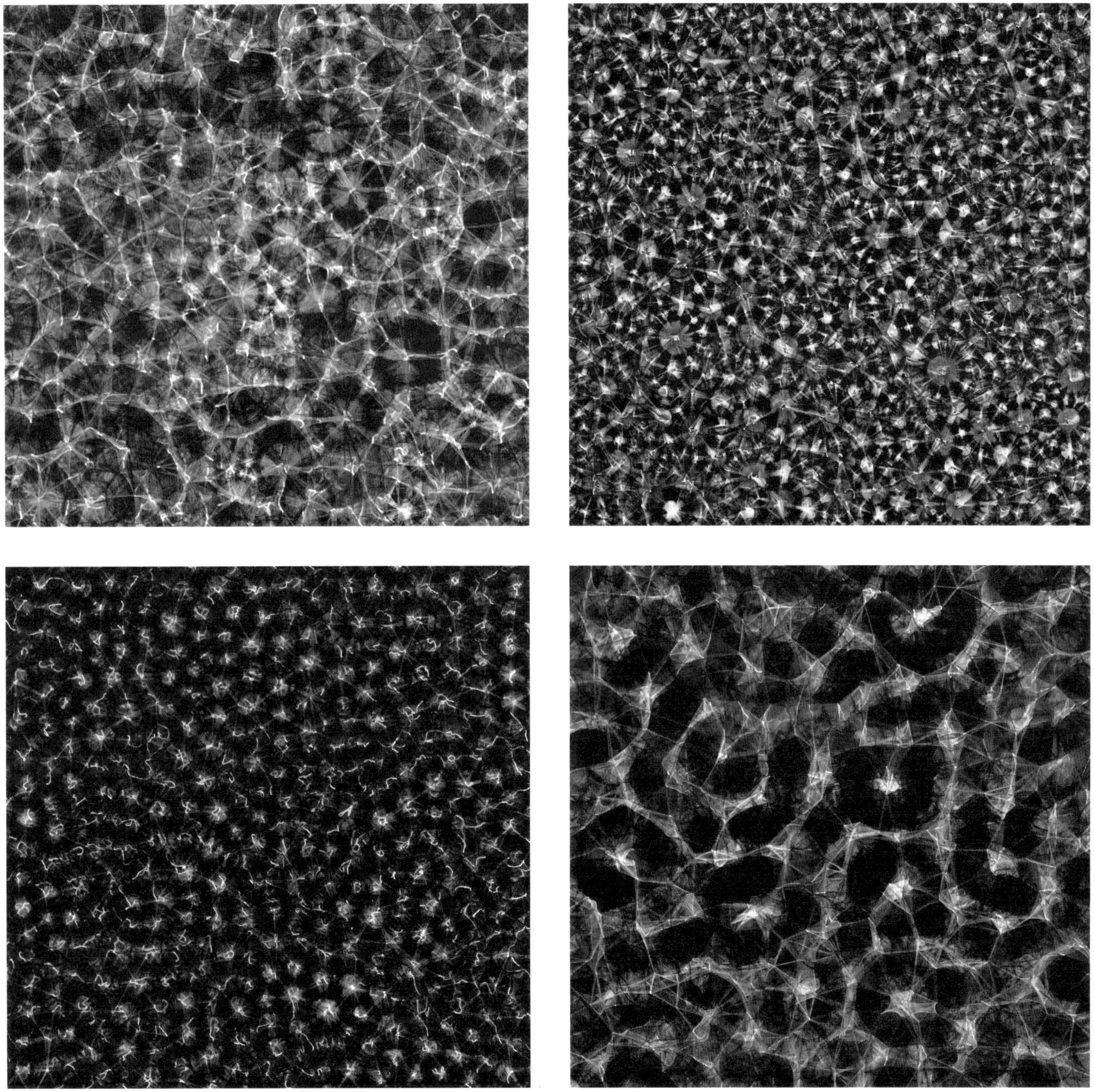

Images captured from different software interpretations of *Process 7*

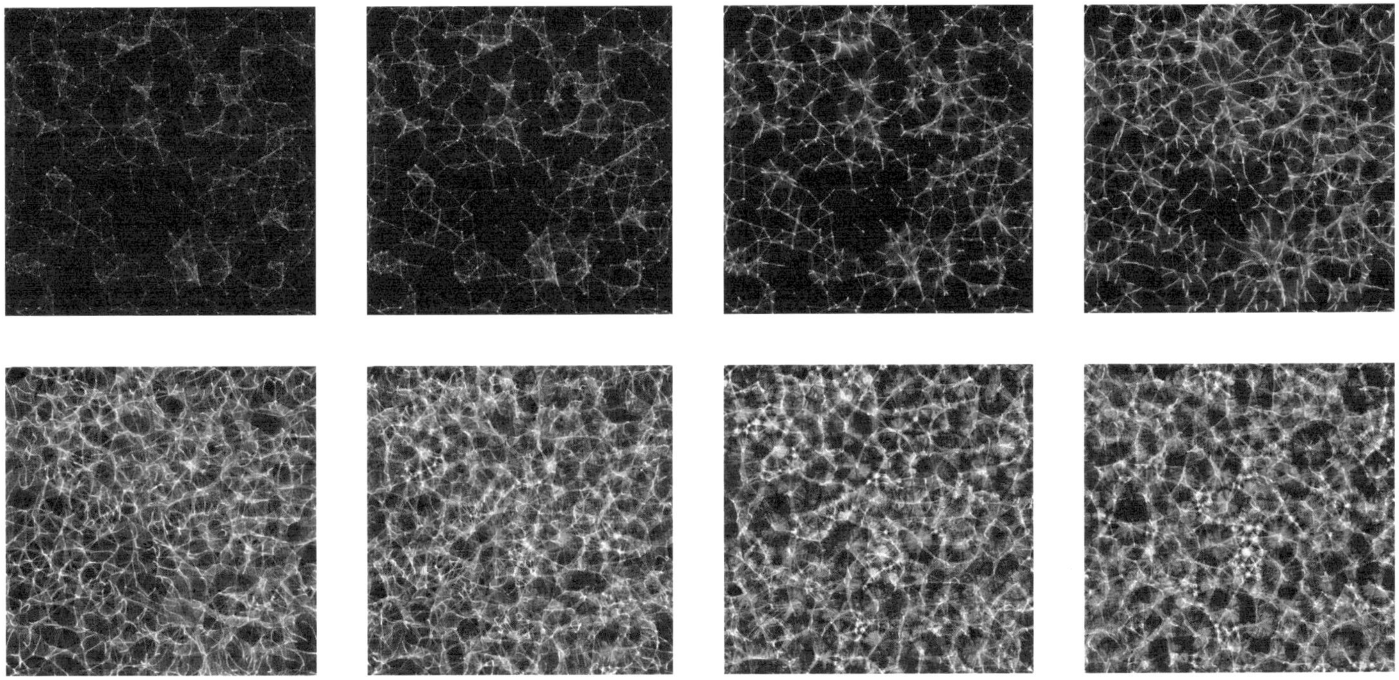

Image sequence from a software interpretation of *Process 7*

Process 8

A rectangular surface densely filled with instances of Element 2, each with a different size, speed, and direction. Display the intersections by drawing a circle at each point of contact. Set the size of each circle relative to the distance between the centers of the overlapping Elements. Draw the smallest possible circle as black and largest as white, with varying grays representing sizes in between.

Process 8, 2005
Text, unique custom
software, computer,
documentation prints
Dimensions variable

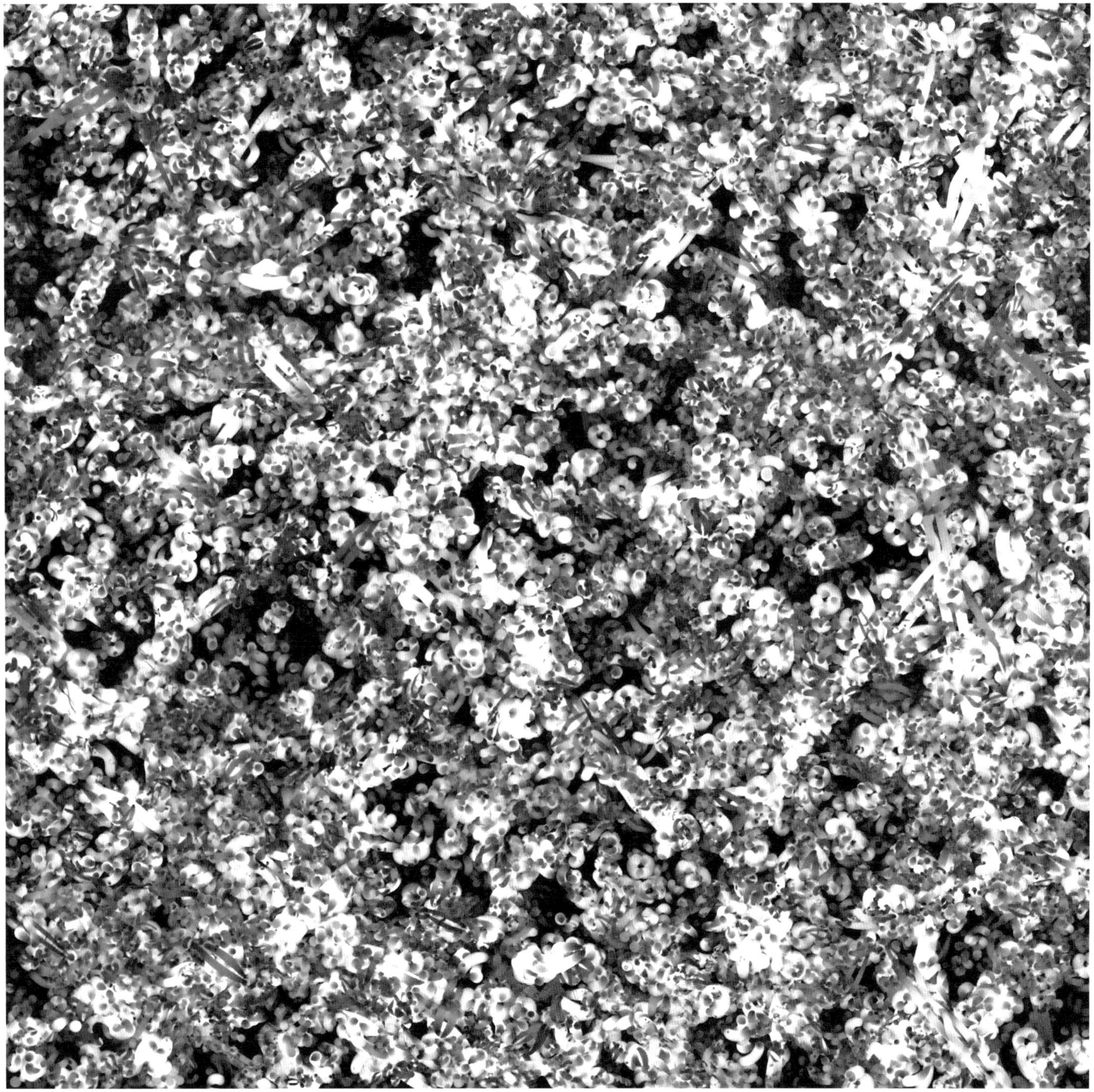

Process 8 (A), 2010
C print
Edition of 8 + 2 AP
50cm x 50cm

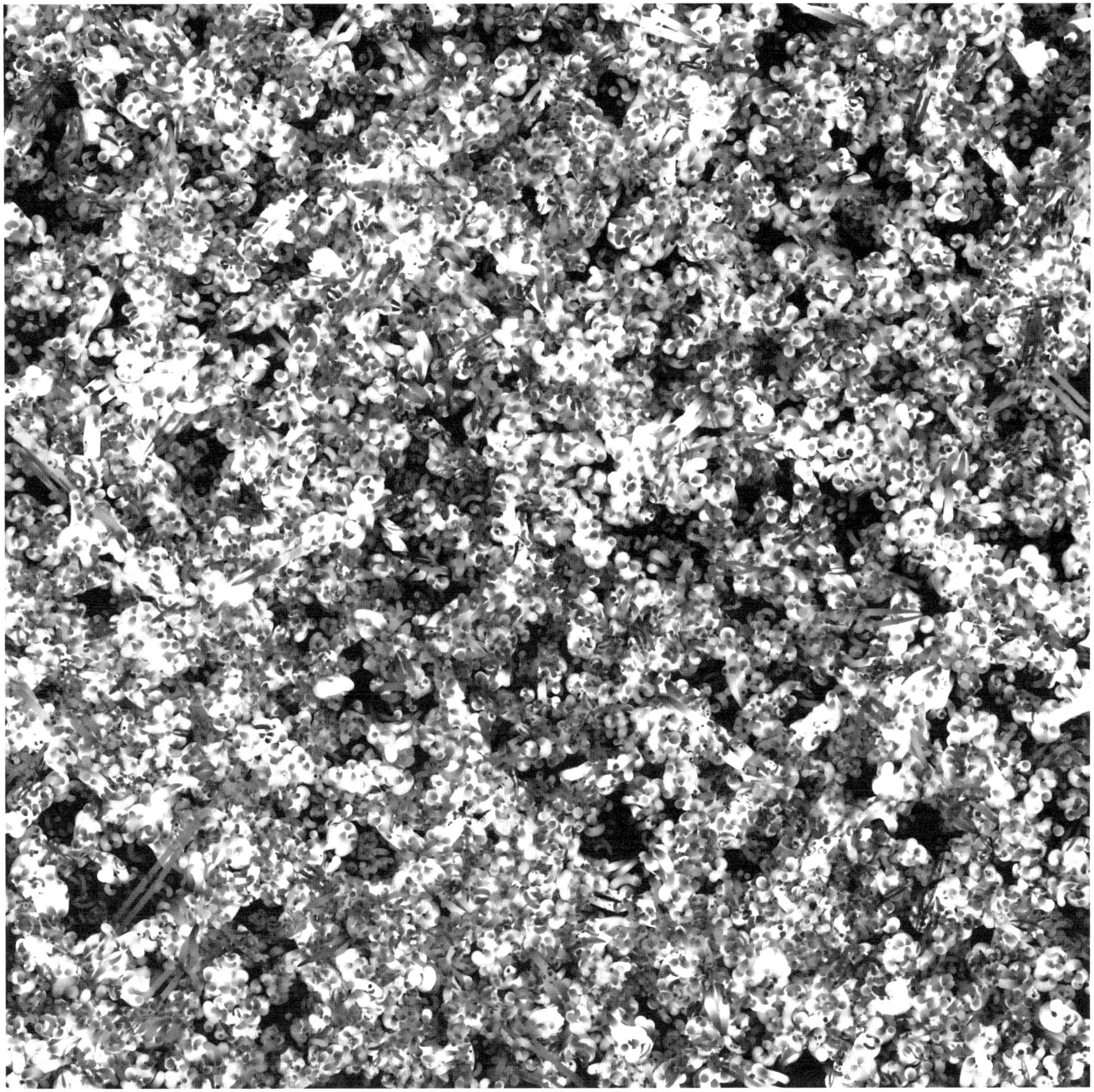

Process 8 (B), 2010
C print
Edition of 8 + 2 AP
50cm x 50cm

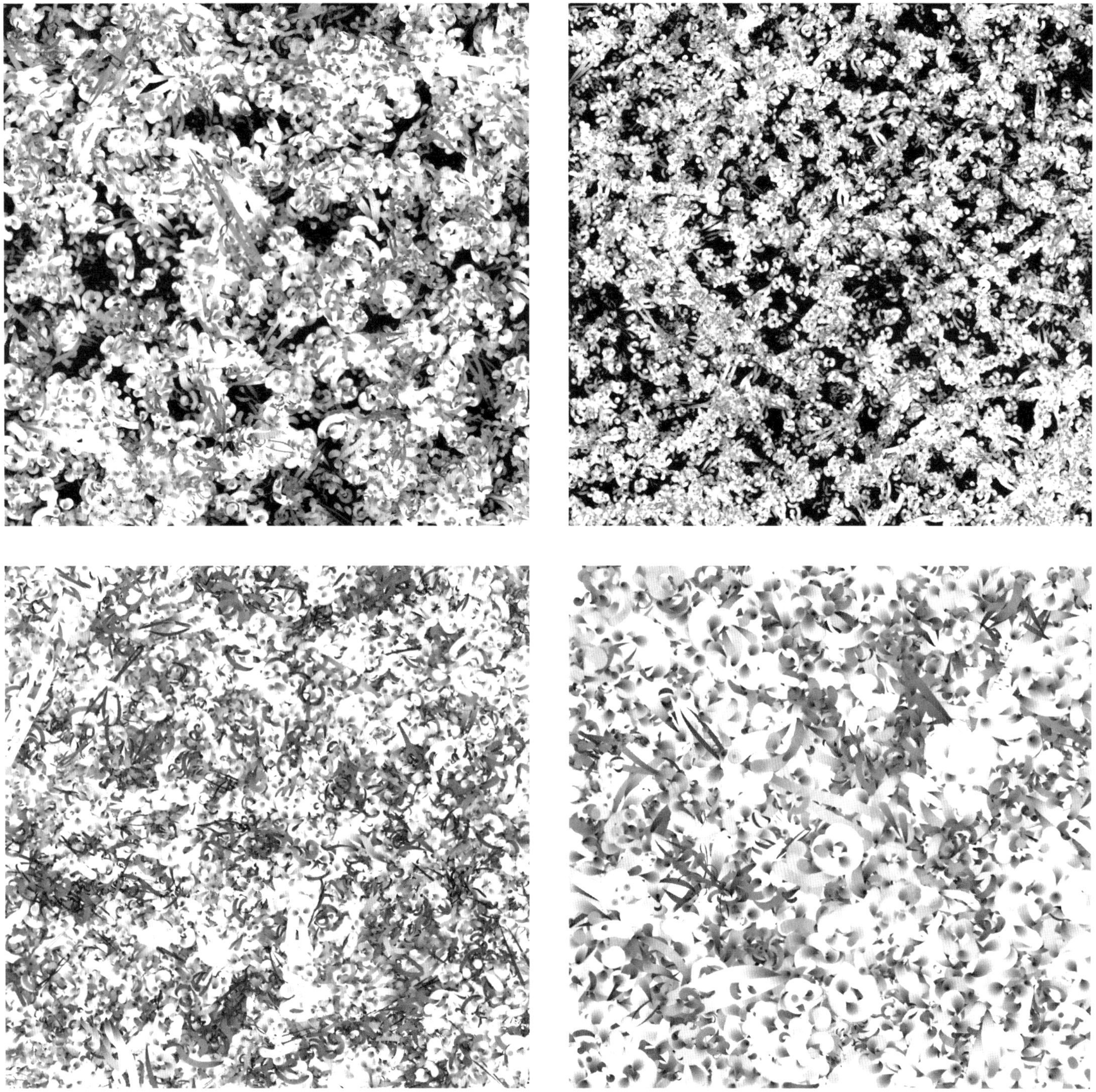

Images captured from different software interpretations of *Process 8*

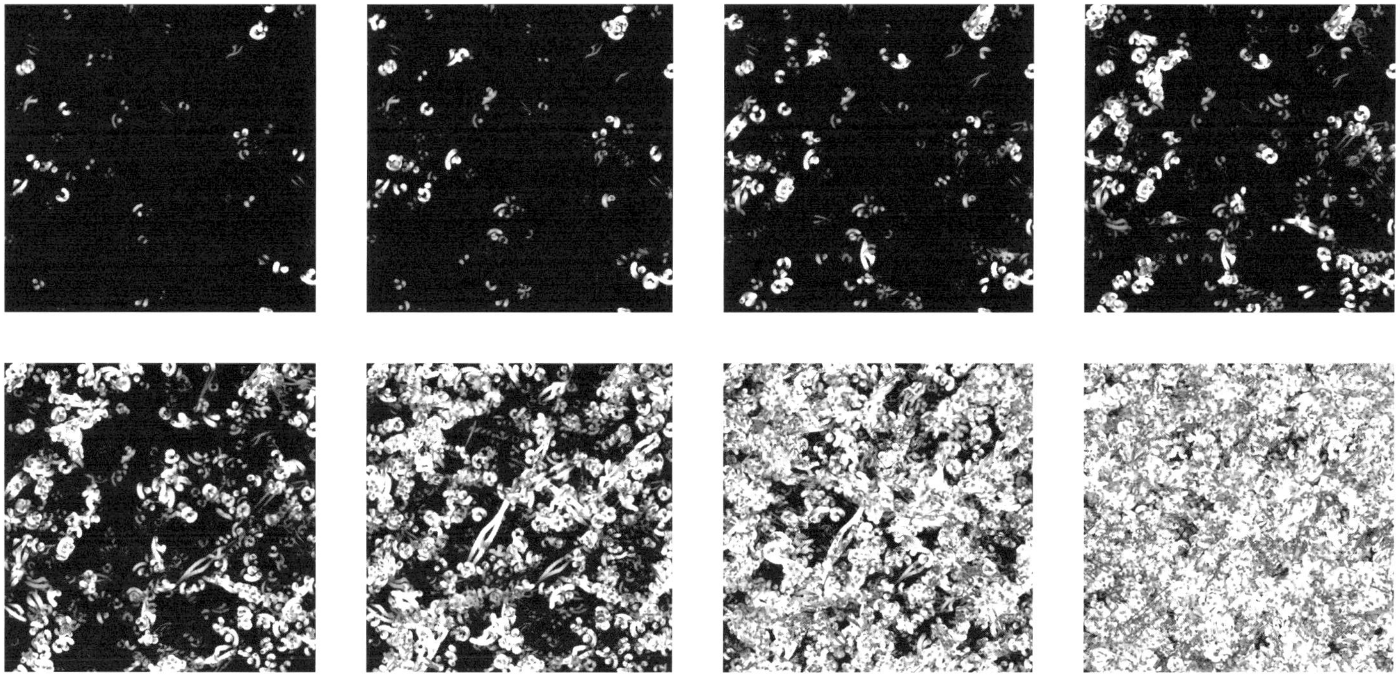

Image sequence from a software interpretation of *Process 8*

Process 9

Position three large circles on a rectangular surface. Set the center of each circle as the origin for a large group of Element 2. When an Element moves beyond the edge of its circle, return to the origin. Display the intersections by drawing a circle at each point of contact. Set the size of each circle relative to the distance between the centers of the overlapping Elements. Draw the smallest possible circle as white and largest as black, with varying grays representing sizes in between.

Process 9, 2005
Text, unique custom
software, computer,
documentation prints
Dimensions variable

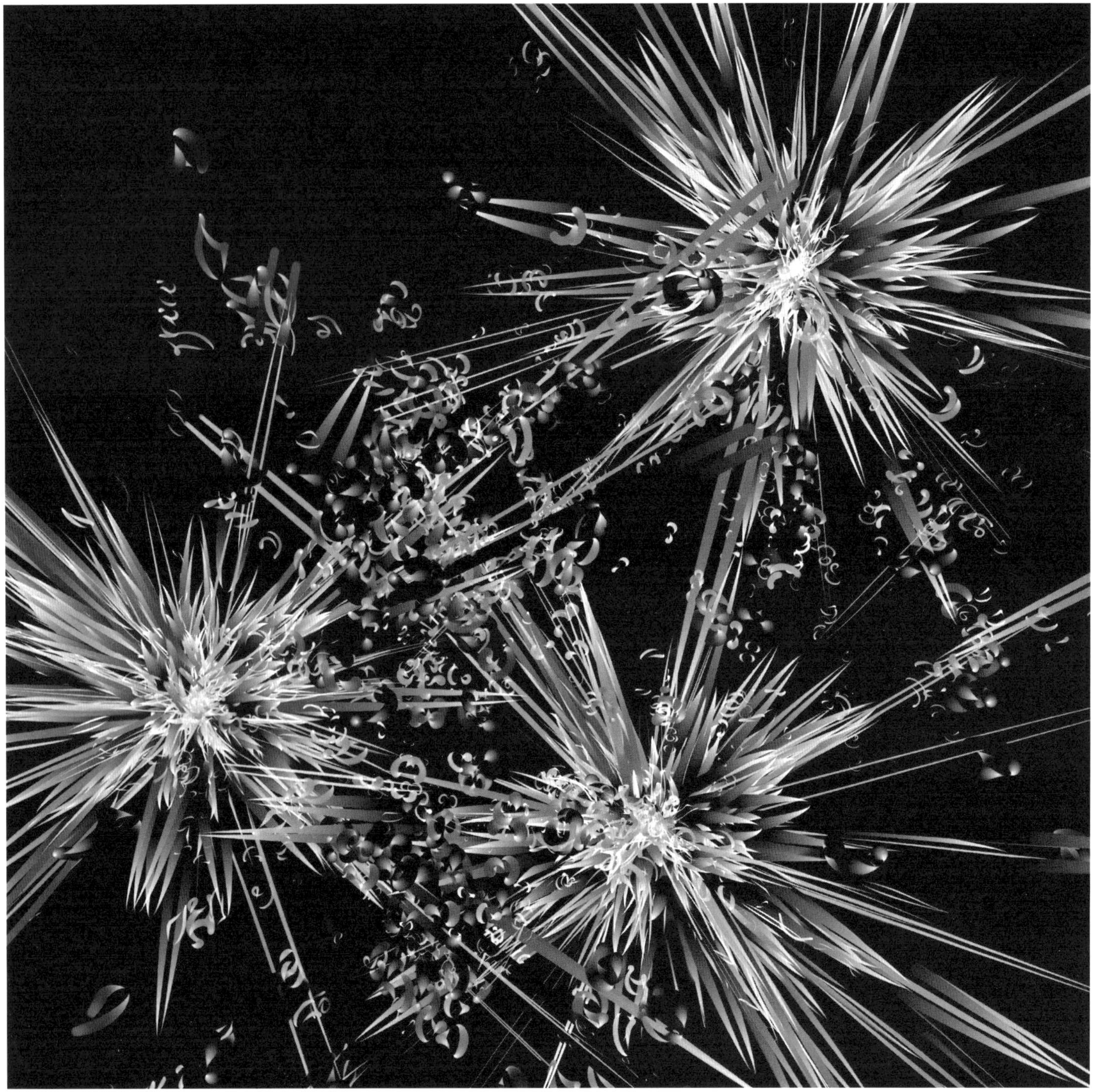

Process 9 (A), 2010
C print
Edition of 8 + 2 AP
50cm x 50cm

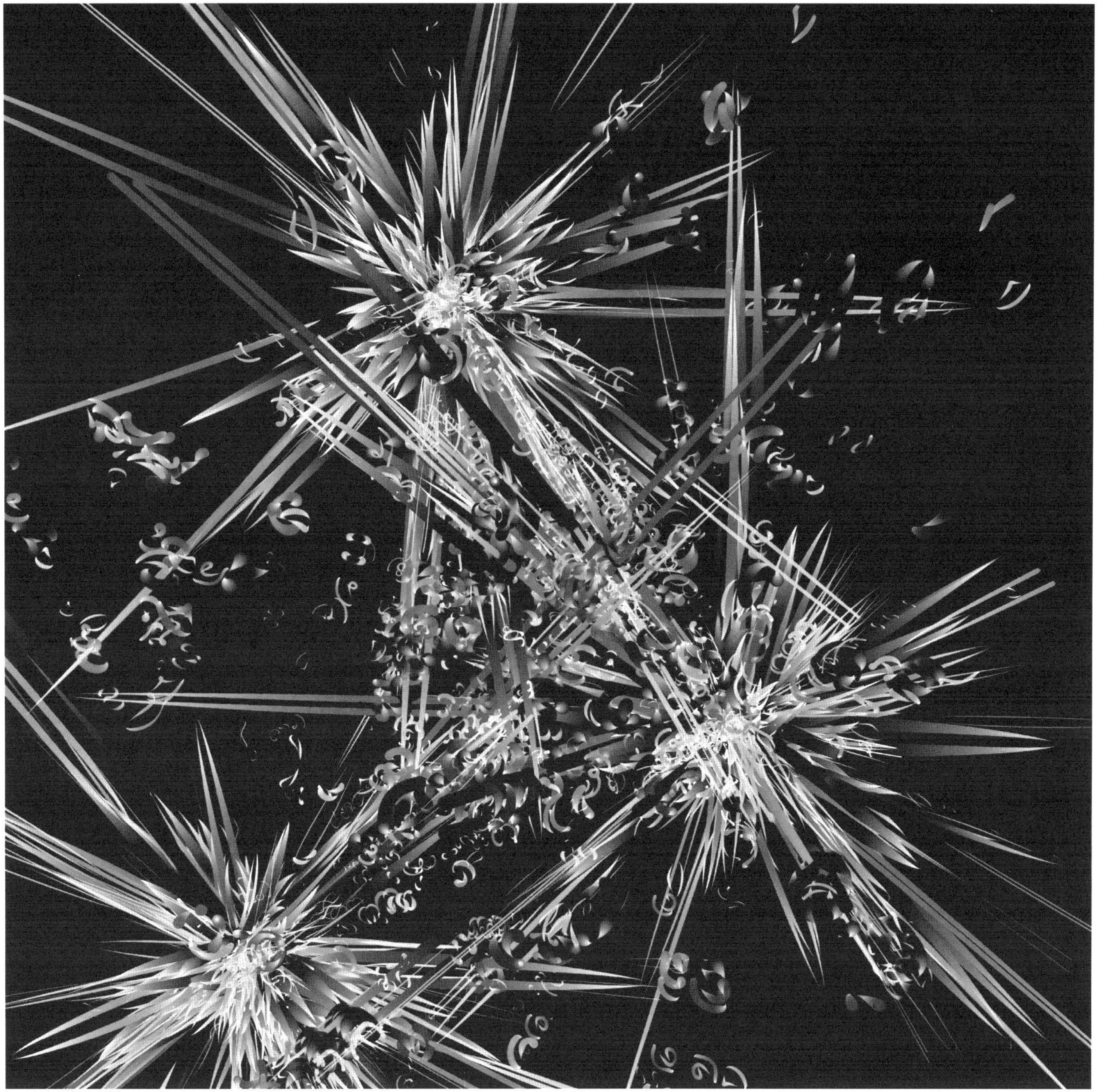

Process 9 (B), 2010
C print
Edition of 8 + 2 AP
50cm x 50cm

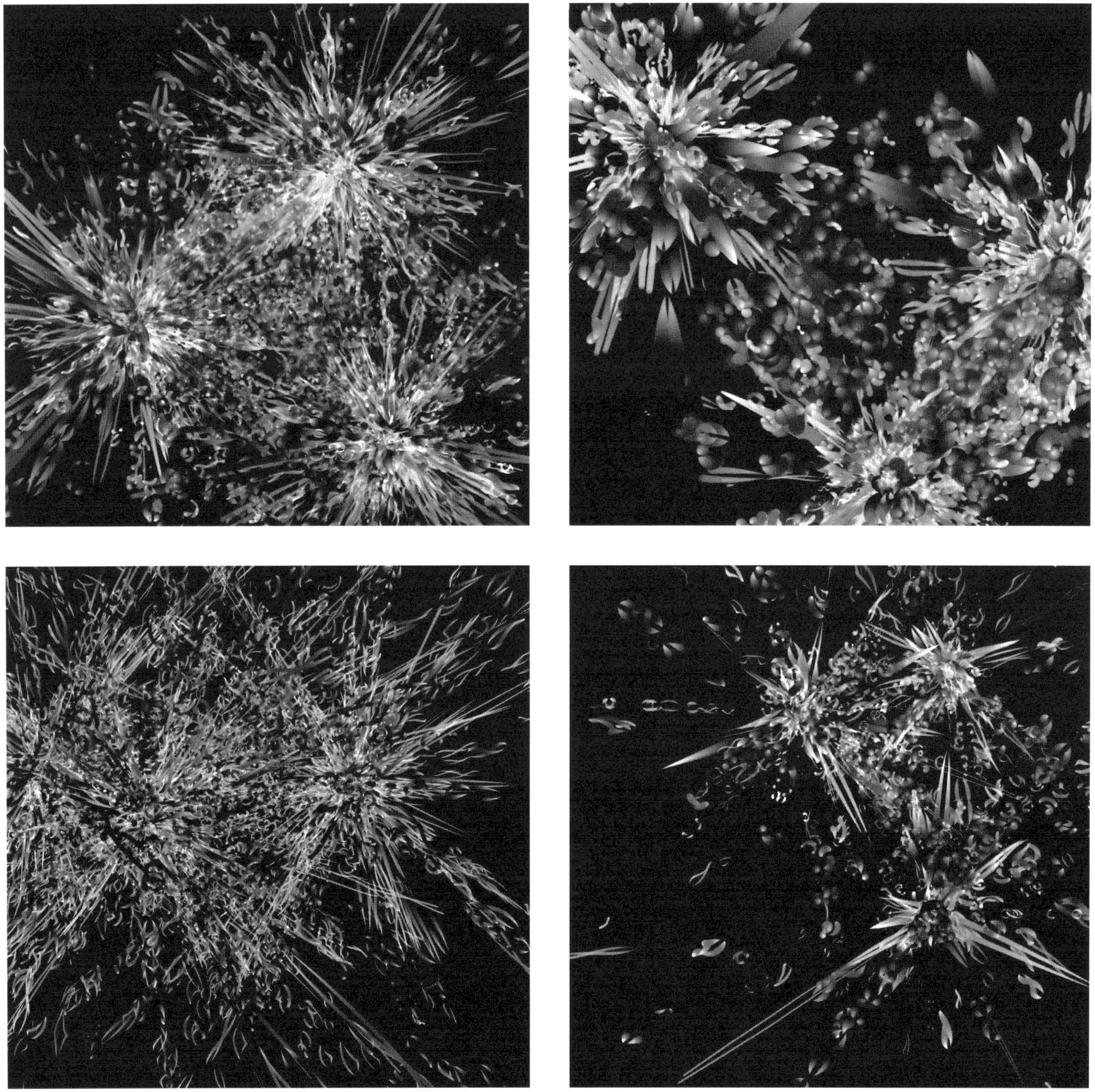

Images captured from different software interpretations of *Process 9*

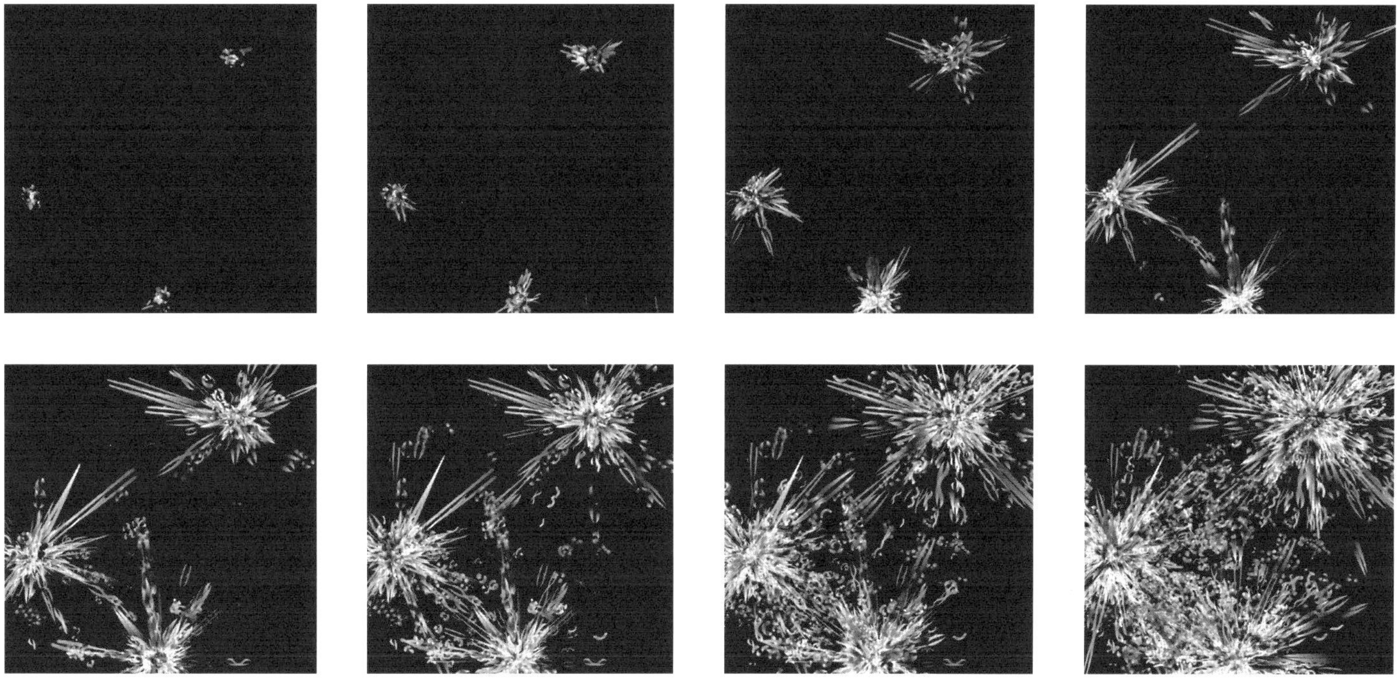

Image sequence from a software interpretation of *Process 9*

Process 10

Position a circle at the center of a rectangular surface. Set the center of the circle as the origin for a large group of Element 1. When an Element moves beyond the edge of its circle, return to the origin. Draw a line from the centers of Elements that are touching. Set the value of the shortest possible line to black and the longest to white, with varying grays representing values in between.

Process 10, 2005
Text, unique custom software, computer, documentation prints
Dimensions variable

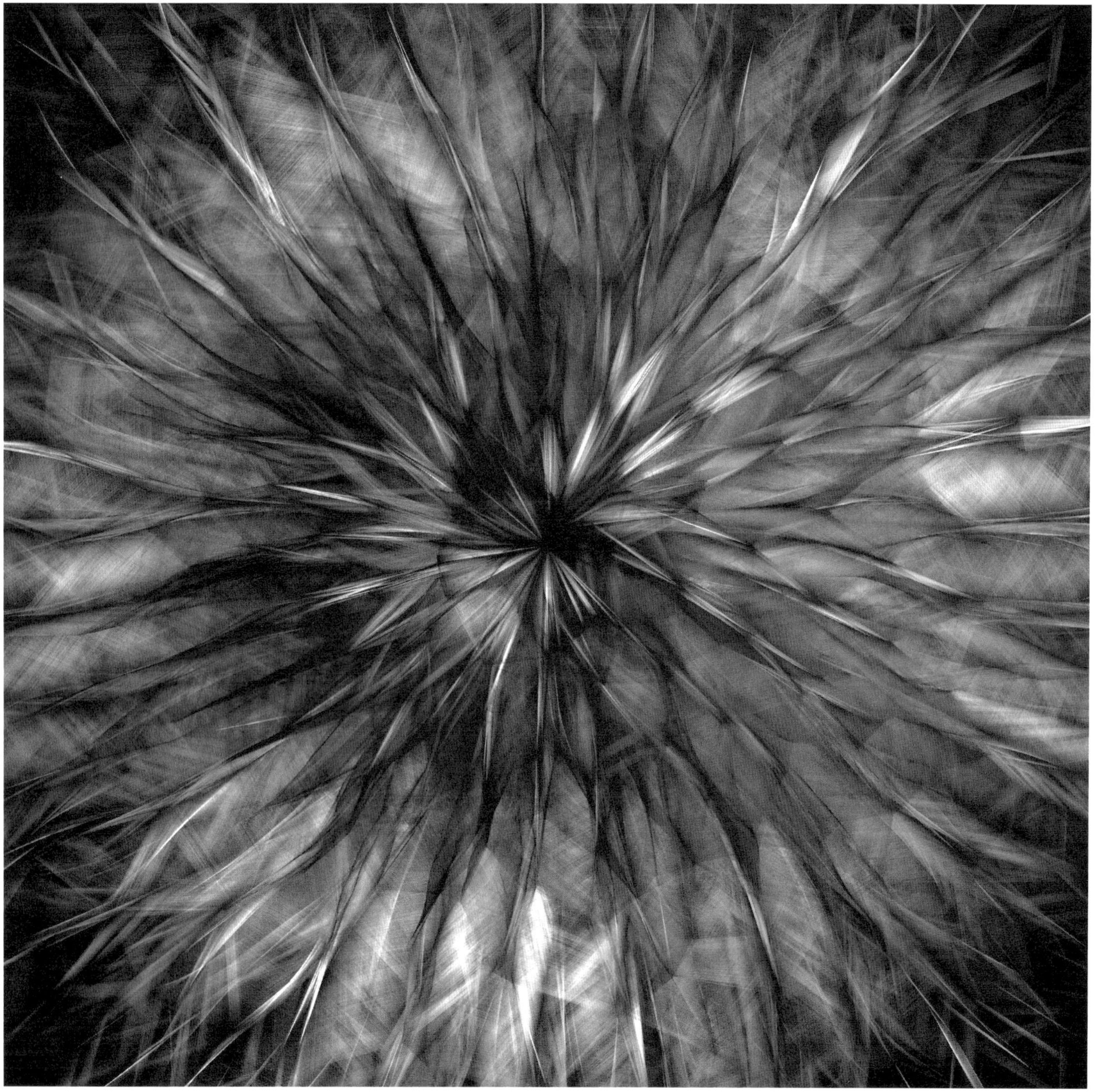

Process 10 (A), 2010
C print
Edition of 8 + 2 AP
50cm x 50cm

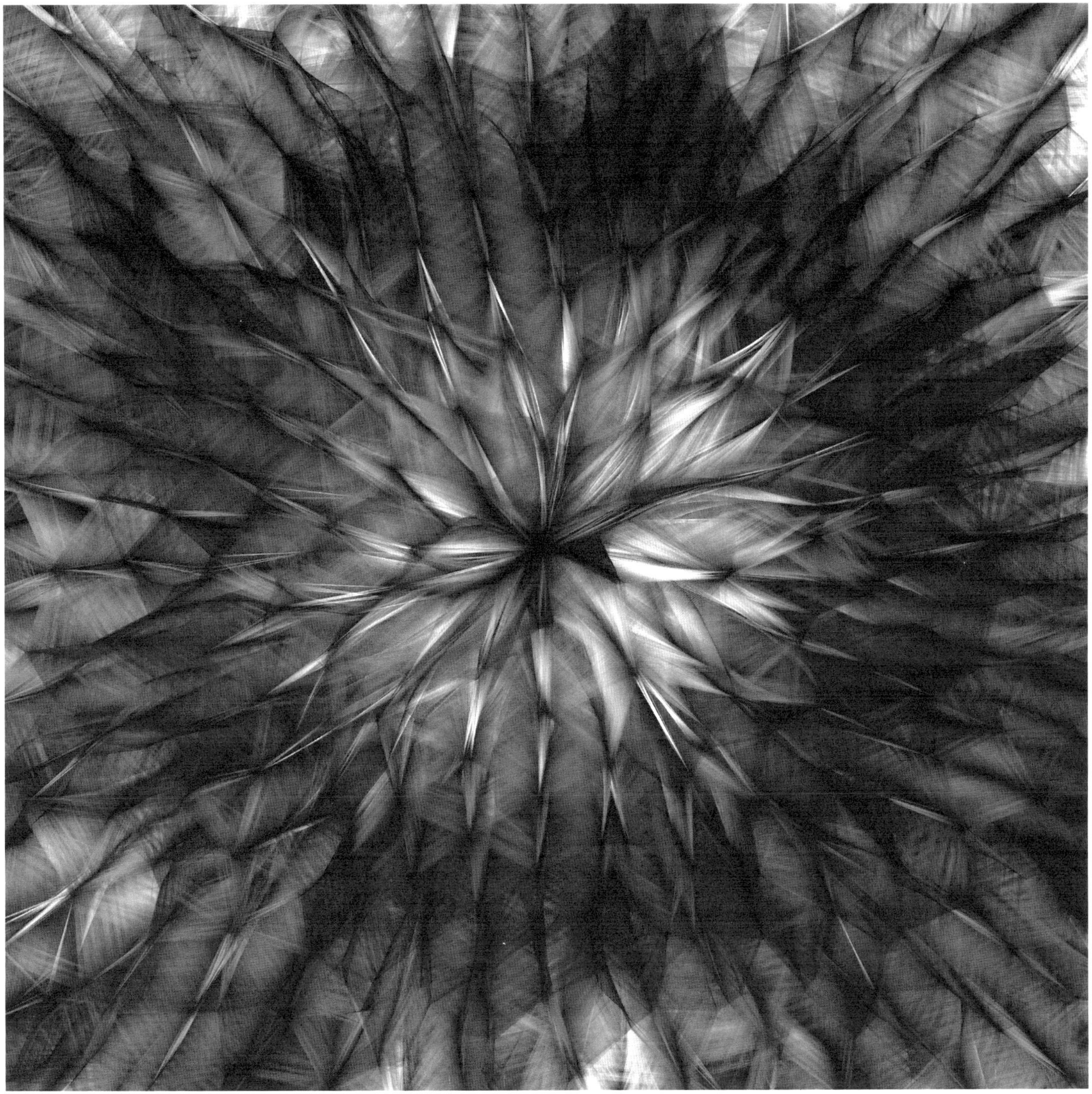

Process 10 (B), 2010
C print
Edition of 8 + 2 AP
50cm x 50cm

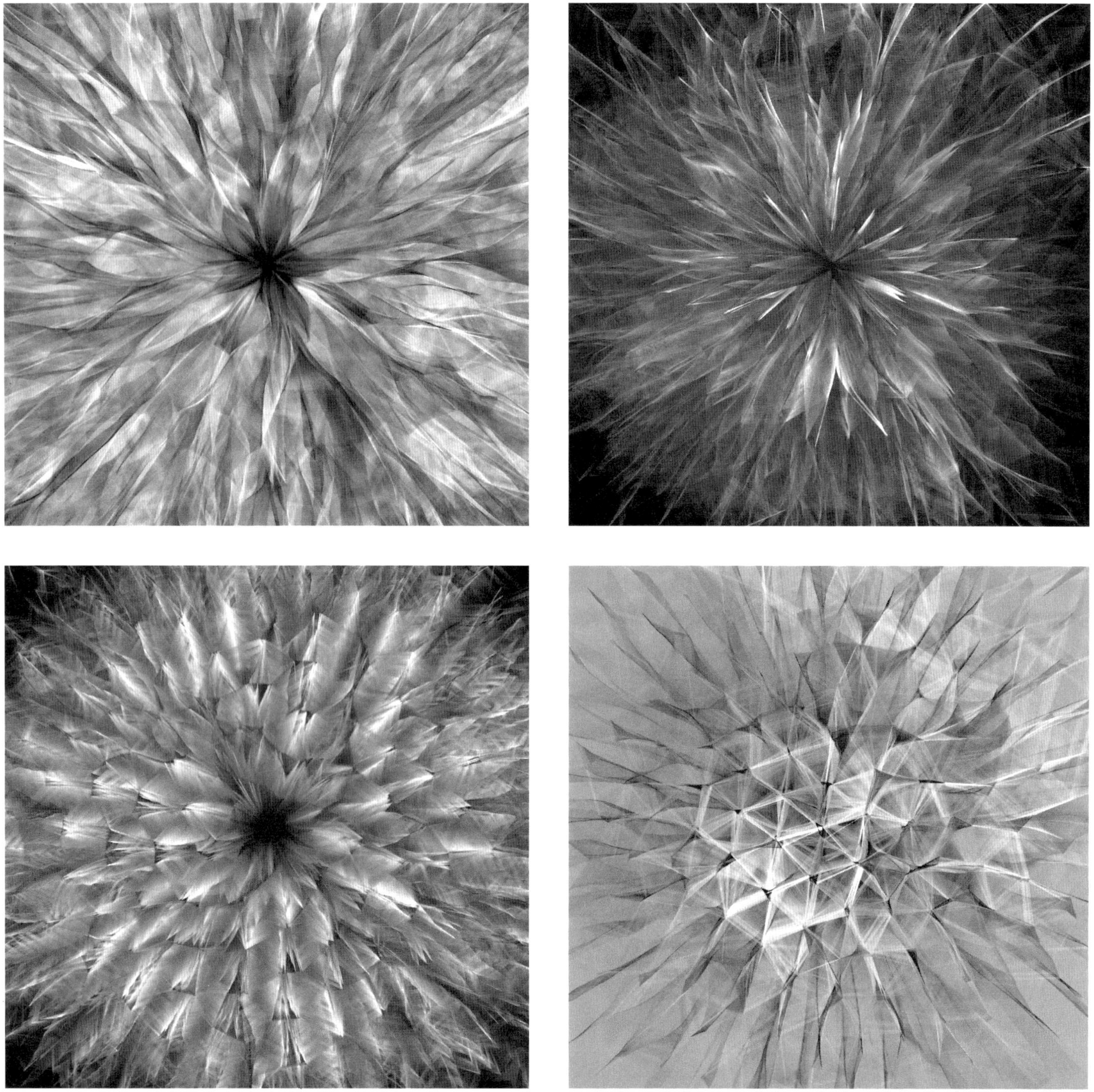

Images captured from different software interpretations of *Process 10*

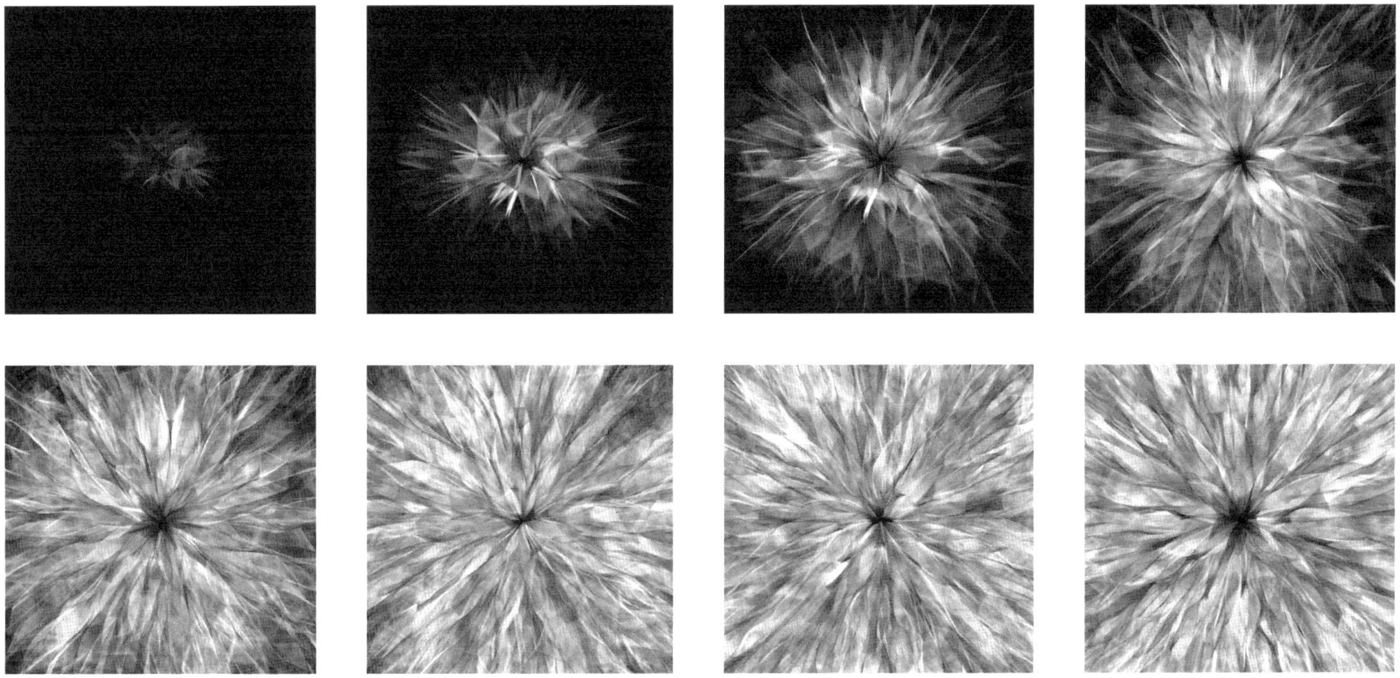

Image sequence
from a software
interpretation
of *Process 10*

Process 11

A rectangular surface filled with instances of Element 2, each with a different size, speed, and direction. Display the intersections by drawing a circle at each point of contact. Set the size of one circle to be relative to the distance between the centers of the overlapping Elements and make the other circle tiny. Draw the smallest possible circle as white and largest as black, with varying grays representing sizes in between.

Process 11, 2006
Text, unique custom software, computer, documentation prints
Dimensions variable

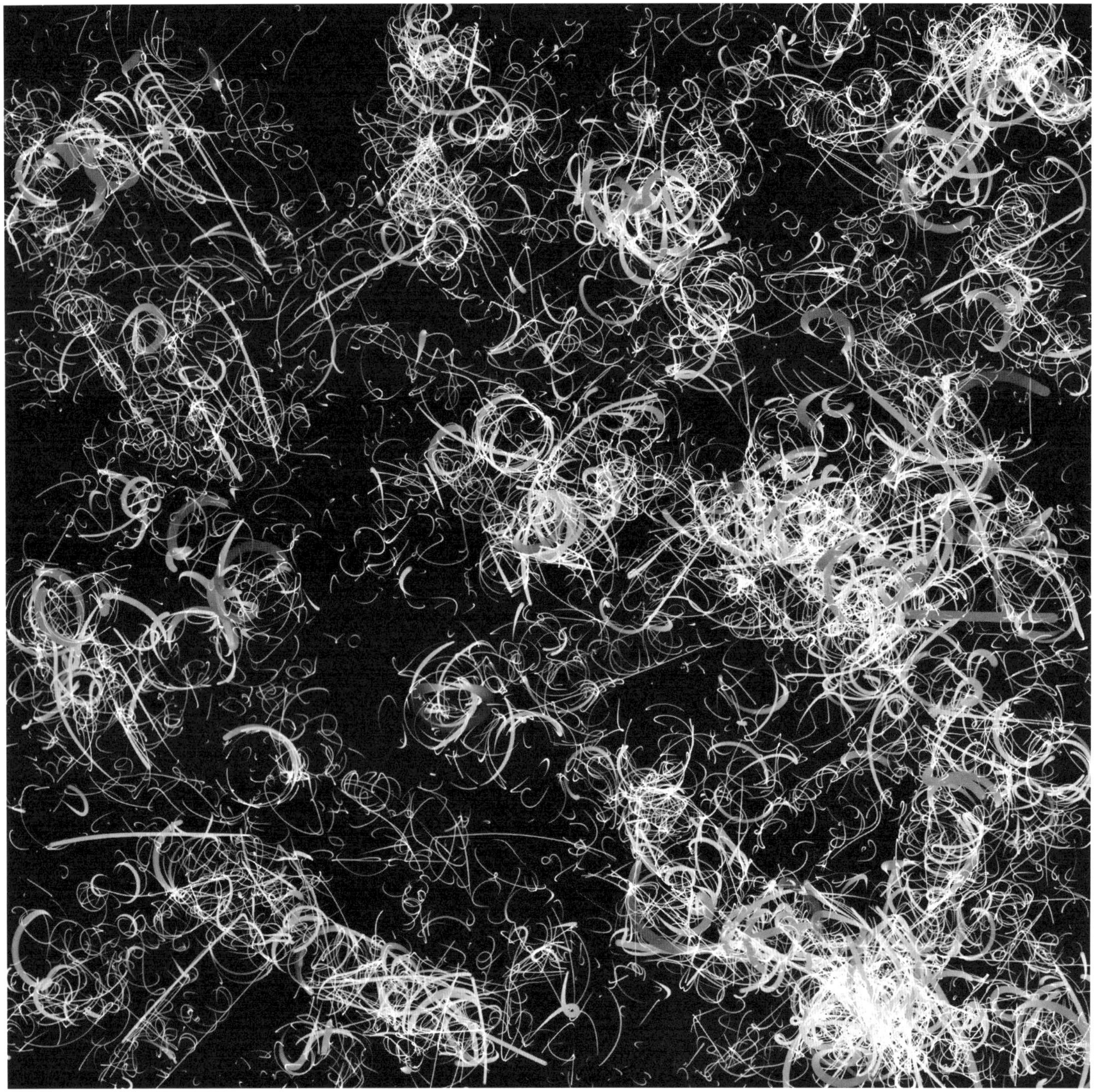

Process 11 (A), 2010
C print
Edition of 8 + 2 AP
50cm x 50cm

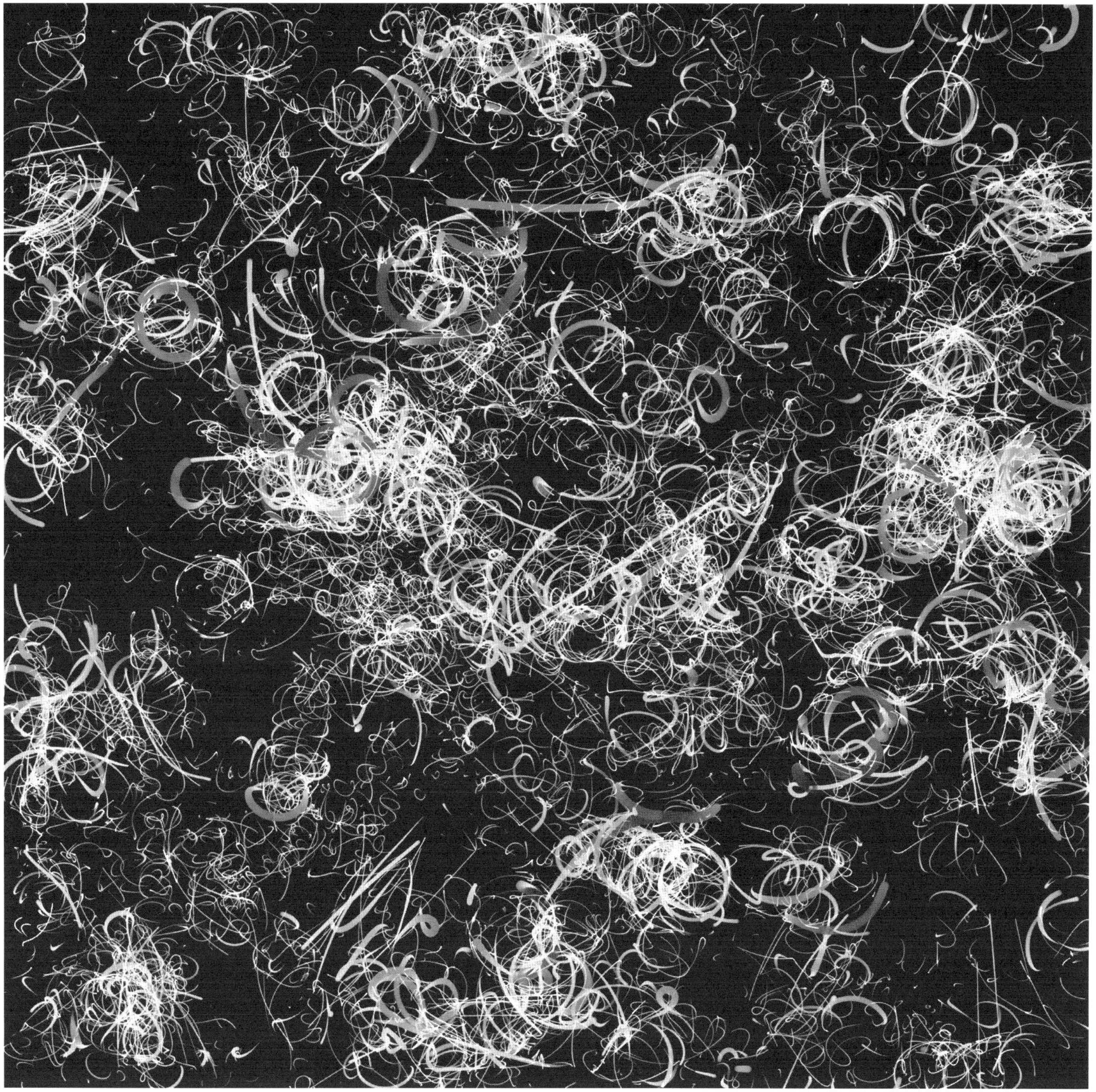

Process 11 (B), 2010
C print
Edition of 8 + 2 AP
50cm x 50cm

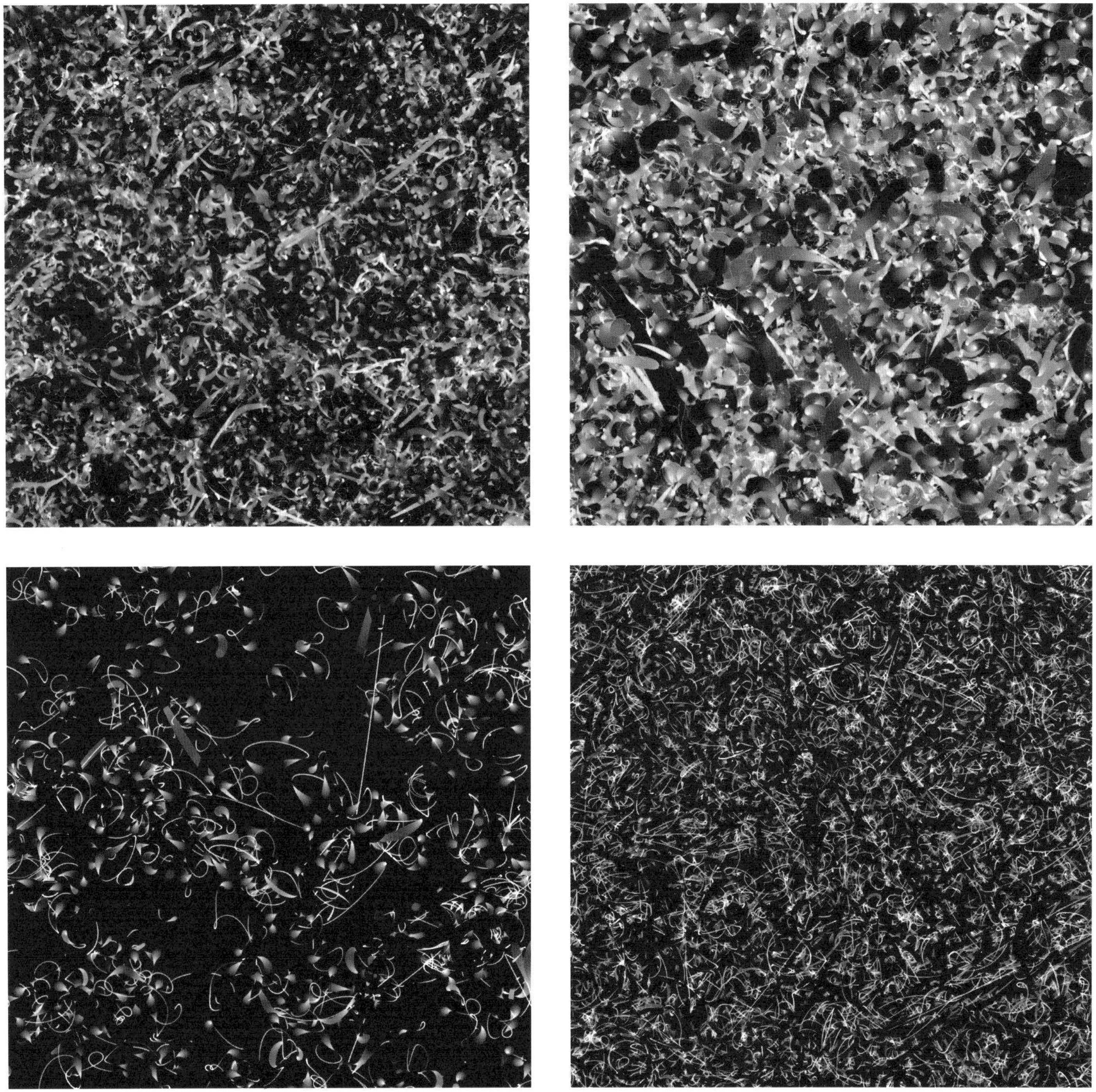

Images captured from different software interpretations of *Process 11*

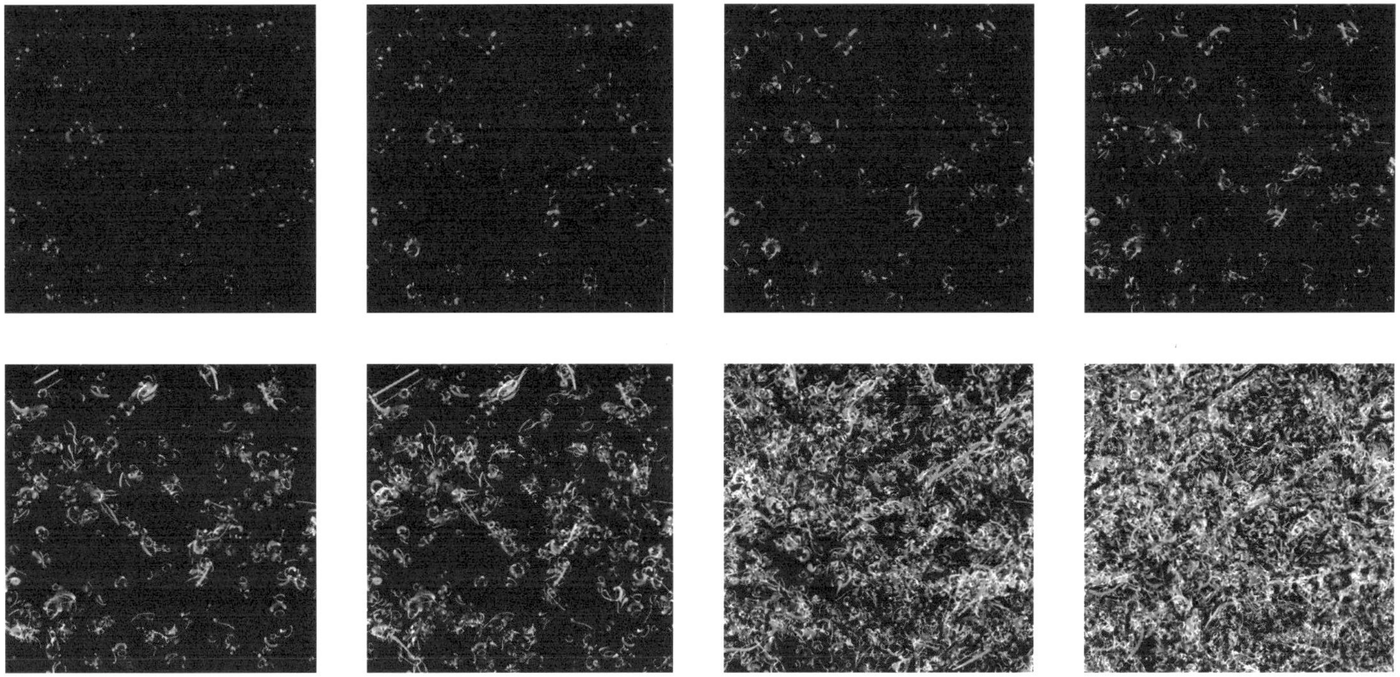

Image sequence
from a software
interpretation
of *Process 11*

Process 12

A rectangular surface filled with instances of Element 3, each with a different size and gray value. Draw a dot at the center of each line. Draw a quadrilateral connecting the endpoints of each pair of Elements that are touching. Increase the opacity of the dot and quadrilateral while the Elements are touching and decrease while they are not.

Process 12, 2006
Text, unique custom software, computer, documentation prints
Dimensions variable

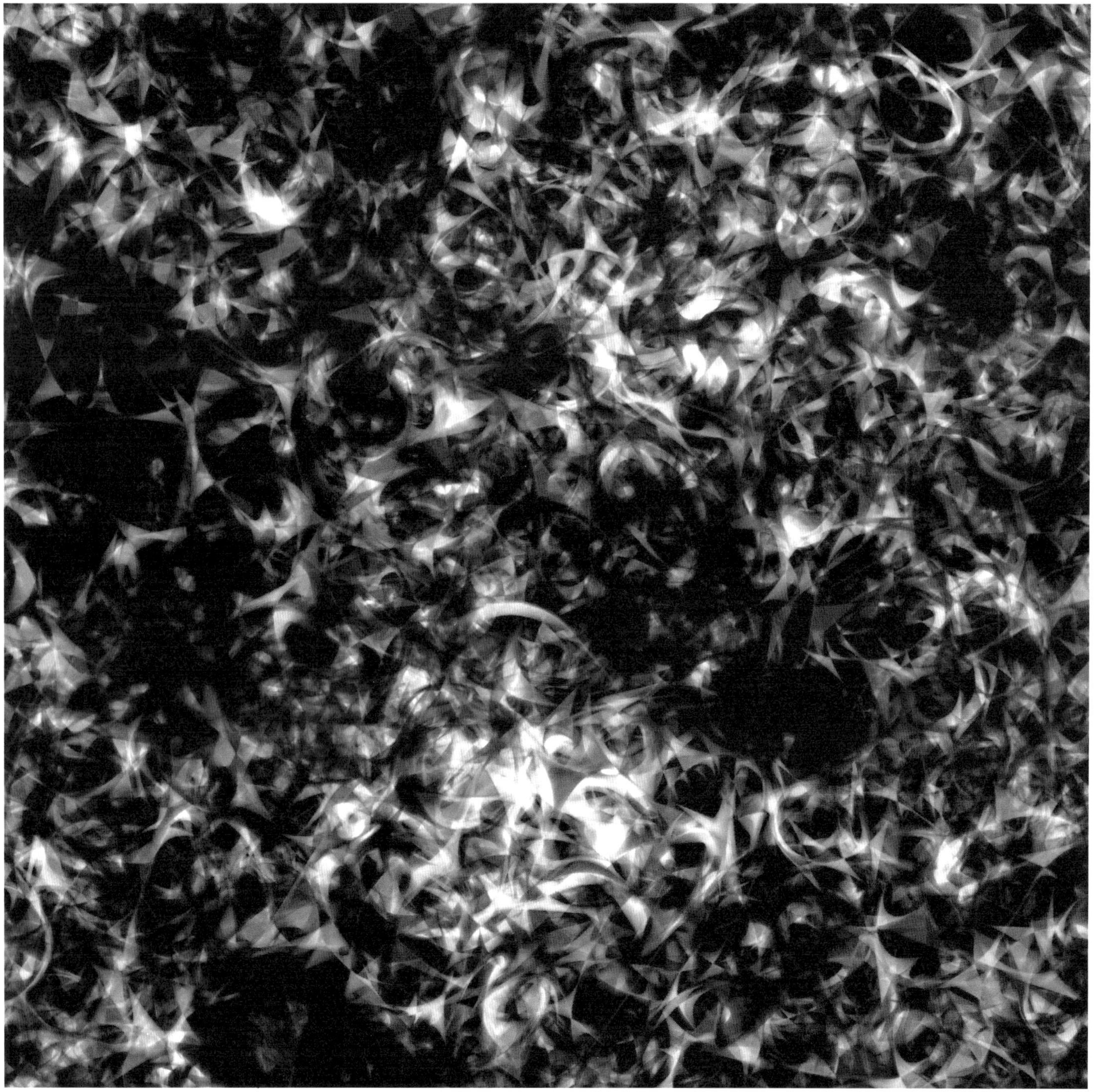

Process 12 (A), 2010
C print
Edition of 8 + 2 AP
50cm x 50cm

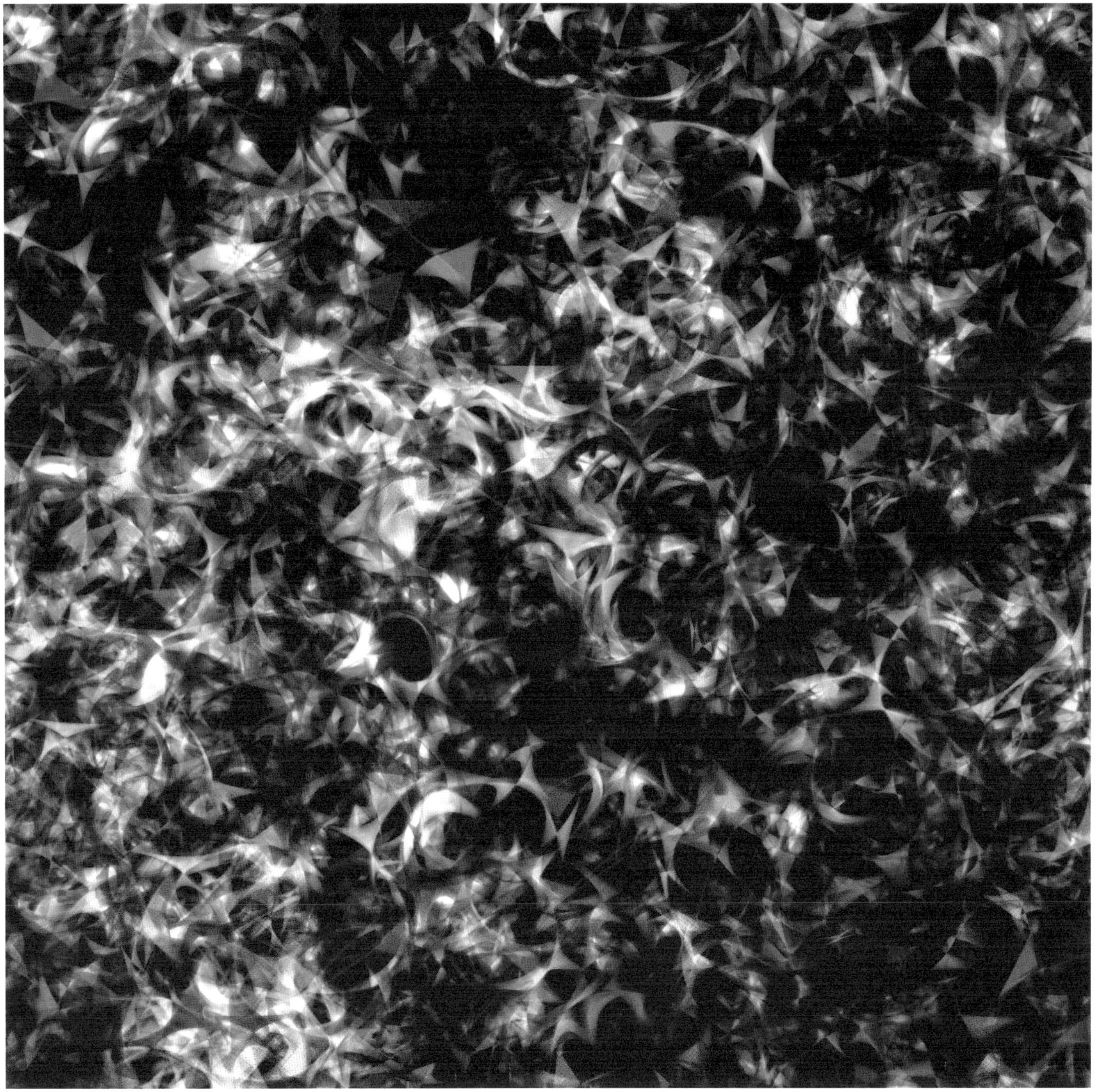

Process 12 (B), 2010
C print
Edition of 8 + 2 AP
50cm x 50cm

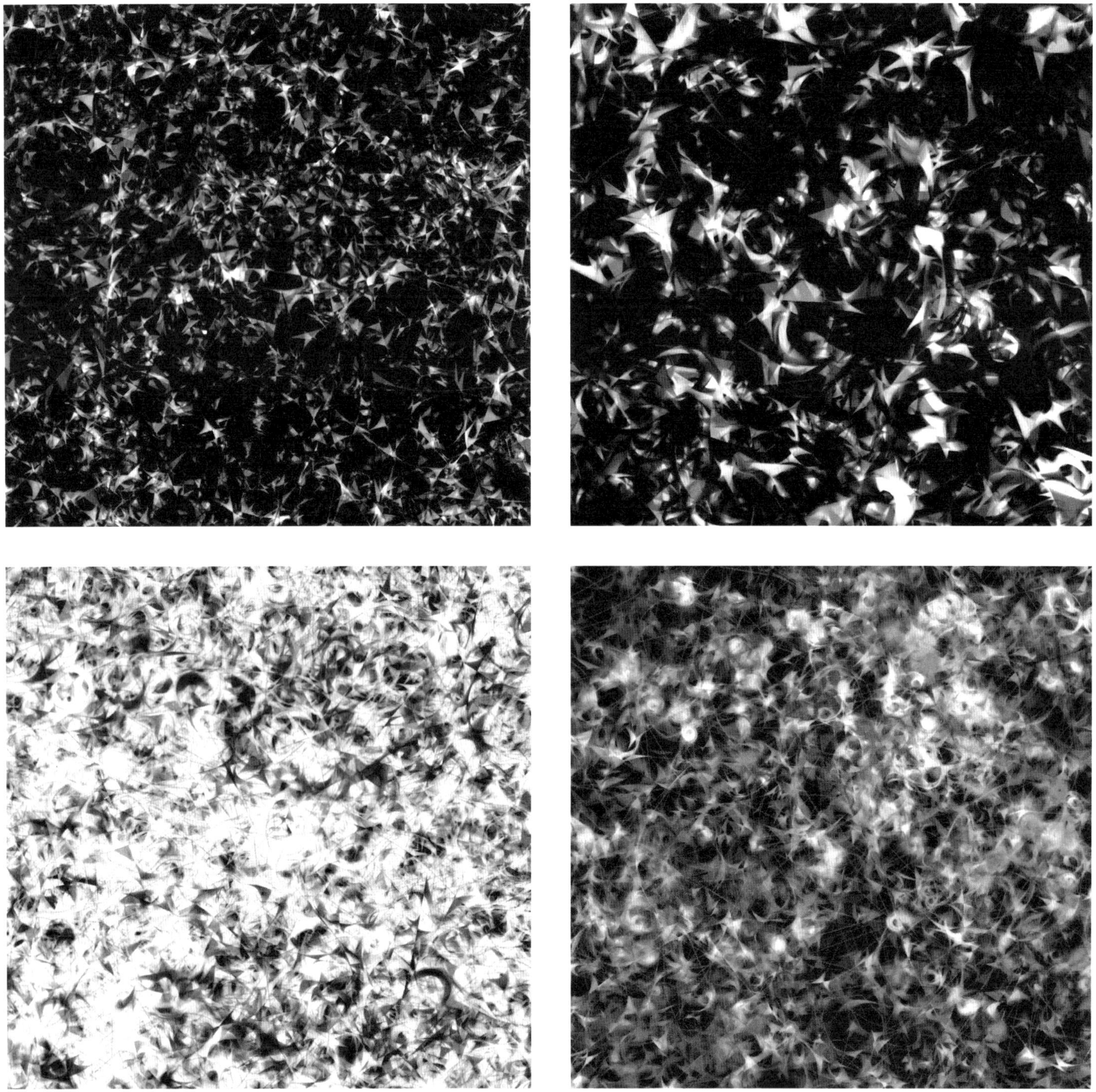

Images captured from different software interpretations of *Process 12*

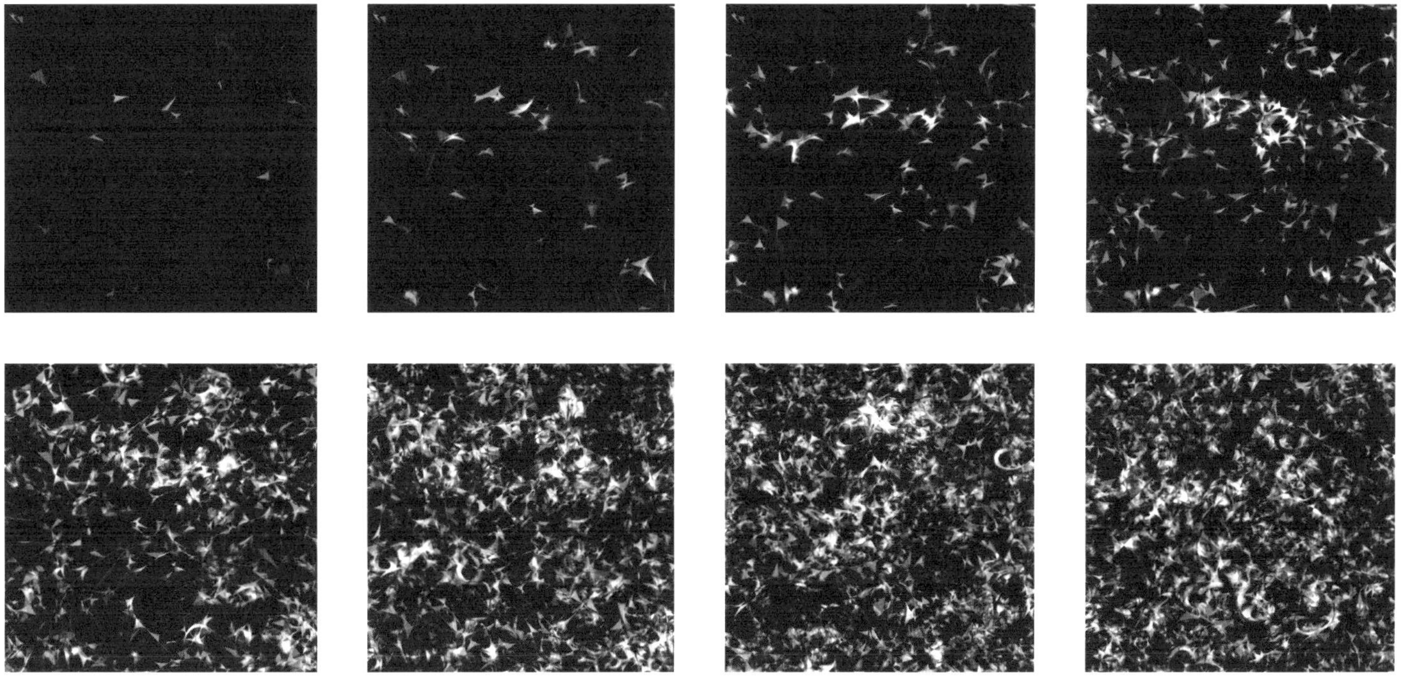

Image sequence
from a software
interpretation
of *Process 12*

Process 13

Bisect a rectangular surface and define the dividing line as the origin for a large group of Element 1. When each Element moves beyond the surface, move its position back to the origin. Draw a line from the centers of Elements that are touching. Set the value of the shortest possible line to black and the longest to white, with varying grays representing values in between.

Process 13, 2010
Text, unique custom software, computer, documentation prints
Dimensions variable

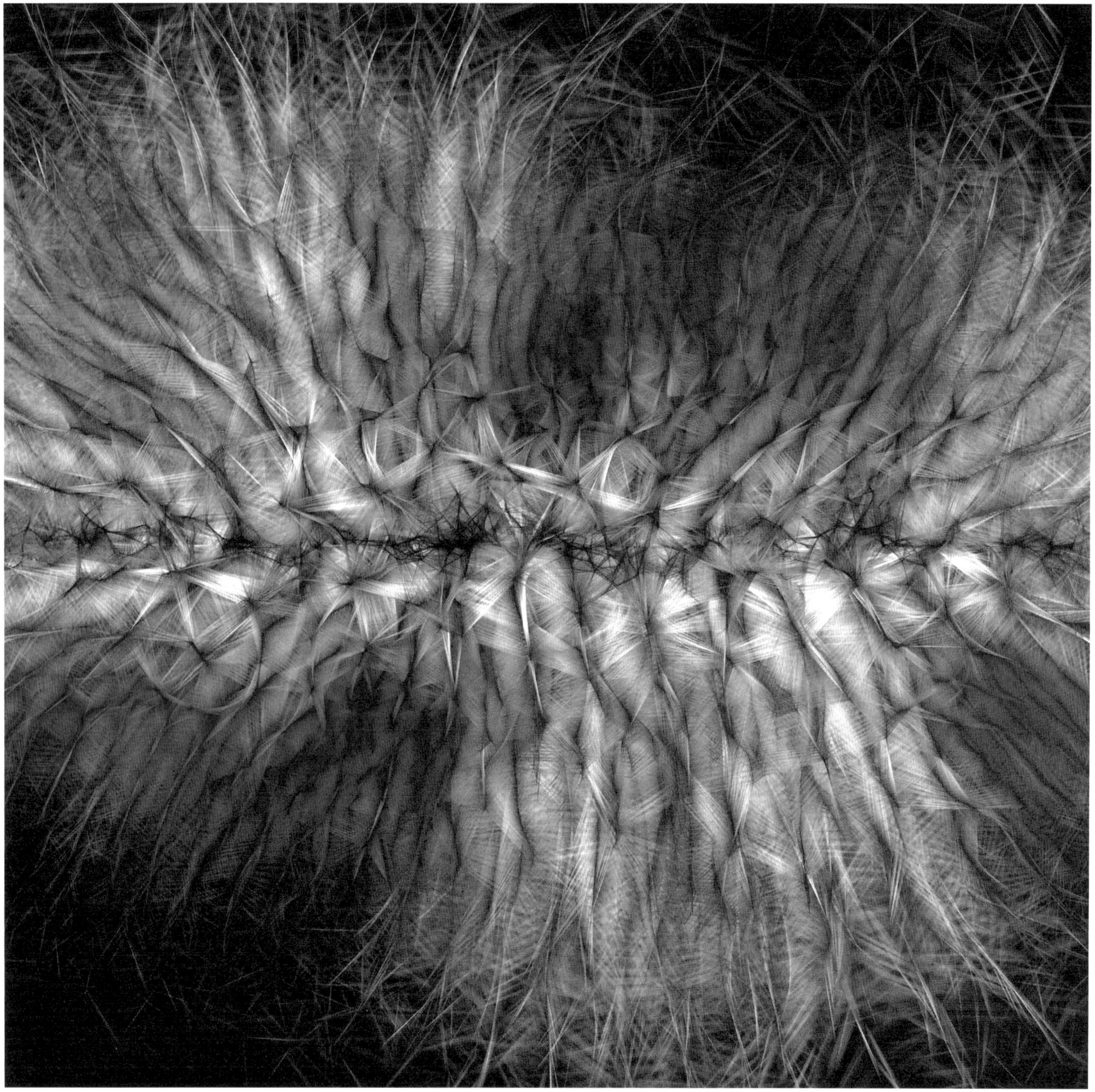

Process 13 (A), 2010
C print
Edition of 8 + 2 AP
50cm x 50cm

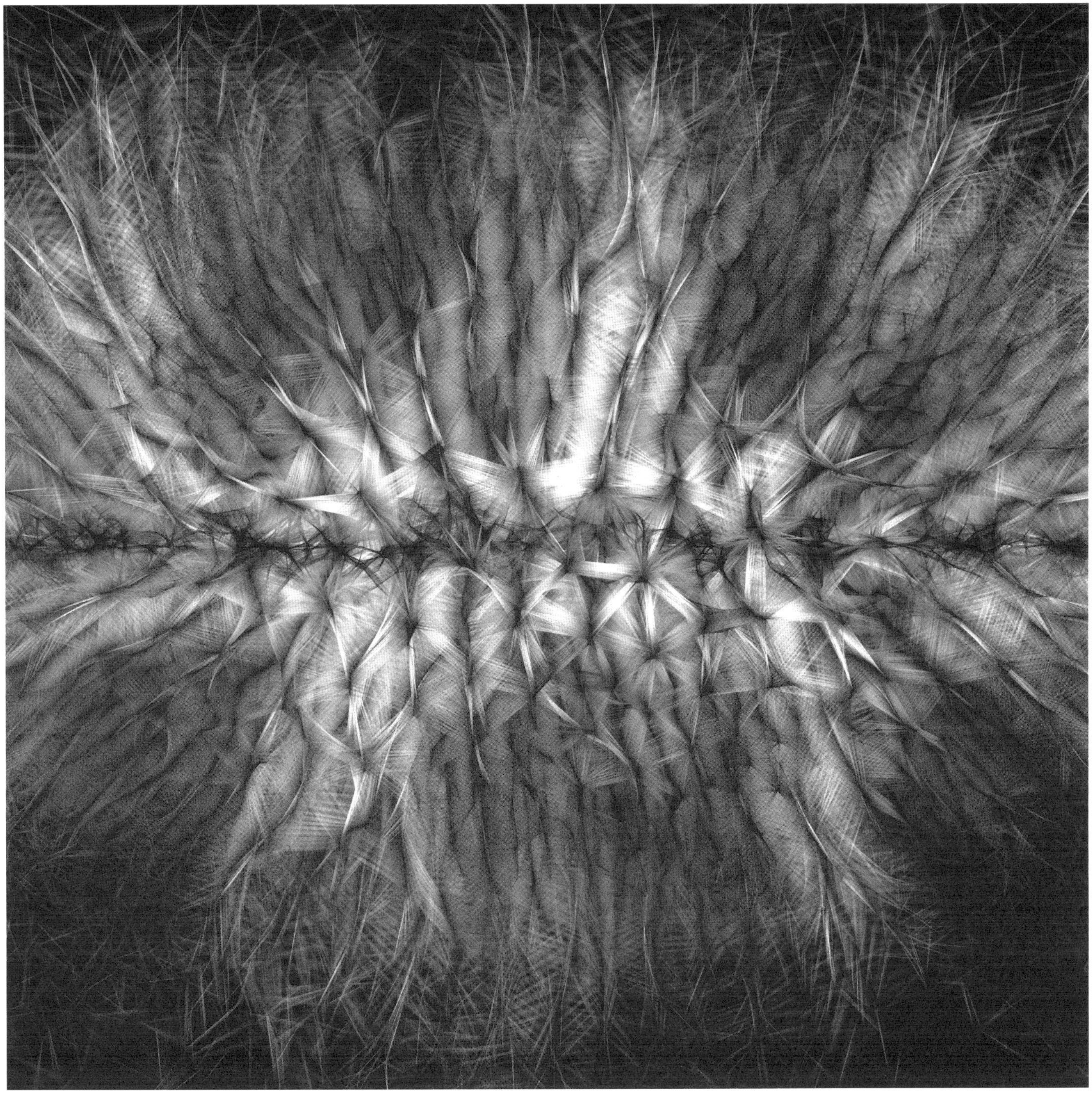

Process 13 (B), 2010
C print
Edition of 8 + 2 AP
50cm x 50cm

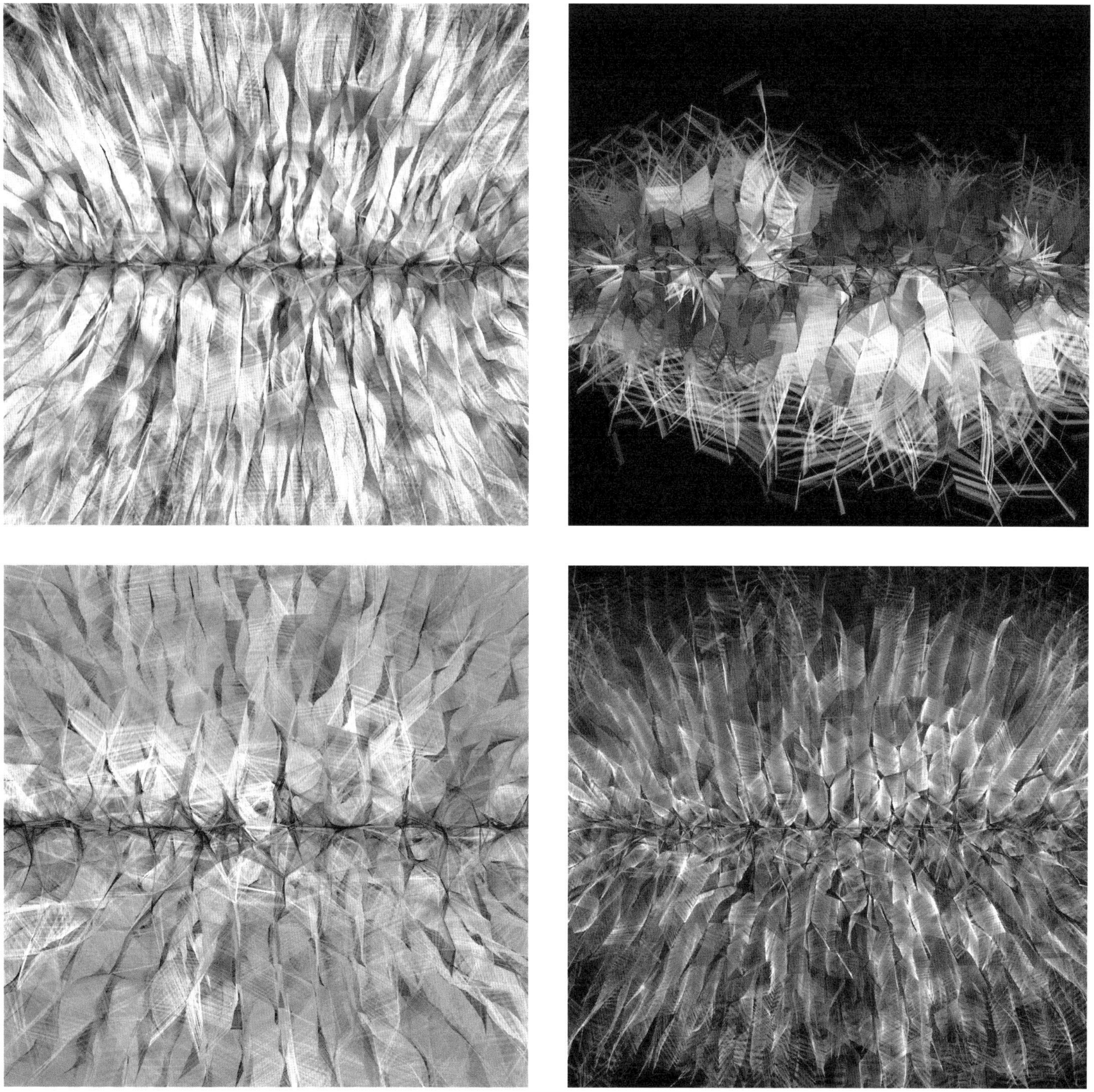

Images captured from different software interpretations of *Process 13*

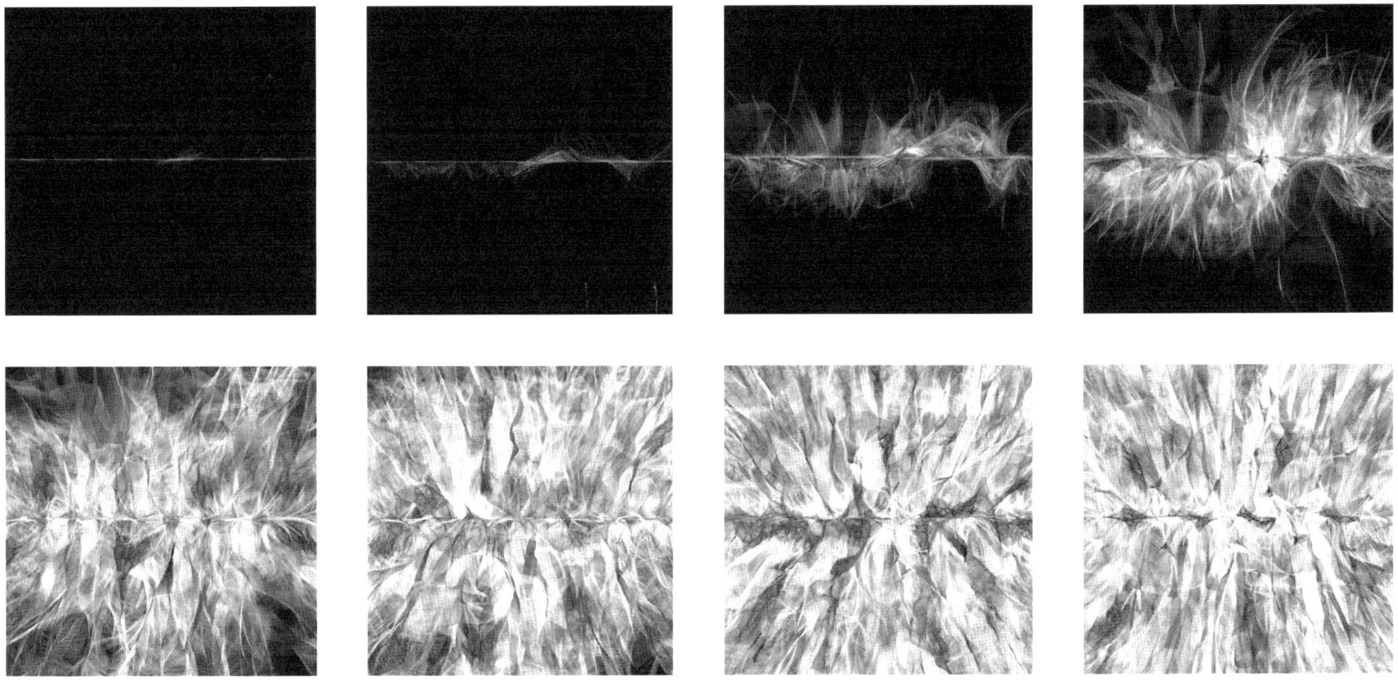

Image sequence from a software interpretation of *Process 13*

Process 14

A rectangular surface filled with instances of Element 4, each with a different size and direction. Display the intersections by drawing a circle at each point of contact. Set the size of each circle relative to the distance between the centers of the overlapping Elements. Draw the smallest possible circle as white and the largest as black, with varying grays representing sizes in between.

Process 14, 2008
Text, unique custom software, computer, documentation prints
Dimensions variable

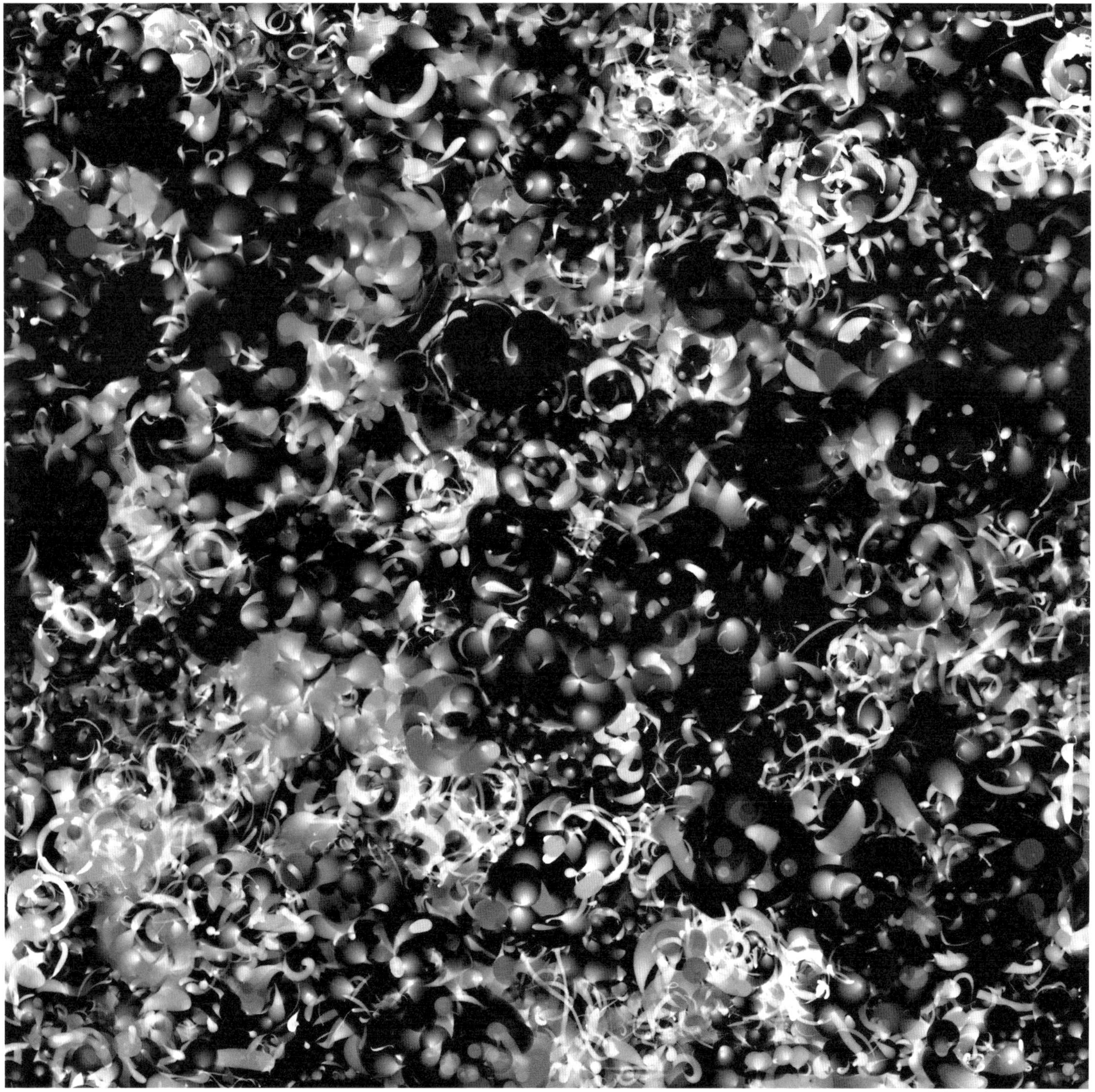

Process 14 (A), 2010
C print
Edition of 8 + 2 AP
50cm x 50cm

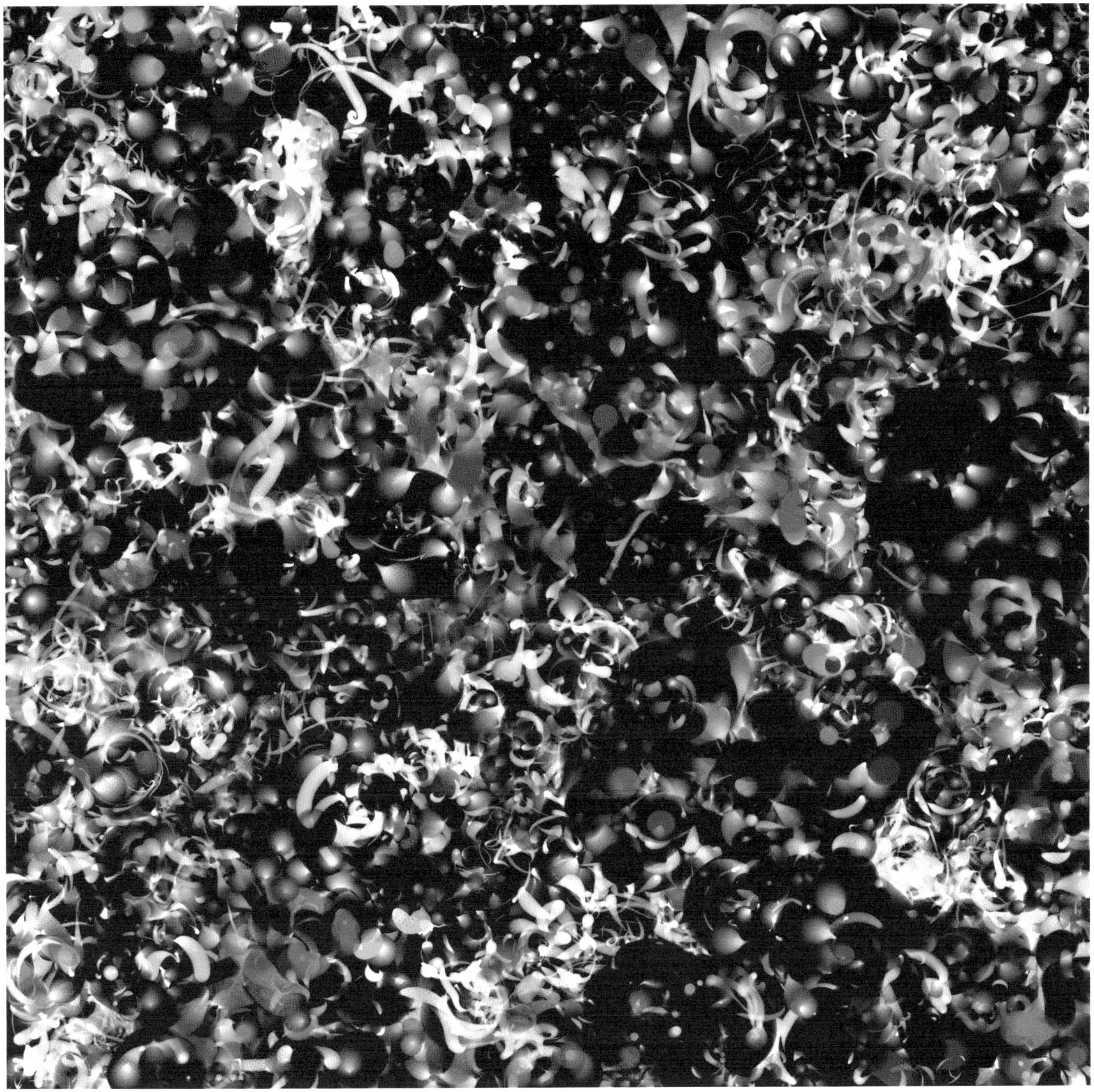

Process 14 (B), 2010
C print
Edition of 8 + 2 AP
50cm x 50cm

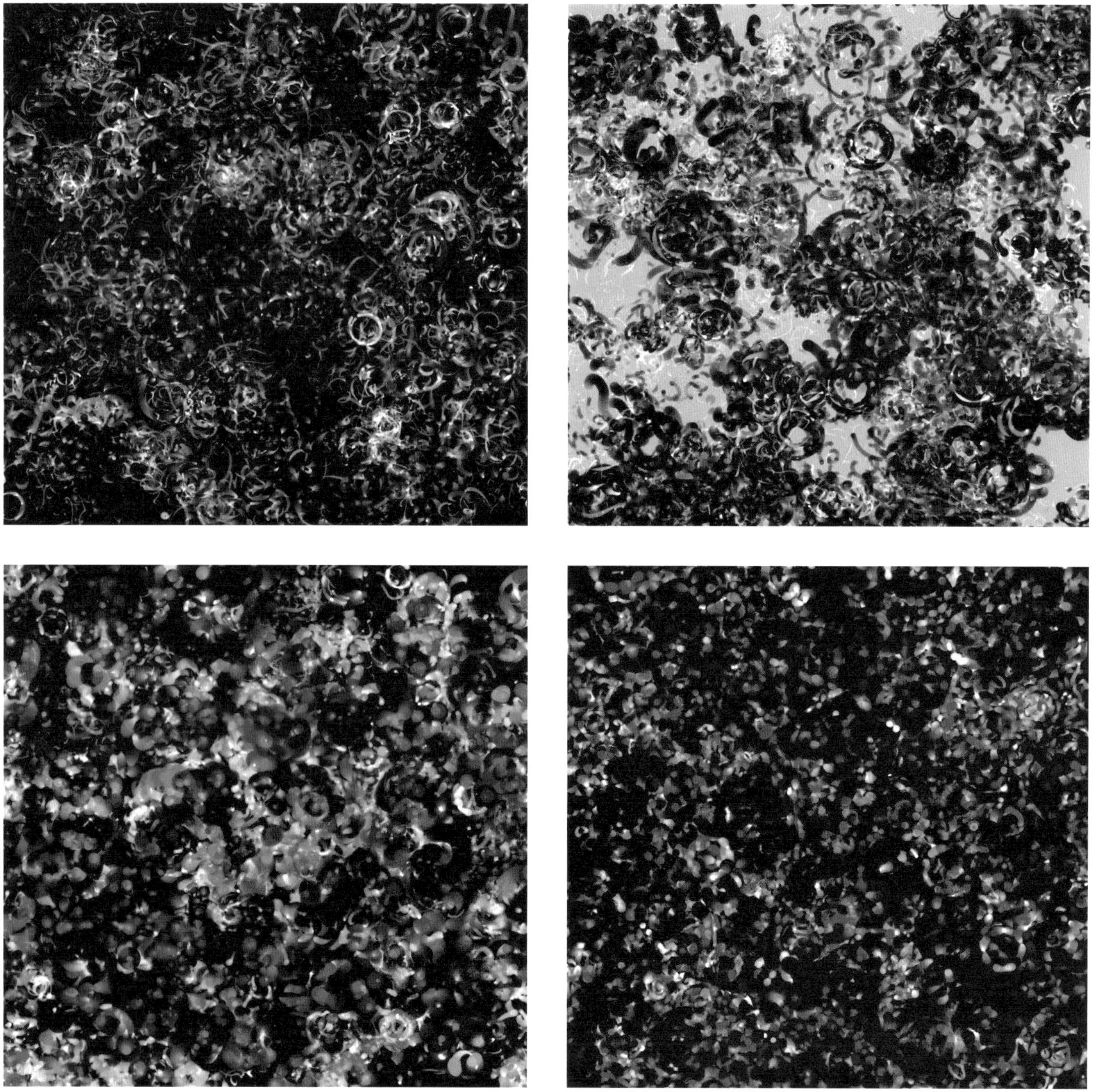

Images captured from different software interpretations of *Process 14*

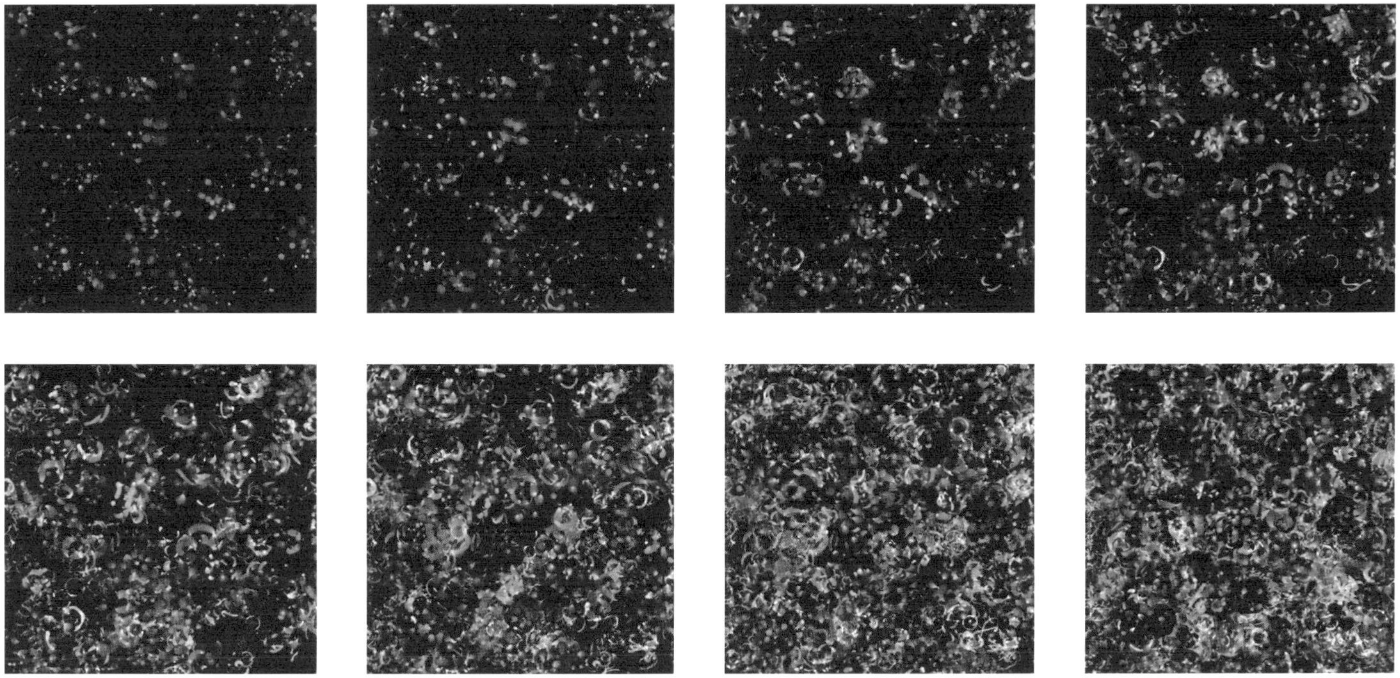

Image sequence
from a software
interpretation
of *Process 14*

Process 15

A rectangular surface filled with instances of Element 3, each with a different size and gray value. Draw a small, transparent circle at the midpoint of each Element. Increase the circle's opacity while its Element is touching another Element and decrease while it is not.

Process 15, 2006
Text, unique custom software, computer, documentation prints
Dimensions variable

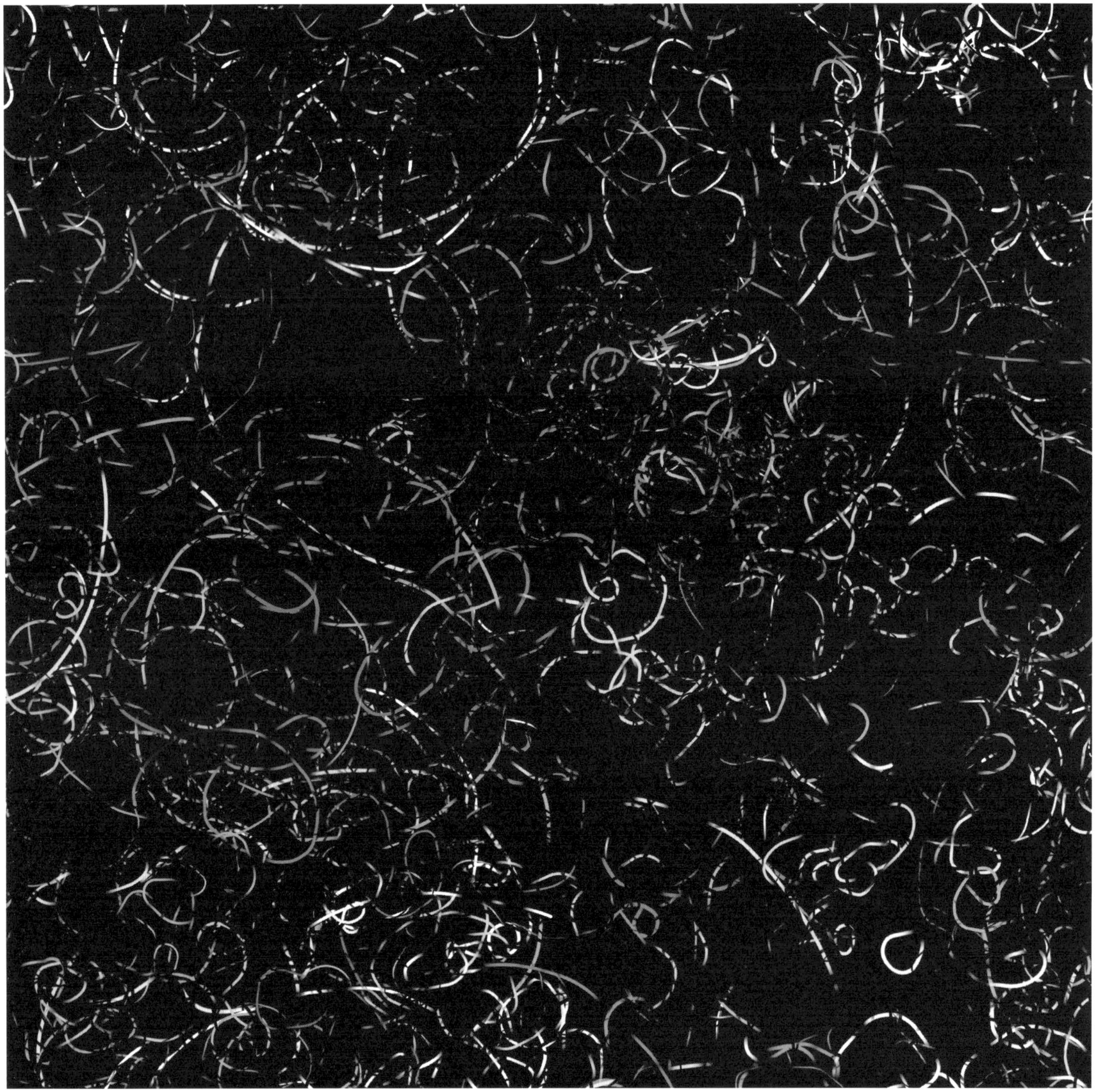

Process 15 (A), 2010
C print
Edition of 8 + 2 AP
50cm x 50cm

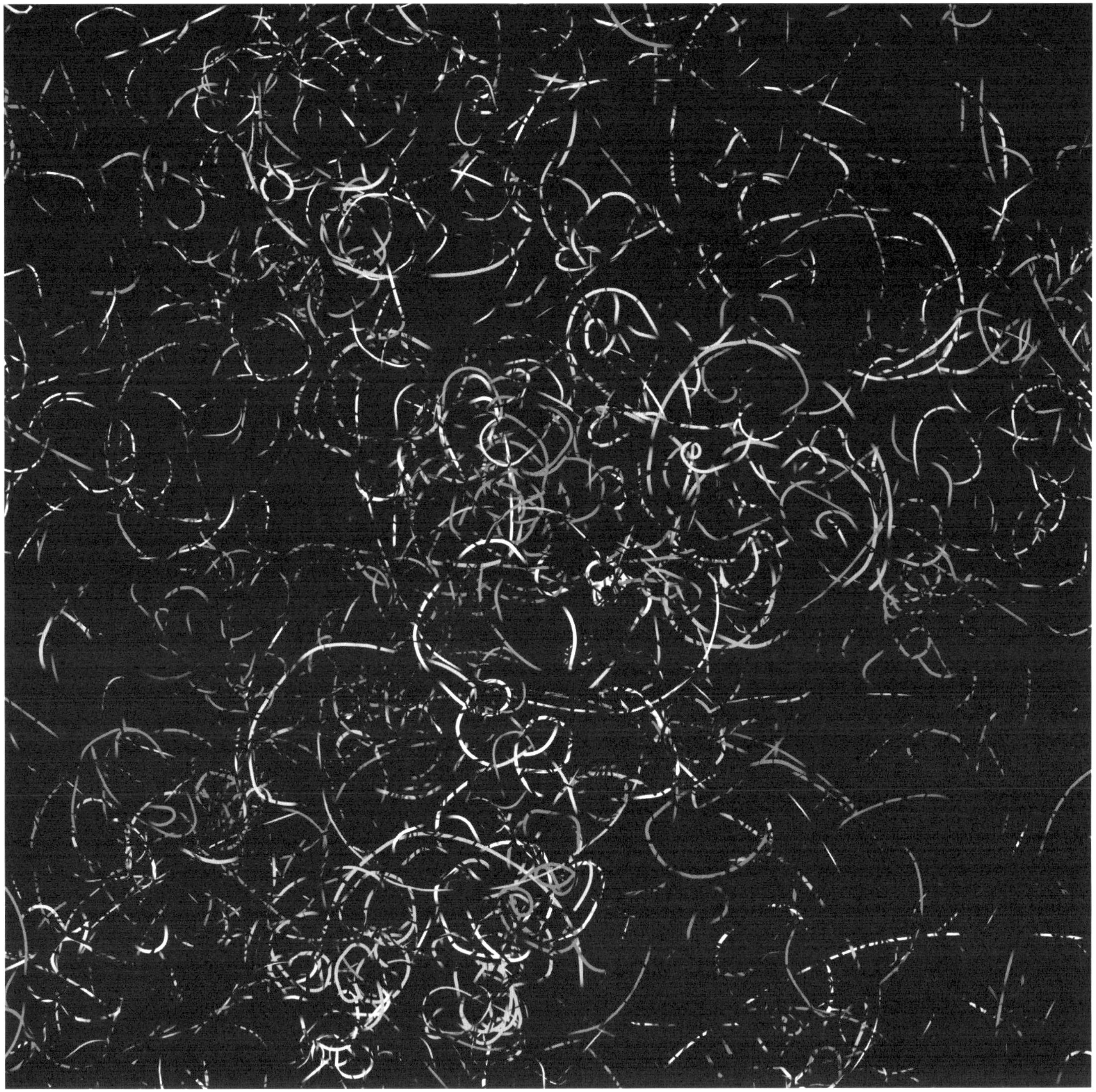

Process 15 (B), 2010
C print
Edition of 8 + 2 AP
50cm x 50cm

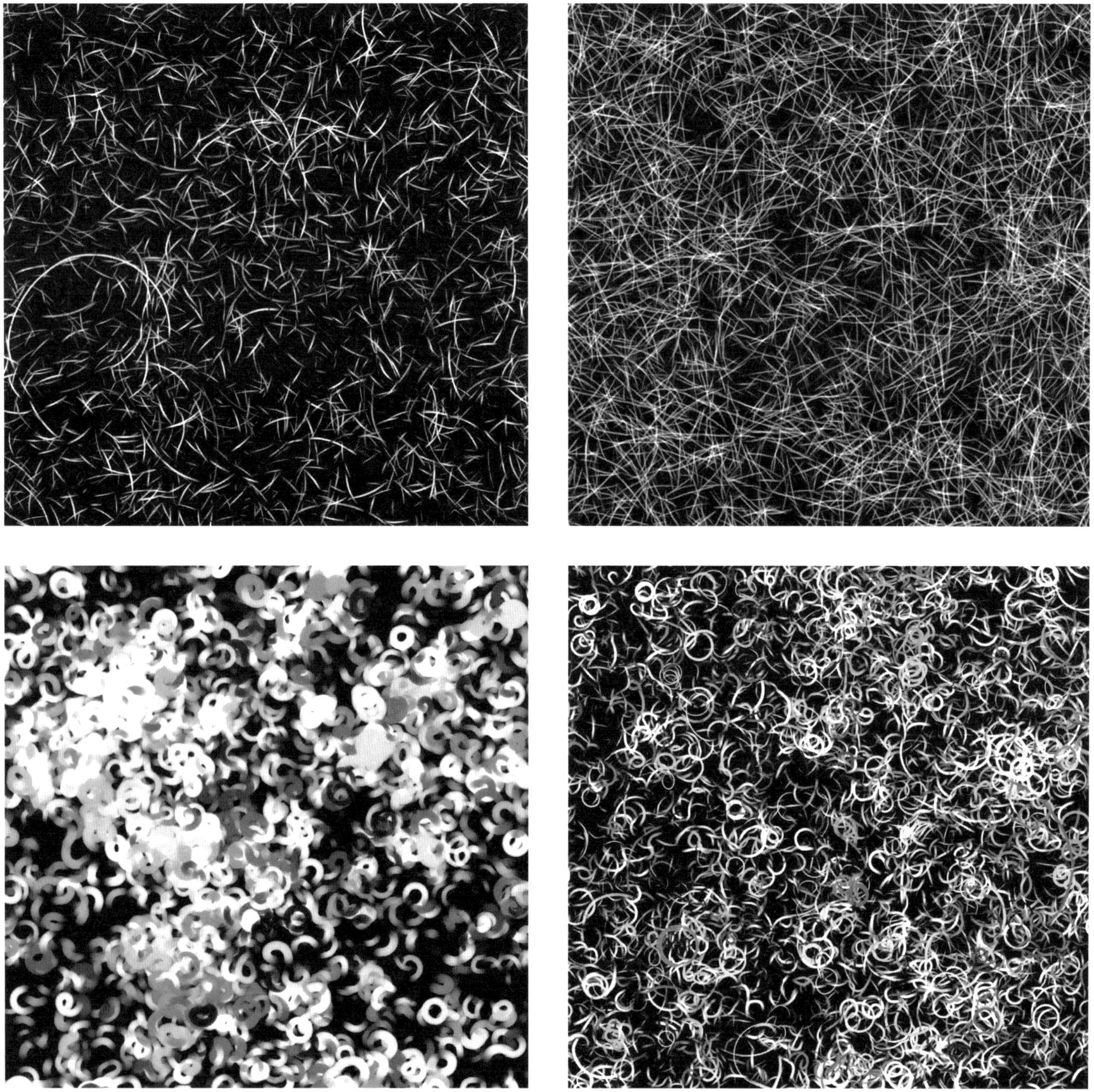

Images captured from
different software
interpretations of
Process 15

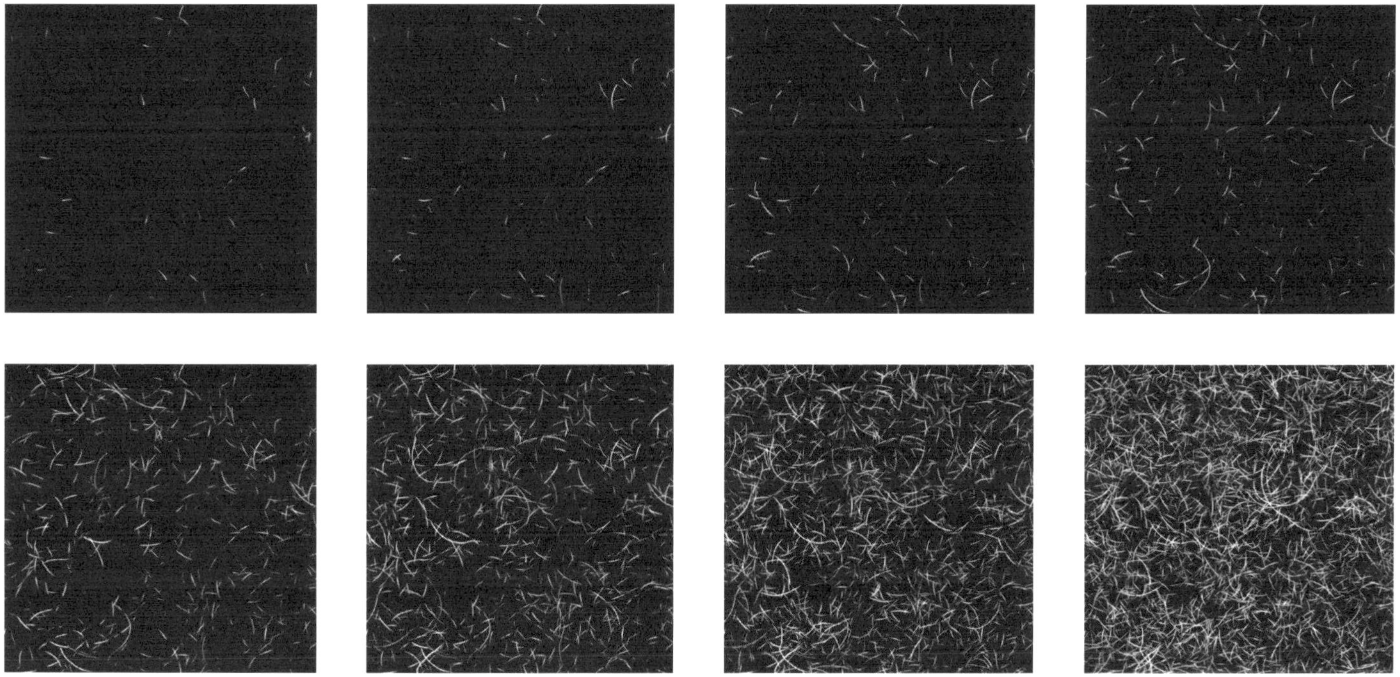

Image sequence
from a software
interpretation
of *Process 15*

Process 16

A rectangular surface filled with instances of Element 3, each with a different size and gray value. Draw a tiny, transparent circle at the midpoint of each Element. Increase a circle's size and opacity while its Element is touching another Element and decrease while it is not.

Process 16, 2006
Text, unique custom software, computer, documentation prints
Dimensions variable

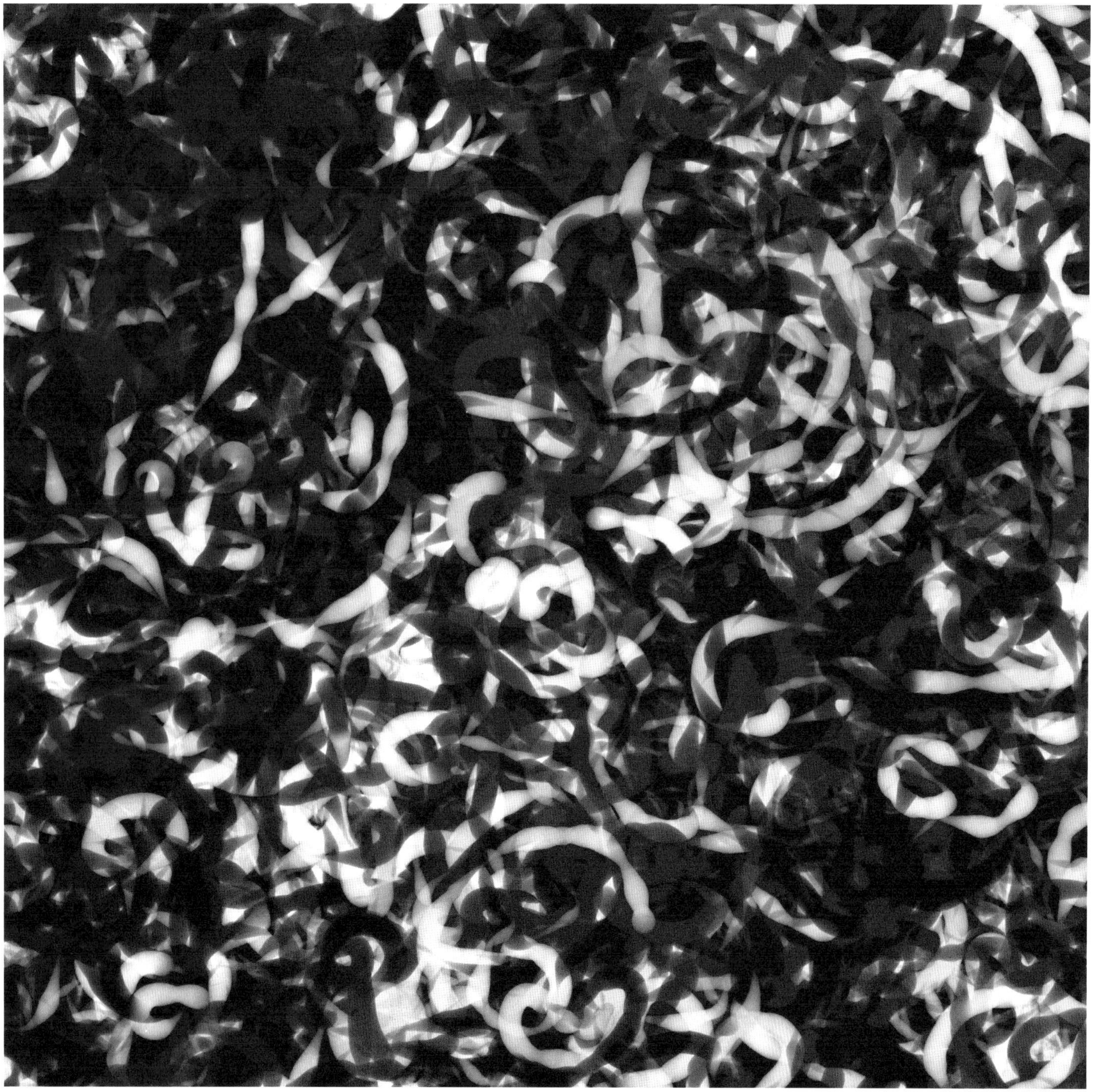

Process 16 (A), 2010
C print
Edition of 8 + 2 AP
50cm x 50cm

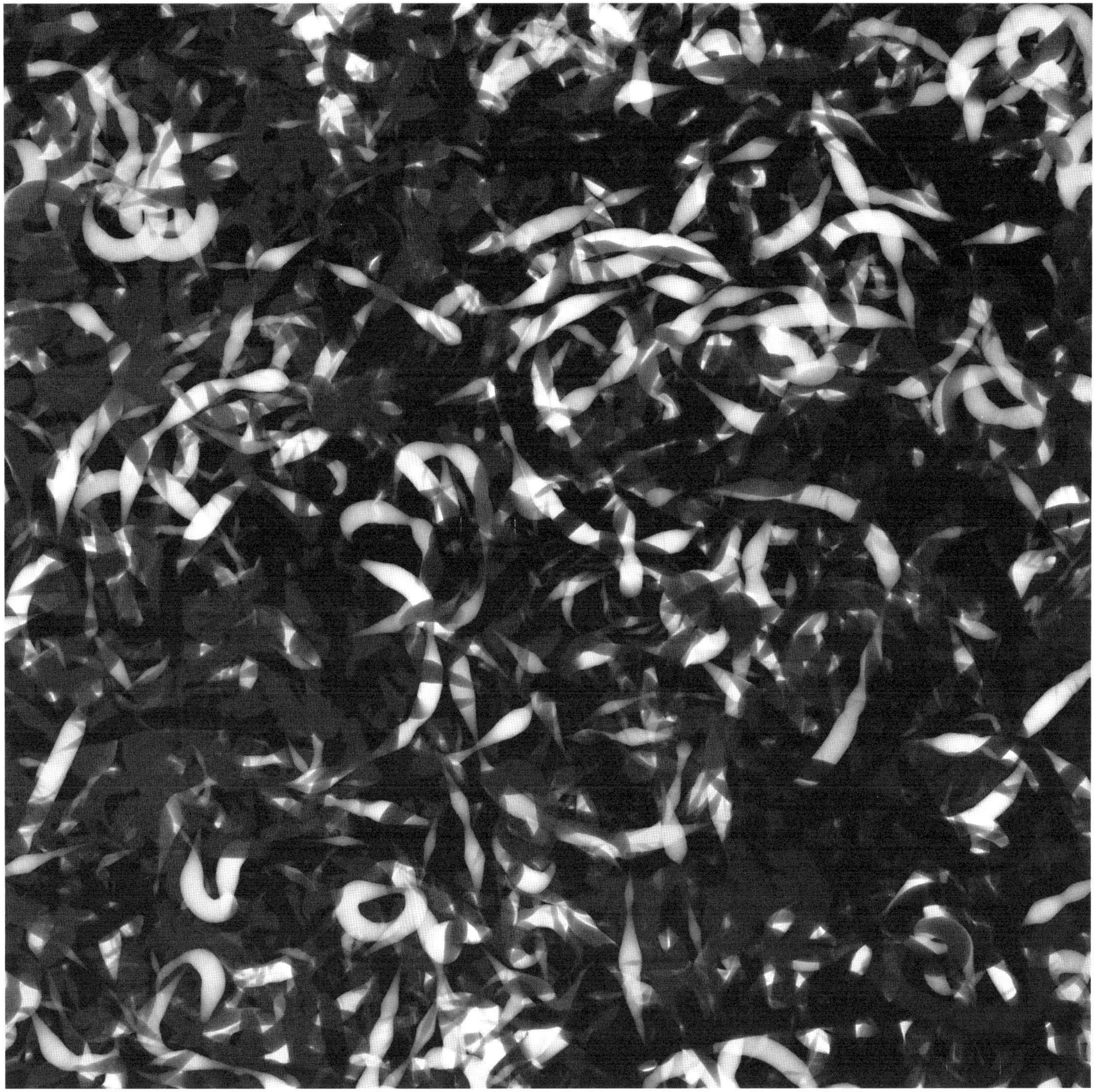

Process 16 (B), 2010
C print
Edition of 8 + 2 AP
50cm x 50cm

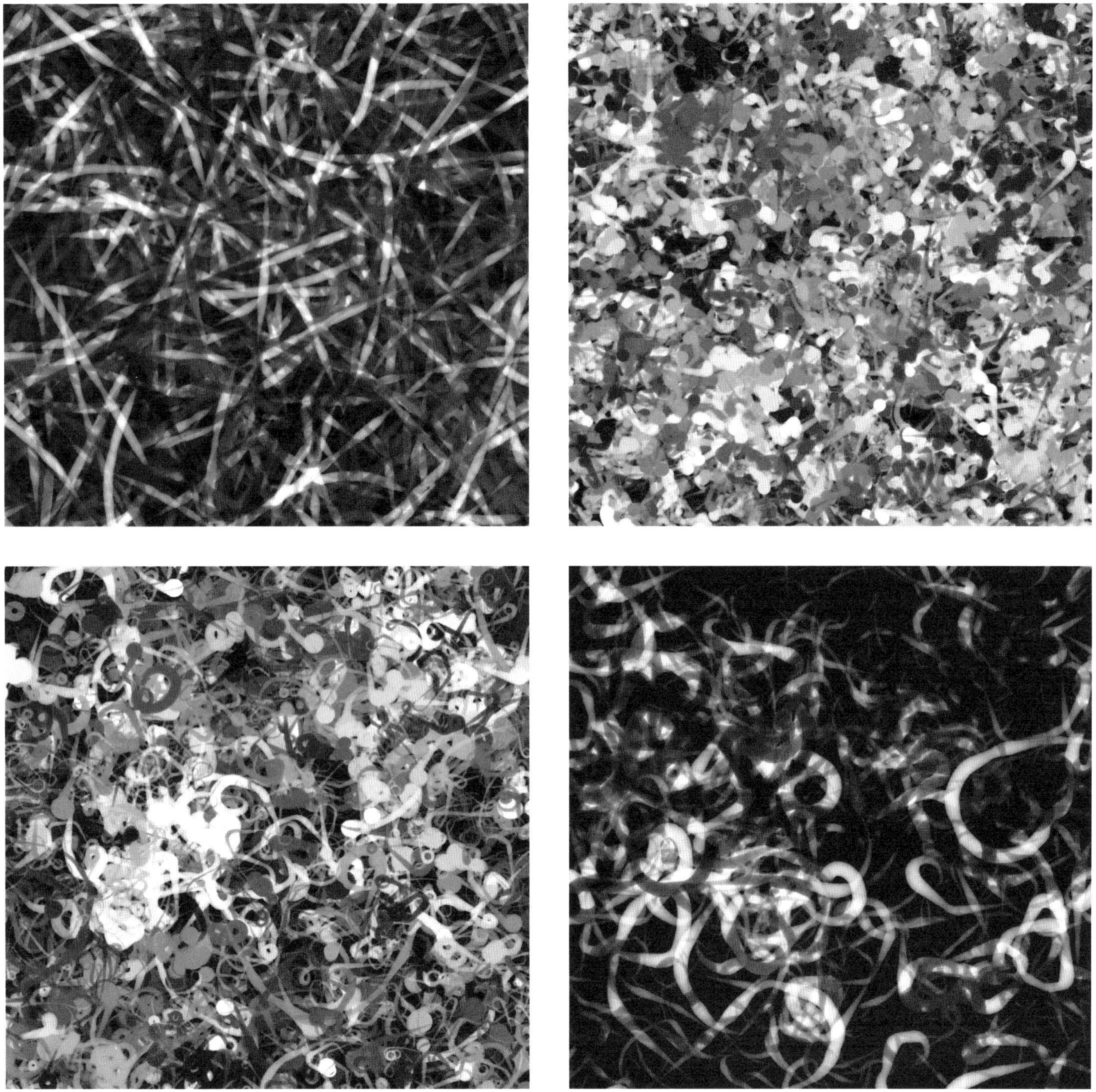

Images captured from different software interpretations of *Process 16*

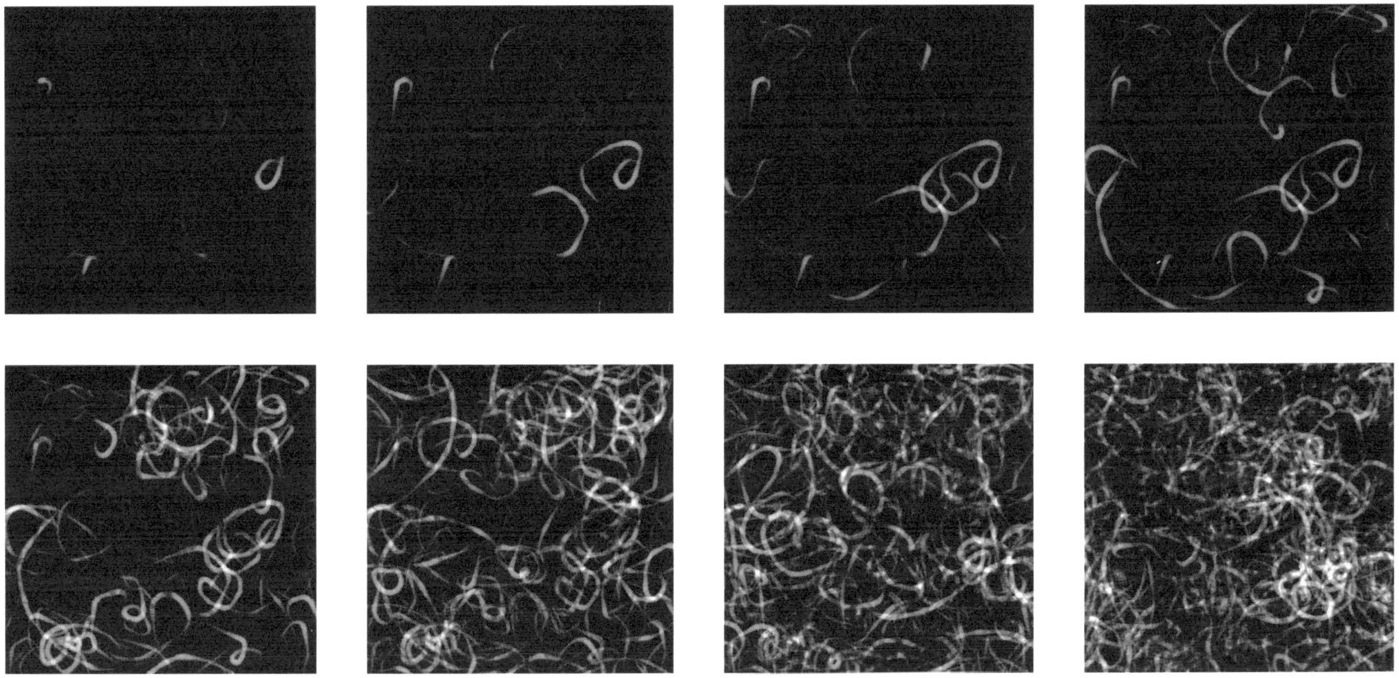

Image sequence
from a software
interpretation
of *Process 16*

Process 17

A rectangular surface filled with instances of Element 5, each with a different size and gray value. Draw a transparent circle at the midpoint of each Element. Increase a circle's size and opacity while its Element is touching another Element and decrease while it is not.

Process 17, 2010
Text, unique custom software, computer, documentation prints
Dimensions variable

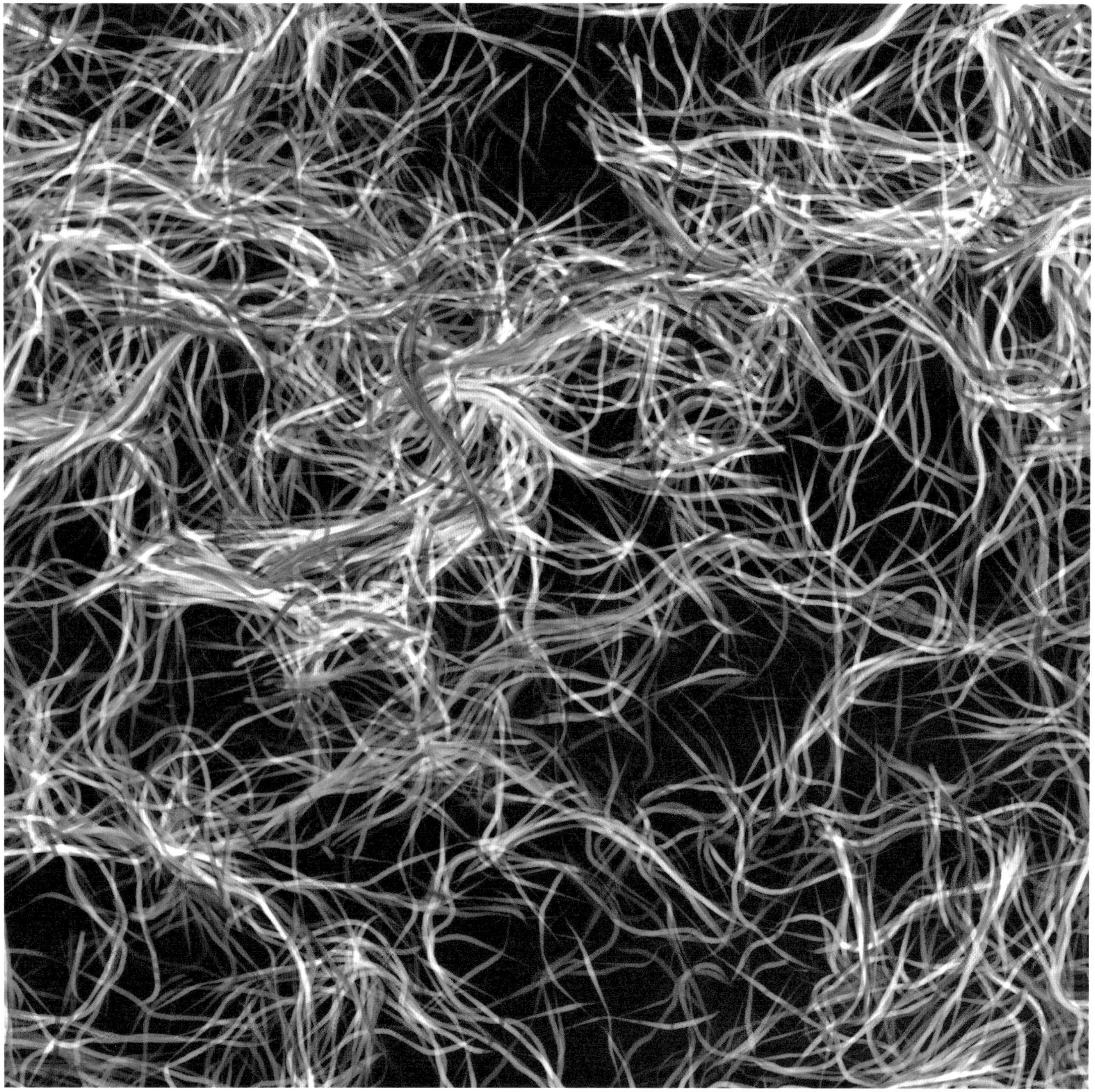

Process 17 (A), 2010
C print
Edition of 8 + 2 AP
50cm x 50cm

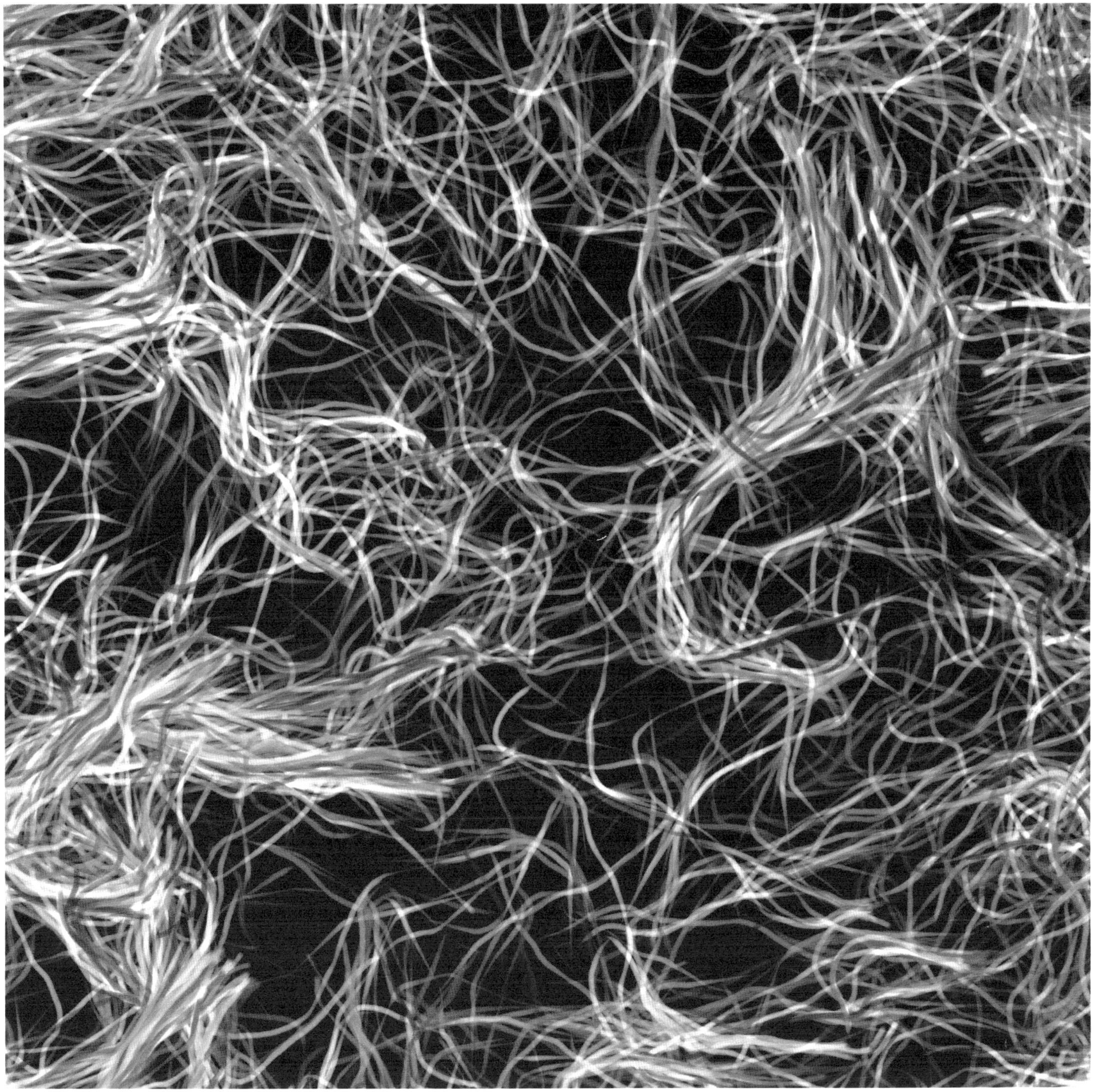

Process 17 (B), 2010
C print
Edition of 8 + 2 AP
50cm x 50cm

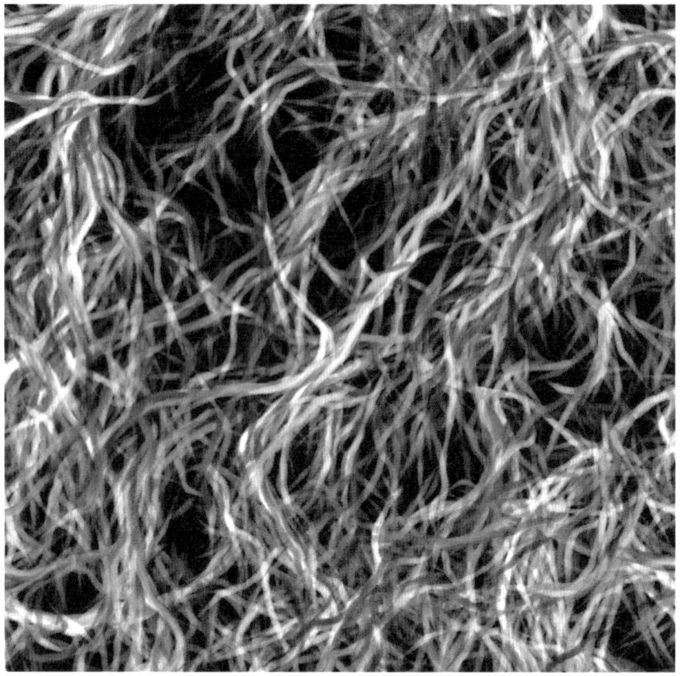

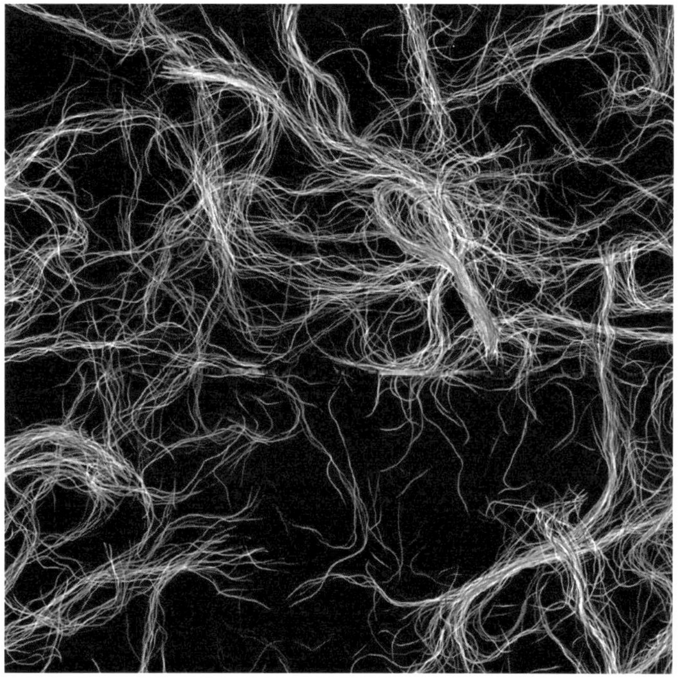

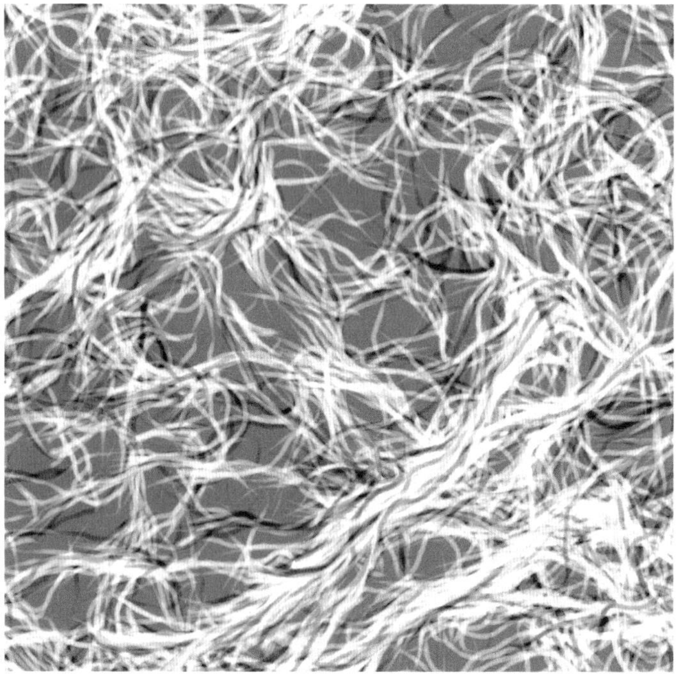

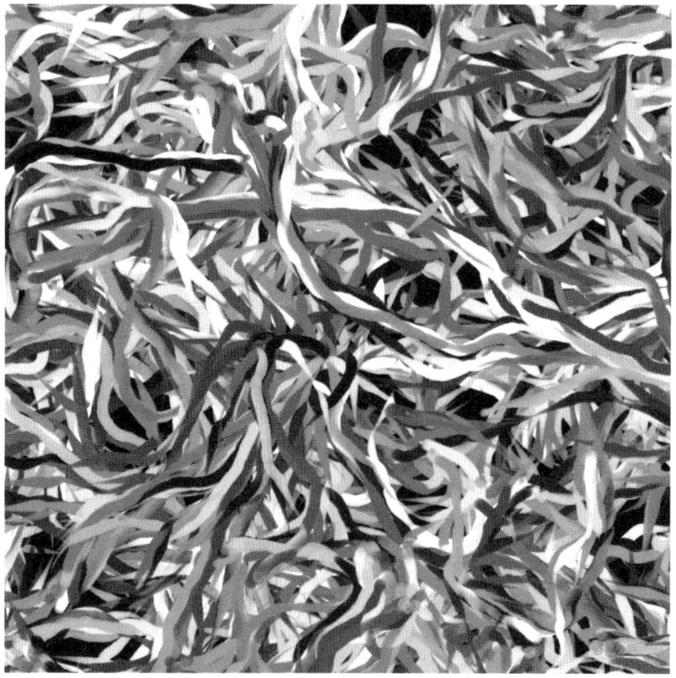

Images captured from different software interpretations of *Process 17*

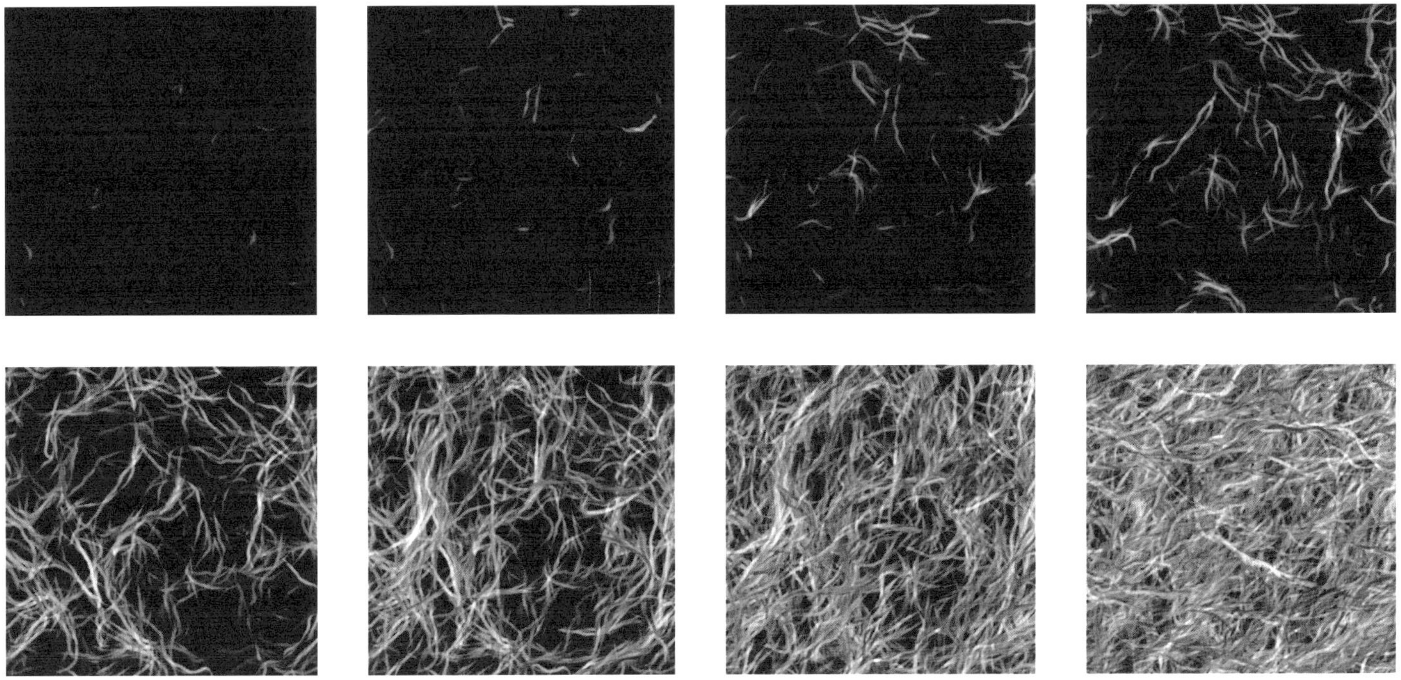

Image sequence
from a software
interpretation
of *Process 17*

Process 18

A rectangular surface filled with instances of Element 5, each with a different size and gray value. Draw a quadrilateral connecting the endpoints of each pair of Elements that are touching. Increase the opacity of the quadrilateral while the Elements are touching and decrease while they are not.

Process 18, 2008
Text, unique custom software, computer, documentation prints
Dimensions variable

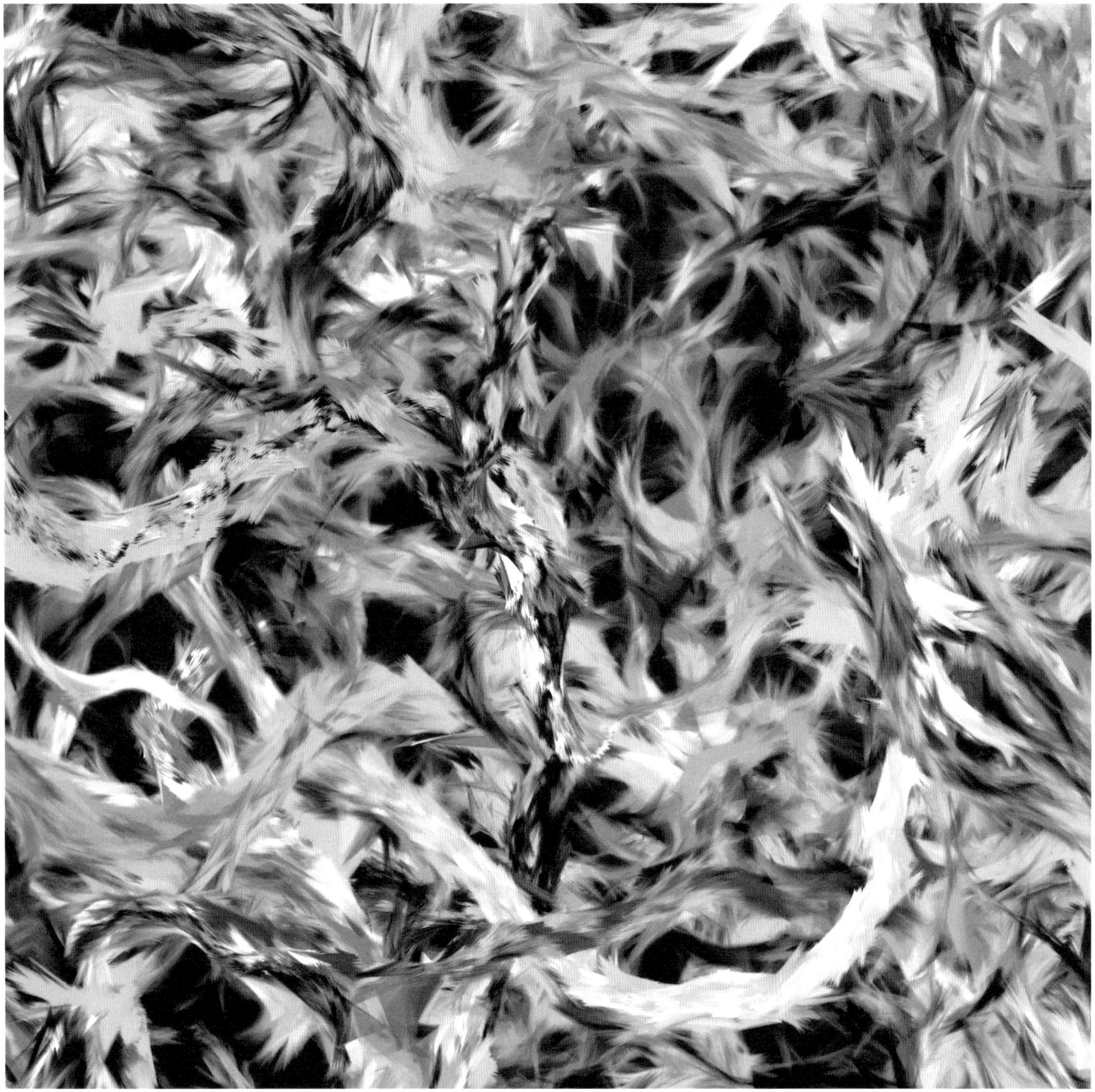

Process 18 (A), 2010
C print
Edition of 8 + 2 AP
50cm x 50cm

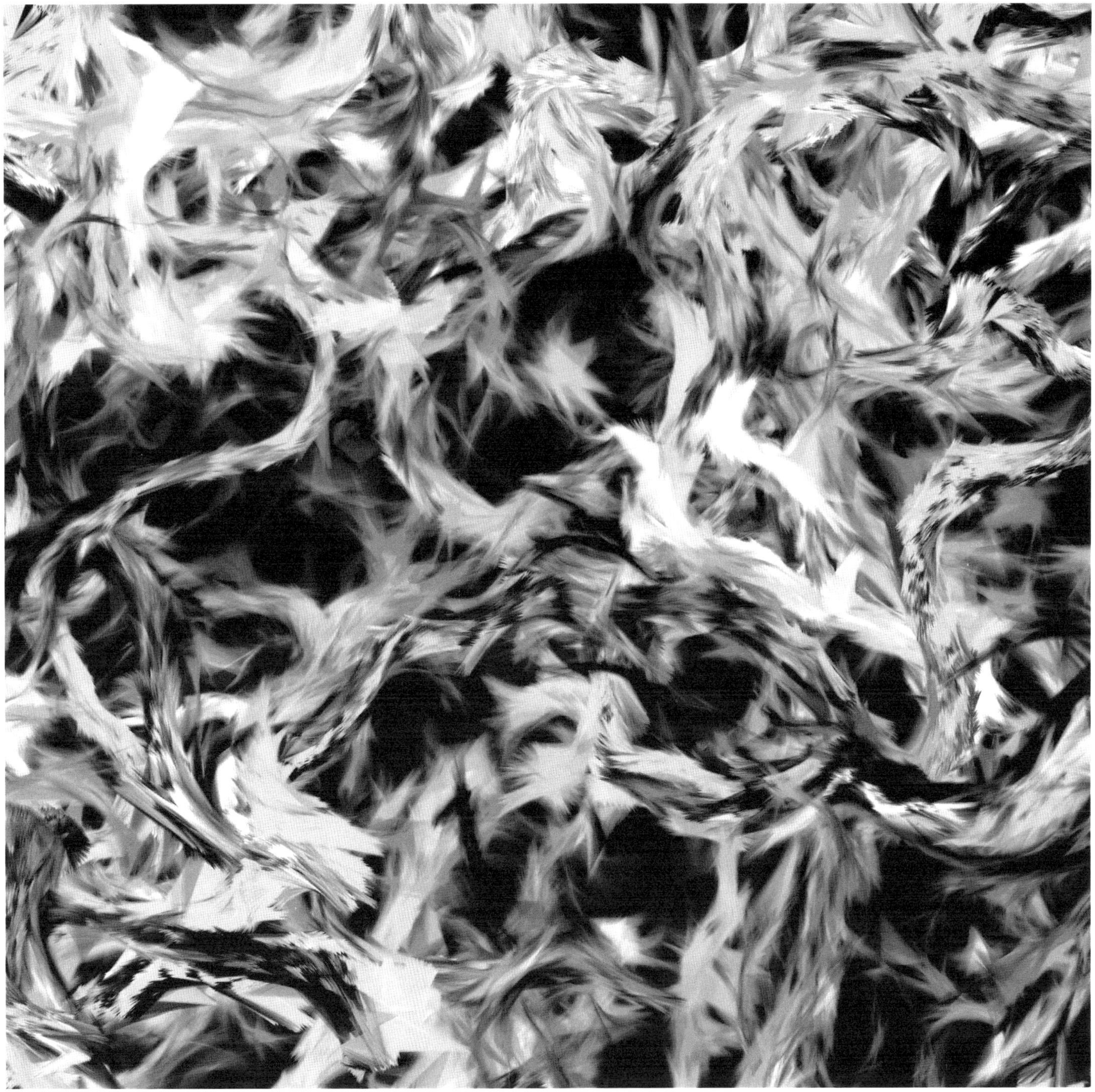

Process 18 (B), 2010
C print
Edition of 8 + 2 AP
50cm x 50cm

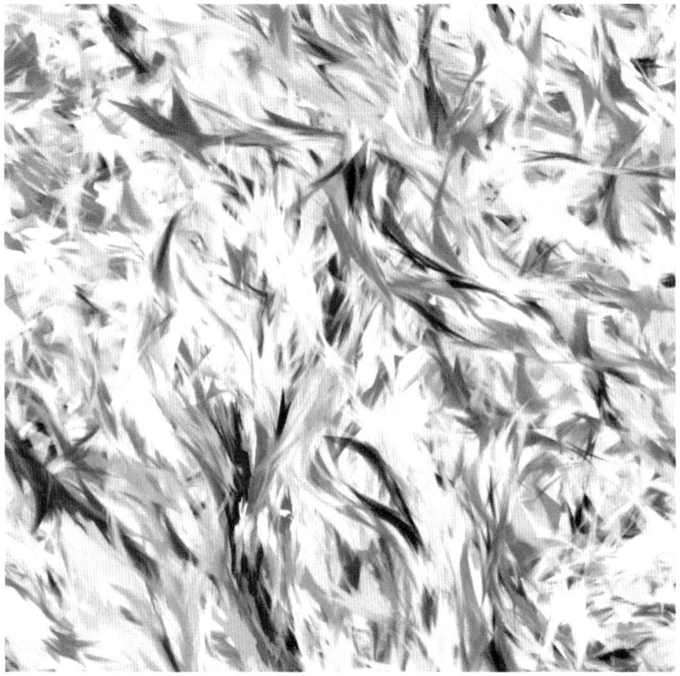

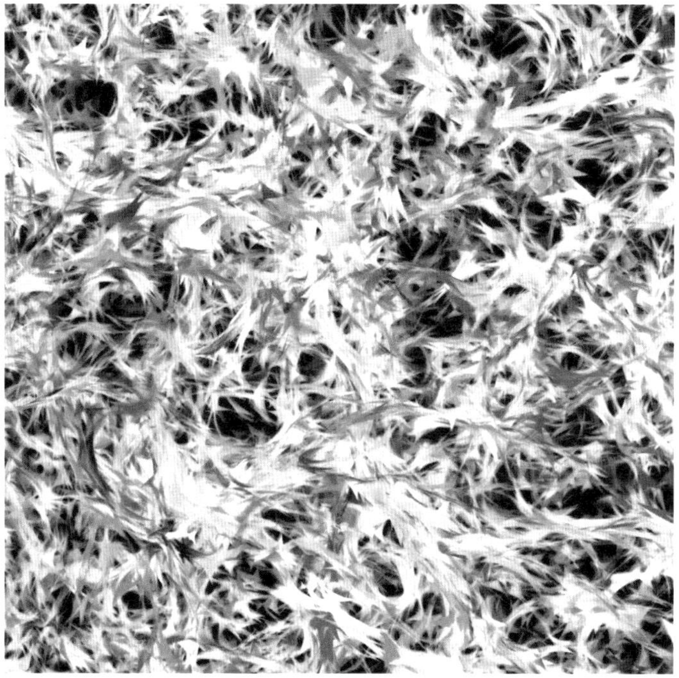

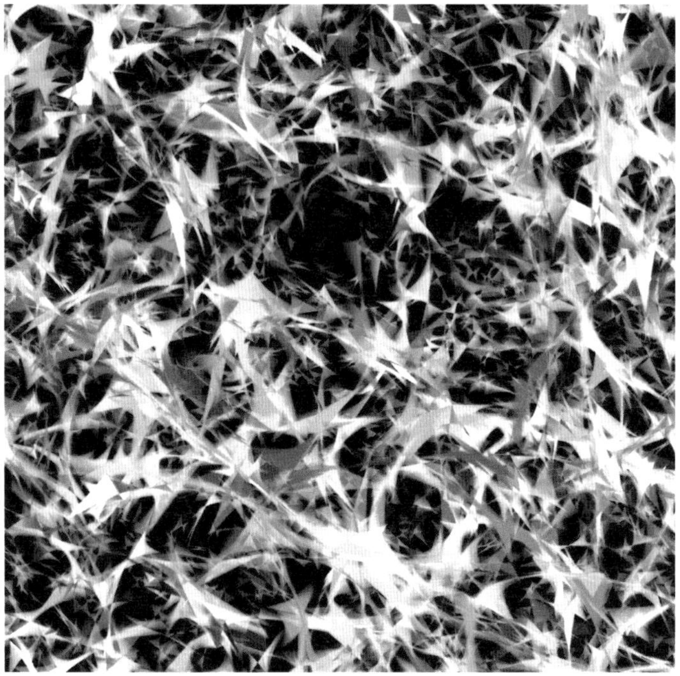

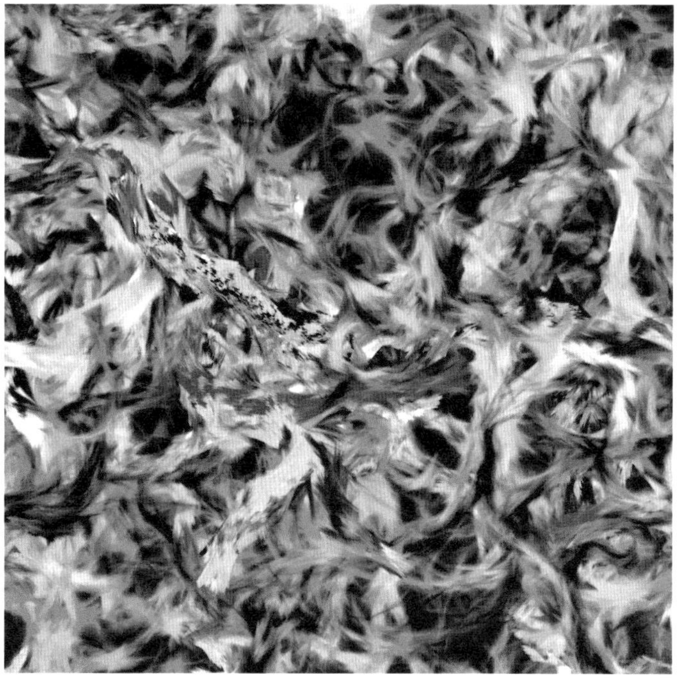

Images captured from different software interpretations of *Process 18*

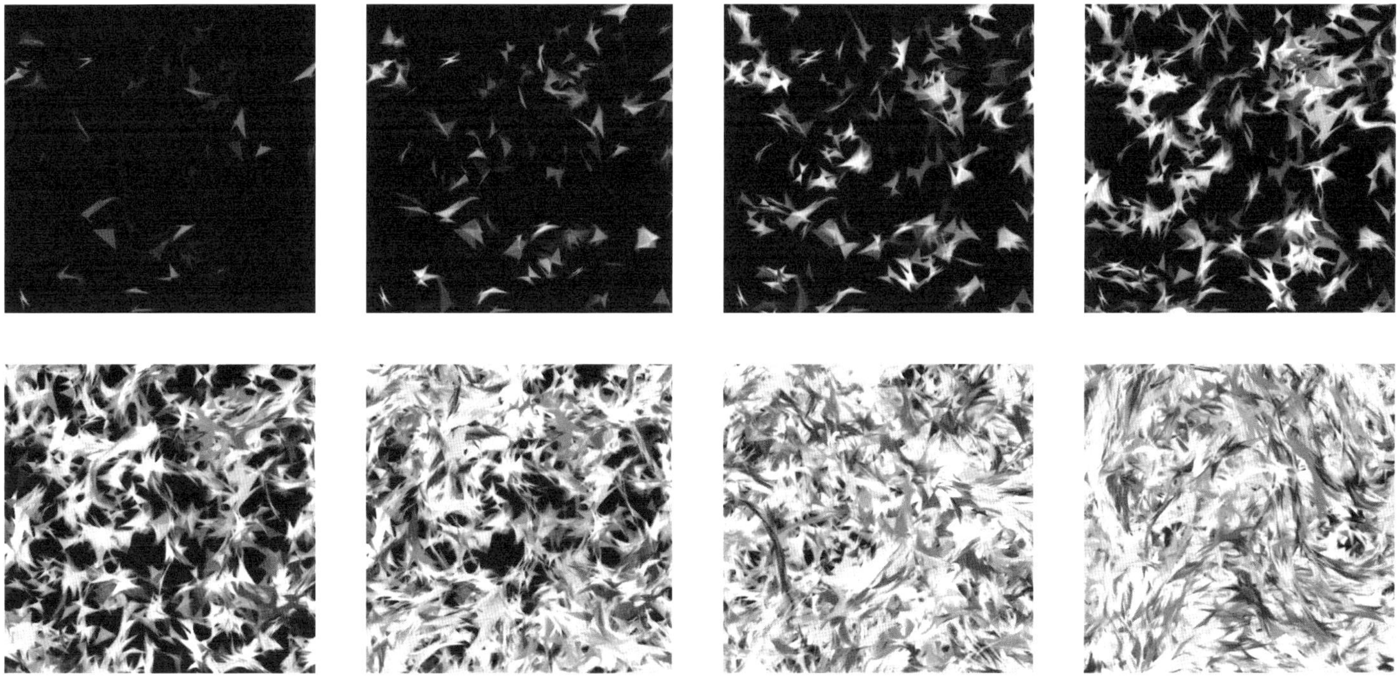

Image sequence from a software interpretation of *Process 18*

Id	0	1	2	3	4	5	6	7	8	9	10	11	12	13	14	15	16	17	18	19	20	21	22	23	24	25	26	27	28
X	224.543	715.448	227.491	313.495	645.691	553.936	285.424	423.861	32.060	407.889	252.081	248.143	393.045	230.626	362.382	11.905	574.063	701.331	670.266	597.968	665.753	163.863	721.900	610.546	311.150	183.390	515.672	447.762	49
Y	247.001	879.651	839.485	291.144	646.339	853.732	862.896	205.989	233.230	168.351	886.406	471.750	494.953	62.905	210.355	228.244	616.653	590.738	659.973	432.679	400.694	43.630	259.418	386.658	143.228	366.307	890.304	533.457	41.
Size	20.000	20.024	20.048	20.072	20.095	20.119	20.143	20.167	20.191	20.215	20.238	20.262	20.286	20.310	20.334	20.358	20.381	20.405	20.429	20.453	20.477	20.501	20.524	20.548	20.572	20.596	20.620	20.644	20.
Angle	1.429	1.000	4.141	0.144	0.716	0.575	1.284	2.289	1.712	6.274	-0.143	4.276	4.988	5.130	1.852	1.013	4.272	4.698	4.270	3.416	0.592	3.841	4.719	1.706	6.283	5.259	6.111	2.589	0.9
Others	2	1	2	1	1	3	1	3	2	3	2	1	3	4	3	2	2	1	2	2	3	2	2	2	4	3	3	4	0

29	30	31	32	33	34	35	36	37	38	39	40	41	42	43	44	45	46	47	48	49	50	51	52	53	54	55	56	57	58
396.477	386.946	655.302	347.761	158.650	743.790	469.508	134.131	481.745	374.062	53.068	195.427	713.998	654.624	600.864	618.949	537.270	50.853	388.051	379.897	715.577	691.771	74.928	423.083	105.749	443.942	566.421	318.827	494.541	553
396.899	468.870	242.406	625.749	466.553	672.639	176.212	63.961	903.938	404.794	601.575	318.928	54.688	61.103	904.833	423.640	391.672	317.668	194.782	830.948	97.351	895.310	461.421	803.348	798.591	224.204	621.904	405.189	205.241	957
20.691	20.715	20.739	20.763	20.787	20.810	20.834	20.858	20.882	20.906	20.930	20.954	20.977	21.001	21.025	21.049	21.073	21.097	21.120	21.144	21.168	21.192	21.216	21.240	21.263	21.287	21.311	21.335	21.359	21.
4.687	5.715	5.395	3.691	6.245	4.722	5.006	0.326	2.454	4.962	4.111	5.291	1.700	1.183	6.283	0.052	1.841	2.123	2.547	2.038	1.556	2.040	3.959	0.062	-0.141	1.131	3.956	4.238	4.023	0.0
1	3	2	2	2	2	2	1	2	1	1	1	1	3	3	2	4	2	1	2	2	1	2	1	3	1	3	2	3	3

59	60	61	62	63	64	65	66	67	68	69	70	71	72	73	74	75	76	77	78	79	80	81	82	83	84	85	86	87	88
388.065	450.679	302.301	18.621	9.702	414.063	258.200	164.499	270.106	658.452	311.906	118.442	545.967	122.723	589.670	639.674	298.152	557.838	282.093	38.254	633.445	615.833	732.555	158.340	158.084	146.754	500.961	351.705	486.060	489
269.422	795.973	319.802	598.880	782.143	518.932	928.179	906.635	405.332	135.555	164.954	545.745	419.988	877.825	48.918	135.766	308.592	58.257	558.723	565.192	176.590	126.686	310.711	12.118	59.367	489.874	650.797	10.258	736.670	962
21.406	21.430	21.454	21.478	21.502	21.526	21.549	21.573	21.597	21.621	21.645	21.669	21.692	21.716	21.740	21.764	21.788	21.812	21.836	21.859	21.883	21.907	21.931	21.955	21.979	22.002	22.026	22.050	22.074	22.
2.471	2.117	1.626	0.988	3.603	3.667	1.410	3.323	3.947	5.719	3.465	4.085	4.929	4.030	3.660	0.845	0.373	5.065	1.500	0.798	1.125	1.925	3.191	2.910	2.630	3.755	4.354	1.825	5.756	4.3
1	1	2	1	2	2	1	3	3	4	3	2	2	2	1	2	1	1	2	1	2	1	1	0	3	2	1	2	3	1

89	90	91	92	93	94	95	96	97	98	99	100	101	102	103	104	105	106	107	108	109	110	111	112	113	114	115	116	117	118
247.620	67.441	13.802	90.058	440.551	473.323	304.838	81.000	639.132	565.547	358.782	18.293	146.797	141.652	489.424	20.374	693.722	701.360	501.661	175.519	548.920	199.259	295.292	571.826	197.116	676.357	550.826	706.220	675.913	43
450.361	388.695	920.408	602.967	200.302	299.997	931.795	350.255	957.216	35.556	856.071	373.701	717.082	254.811	68.709	741.746	721.961	498.173	242.552	181.022	485.018	486.220	364.524	99.587	150.683	260.699	658.625	133.133	379.717	46
22.122	22.145	22.169	22.193	22.217	22.241	22.265	22.288	22.312	22.336	22.360	22.384	22.408	22.431	22.455	22.479	22.503	22.527	22.551	22.574	22.598	22.622	22.646	22.670	22.694	22.718	22.741	22.765	22.789	22.
2.354	0.952	2.805	0.112	2.384	3.059	3.784	-0.023	5.583	0.260	2.642	1.803	0.560	5.878	3.764	5.164	4.325	1.668	3.067	6.011	3.488	0.135	-0.004	1.257	2.792	3.351	4.188	6.141	0.140	3.
4	3	2	1	2	2	2	3	2	2	2	2	1	2	1	2	1	3	3	1	2	1	3	1	3	2	3	1	1	2

119	120	121	122	123	124	125	126	127	128	129	130	131	132	133	134	135	136	137	138	139	140	141	142	143	144	145	146	147	14
273.211	703.189	179.705	604.988	652.285	301.076	187.339	12.952	539.621	577.130	328.871	441.982	536.933	580.161	653.693	101.314	249.295	173.896	297.318	598.158	415.725	303.731	742.595	741.993	468.844	336.295	17.922	67.035	451.664	41
10.473	564.865	150.969	778.100	385.073	342.530	845.108	724.445	96.675	926.339	13.290	141.516	463.533	757.866	617.420	471.554	904.980	484.918	50.440	533.651	225.592	844.763	695.994	408.686	883.644	425.298	625.943	79.931	855.471	36
22.837	22.861	22.884	22.908	22.932	22.956	22.980	23.004	23.027	23.051	23.075	23.099	23.123	23.147	23.170	23.194	23.218	23.242	23.266	23.290	23.313	23.337	23.361	23.385	23.409	23.433	23.456	23.480	23.504	23
3.633	2.928	3.495	2.370	3.345	0.152	4.194	1.548	0.836	1.132	4.613	4.613	4.614	2.249	6.259	2.781	5.032	0.167	4.308	5.866	5.418	3.611	3.367	1.805	5.552	4.302	0.555	0.318	2.080	0.
1	2	3	0	1	4	3	2	1	2	2	2	1	2	1	3	1	1	2	3	2	0	1	1	2	3	0	1	2	2

149	150	151	152	153	154	155	156	157	158	159	160	161	162	163	164	165	166	167	168	169	170	171	172	173	174	175	176	177	17
598.872	452.157	177.060	570.453	403.738	388.902	178.877	513.504	618.659	50.935	505.891	319.363	530.319	383.239	247.628	143.488	693.821	528.397	457.516	339.244	458.441	401.904	370.772	164.390	548.567	147.591	704.185	383.271	11.870	64
708.373	663.721	68.100	782.881	733.506	177.188	329.722	82.145	160.973	29.416	107.631	383.730	284.282	861.224	297.747	778.806	295.445	436.847	118.170	540.852	815.707	816.771	71.335	685.639	18.157	920.847	81.889	620.543	463.158	11
23.552	23.576	23.600	23.623	23.647	23.671	23.695	23.719	23.743	23.766	23.790	23.814	23.838	23.862	23.886	23.909	23.933	23.957	23.981	24.005	24.029	24.052	24.076	24.100	24.124	24.148	24.172	24.195	24.219	24
0.184	1.109	2.542	2.632	4.205	2.770	5.037	0.192	0.470	3.654	3.735	3.932	6.145	4.701	3.594	2.902	0.203	4.902	0.967	5.385	5.937	0.762	0.625	0.414	4.276	3.525	2.560	5.239	1.378	0.
1	0	3	1	0	4	3	0	2	3	2	2	4	1	2	1	1	2	3	3	3	2	2	1	1	3	2	2	0	2

179	180	181	182	183	184	185	186	187	188	189	190	191	192	193	194	195	196	197	198	199	200	201	202	203	204	205	206	207	20
299.485	146.861	420.448	656.876	12.521	556.200	222.811	733.697	544.074	546.548	397.120	668.842	720.433	151.143	333.726	424.910	659.243	310.970	45.552	704.262	60.883	323.078	271.580	274.993	217.662	467.053	14.105	90.650	528.043	60
737.148	944.372	353.124	783.832	245.782	354.067	473.012	361.595	147.477	427.848	425.627	597.762	115.793	80.080	571.396	342.536	723.144	492.922	921.501	853.323	481.960	615.456	323.909	888.401	402.082	270.444	359.682	819.639	230.048	92
24.267	24.291	24.315	24.338	24.362	24.386	24.410	24.434	24.458	24.482	24.505	24.529	24.553	24.577	24.601	24.625	24.648	24.672	24.696	24.720	24.744	24.768	24.791	24.815	24.839	24.863	24.887	24.911	24.934	24
4.217	-0.000	5.319	2.341	2.753	1.328	0.641	1.789	6.052	0.095	1.512	4.949	2.298	5.047	1.475	2.575	2.609	0.654	4.667	4.392	-0.028	3.128	3.703	2.331	2.307	0.663	5.756	5.480	0.667	4.
2	3	3	3	3	2	1	4	1	4	0	2	3	4	2	3	2	2	3	2	2	1	1	2	3	1	2	1	1	3

209	210	211	212	213	214	215	216	217	218	219	220	221	222	223	224	225	226	227	228	229	230	231	232	233	234	235	236	237	23
487.041	343.934	334.037	686.079	636.165	105.324	438.555	491.735	651.356	161.212	323.861	697.204	298.343	368.614	246.701	85.385	42.402	15.060	744.783	541.247	458.621	202.361	58.617	676.551	86.096	259.405	419.598	372.848	273.684	46
260.058	752.971	958.201	579.620	913.749	53.237	608.380	576.566	513.410	160.674	906.319	809.928	898.007	132.679	45.401	483.905	121.185	877.900	12.832	227.371	621.999	505.506	779.971	195.157	785.340	143.140	957.295	488.299	612.346	60
24.982	25.006	25.030	25.054	25.077	25.101	25.125	25.149	25.173	25.197	25.221	25.244	25.268	25.292	25.316	25.340	25.364	25.387	25.411	25.435	25.459	25.483	25.507	25.530	25.554	25.578	25.602	25.626	25.650	25
4.519	5.613	3.695	2.189	4.104	4.377	3.822	4.369	3.554	3.140	2.050	6.148	1.912	4.781	5.325	4.641	4.646	1.092	0.136	1.782	4.920	-0.261	5.465	1.908	1.090	1.788	4.903	0.000	0.838	1.
3	4	2	4	2	1	3	2	3	3	1	3	3	2	4	2	2	2	1	3	3	2	2	2	2	4	3	4	3	3

239	240	241	242	243	244	245	246	247	248	249	250	251	252	253	254	255	256	257	258	259	260	261	262	263	264	265	266	267	26
377.299	405.522	377.477	581.578	671.869	15.807	54.010	636.531	209.815	604.361	207.936	699.634	590.513	334.553	208.102	480.754	228.733	371.216	430.173	569.222	502.624	660.726	63.153	383.048	710.285	278.931	593.982	219.864	439.968	54
891.252	761.239	784.449	357.056	333.073	544.330	653.087	363.079	886.783	35.657	89.092	269.314	381.799	927.619	959.876	356.535	127.698	529.885	529.865	642.482	554.941	540.874	579.949	50.550	241.199	348.613	656.861	665.289	494.086	33
25.697	25.721	25.745	25.769	25.793	25.816	25.840	25.864	25.888	25.912	25.936	25.959	25.983	26.007	26.031	26.055	26.079	26.103	26.126	26.150	26.174	26.198	26.222	26.246	26.269	26.293	26.317	26.341	26.365	26
2.881	2.610	6.121	1.116	2.447	0.408	2.039	3.397	5.162	1.122	2.481	5.023	-0.368	5.564	0.585	2.214	3.164	0.182	3.979	-0.358	2.896	1.490	6.095	4.334	2.708	2.978	2.900	5.683	0.737	0.
3	1	3	4	0	1	0	0	3	2	2	1	4	3	2	4	3	4	2	3	3	2	1	3	3	3	3	4	1	2

269	270	271	272	273	274	275	276	277	278	279	280	281	282	283	284	285	286	287	288	289	290	291	292	293	294	295	296	297	29
62.721	463.953	589.302	386.438	453.148	304.703	499.410	414.571	93.664	221.234	513.109	393.611	616.427	487.256	411.107	349.377	318.326	83.603	11.696	279.990	564.423	689.668	420.847	477.385	489.499	635.118	235.566	668.565	428.982	30
542.458	748.814	214.257	662.929	429.999	876.808	941.091	312.724	577.884	781.246	173.835	705.605	267.024	11.129	13.438	699.551	266.970	373.693	107.929	639.092	123.492	109.943	410.482	642.817	422.860	780.371	323.124	113.663	851.194	80
26.412	26.436	26.460	26.484	26.508	26.532	26.555	26.579	26.603	26.627	26.651	26.675	26.698	26.722	26.746	26.770	26.794	26.818	26.841	26.865	26.889	26.913	26.937	26.961	26.985	27.008	27.032	27.056	27.080	27
2.164	0.199	3.850	4.324	5.473	4.863	1.286	2.908	0.810	0.075	2.100	0.077	4.181	4.180	0.351	0.756	5.256	0.894	2.646	1.300	3.905	2.423	2.154	6.190	1.305	3.766	2.421	3.093	4.267	2.
2	1	3	3	3	2	2	2	1	2	4	3	2	2	3	4	2	3	2	1	2	1	1	3	2	2	0	3	3	3

299	300	301	302	303	304	305	306	307	308	309	310	311	312	313	314	315	316	317	318	319	320	321	322	323	324	325	326	327	32
29.033	449.387	170.709	539.008	493.861	71.015	724.376	300.773	508.950	117.781	354.641	270.875	180.518	126.379	514.572	214.816	564.837	576.420	151.303	114.226	657.068	684.142	189.089	525.961	685.914	520.947	657.191	84.942	340.504	22
903.964	85.403	620.287	174.063	326.998	921.106	584.315	124.408	794.491	820.847	269.583	533.847	861.062	523.036	259.693	296.994	382.462	808.247	630.939	954.354	697.906	235.009	87.274	197.671	180.438	408.631	305.712	739.459	366.112	34
27.128	27.151	27.175	27.199	27.223	27.247	27.271	27.294	27.318	27.342	27.366	27.390	27.414	27.437	27.461	27.485	27.509	27.533	27.557	27.580	27.604	27.628	27.652	27.676	27.700	27.723	27.747	27.771	27.795	27
-0.167	6.180	5.507	5.640	2.792	2.122	3.733	3.868	-0.022	2.280	3.870	4.809	1.190	1.325	2.264	3.081	1.194	2.008	4.275	5.480	2.001	-0.134	0.666	1.202	0.401	4.812	5.345	4.680	4.280	2.
2	2	3	2	3	4	3	3	3	3	2	2	3	3	3	0	3	2	3	3	2	2	3	2	2	2	1	1	3	4

329	330	331	332	333	334	335	336	337	338	339	340	341	342	343	344	345	346	347	348	349	350	351	352	353	354	355	356	357	35
725.335	674.915	549.911	331.210	743.631	578.470	484.166	97.943	364.913	290.639	647.313	141.719	51.698	43.138	438.576	519.930	507.091	63.579	415.362	303.396	743.786	644.691	716.216	326.224	635.503	209.006	282.845	261.818	536.222	64
15.967	874.252	402.694	520.555	889.035	422.206	380.571	891.134	815.882	221.643	664.173	289.347	167.352	792.697	635.932	336.480	361.531	410.694	182.568	23.288	379.949	91.924	795.863	138.788	934.121	731.051	823.383	174.505	532.660	82
27.843	27.867	27.890	27.914	27.938	27.962	27.986	28.010	28.033	28.057	28.081	28.105	28.129	28.153	28.176	28.200	28.224	28.248	28.272	28.296	28.319	28.343	28.367	28.391	28.415	28.439	28.462	28.486	28.510	28
1.877	4.138	5.205	2.680	1.067	2.949	3.616	2.284	2.418	-0.000	-0.112	4.152	3.486	3.062	2.822	-0.105	1.626	3.755	0.963	3.723	5.884	0.169	2.296	-0.000	3.985	4.250	4.382	2.301	4.823	4.
2	2	5	1	2	2	4	3	2	3	3	2	2	4	2	4	3	3	2	1	2	2	4	3	3	1	2	2	3	3

359	360	361	362	363	364	365	366	367	368	369	370	371	372	373	374	375	376	377	378	379	380	381	382	383	384	385	386	387	38
467.846	713.220	332.870	111.971	508.256	626.279	584.257	715.555	555.124	205.177	572.924	688.686	256.796	113.135	102.609	540.270	527.397	431.073	431.166	662.403	367.772	318.322	394.058	687.741	257.625	479.342	460.556	415.594	666.095	74
235.667	539.089	289.722	435.432	13.225	330.021	732.199	423.894	205.513	616.458	702.809	618.982	563.235	500.839	861.746	887.264	119.452	63.351	114.233	168.644	102.976	950.298	787.522	12.824	376.543	671.105	955.018	876.273	958.250	56
28.558	28.582	28.605	28.629	28.653	28.677	28.701	28.725	28.749	28.772	28.796	28.820	28.844	28.868	28.892	28.915	28.939	28.963	28.987	29.011	29.035	29.058	29.082	29.106	29.130	29.154	29.178	29.201	29.225	29
6.235	0.845	5.090	2.121	3.977	-0.078	1.248	2.044	3.634	3.767	5.163	4.235	3.901	5.821	2.447	3.506	4.892	3.833	5.418	-0.264	2.188	2.641	3.961	4.621	-0.052	3.299	-0.050	6.068	5.096	1.
2	2	3	2	1	1	1	2	1	2	3	3	2	2	3	3	3	3	2	2	1	4	1	2	2	2	2	2	1	1

389	390	391	392	393	394	395	396	397	398	399	400	401	402	403	404	405	406	407	408	409	410	411	412	413	414	415	416	417	4
744.127	210.600	351.822	326.205	128.645	287.024	118.918	737.073	396.959	619.418	476.886	199.371	607.427	578.492	314.503	145.687	246.816	126.579	231.641	412.427	43.629	605.252	598.866	339.939	733.123	271.987	696.439	323.869	490.560	60
592.296	637.932	143.965	477.190	135.571	150.738	99.570	336.852	342.158	648.542	328.440	178.051	881.949	955.182	229.654	126.862	361.432	899.684	813.650	671.888	96.817	291.839	630.033	780.079	139.554	801.442	472.827	347.274	188.035	59
29.273	29.297	29.321	29.344	29.368	29.392	29.416	29.440	29.464	29.487	29.511	29.535	29.559	29.583	29.607	29.631	29.654	29.678	29.702	29.726	29.750	29.774	29.797	29.821	29.845	29.869	29.893	29.917	29.940	29
5.668	2.899	4.702	1.054	2.595	3.123	1.544	4.177	2.862	-0.032	4.310	3.785	3.522	2.235	3.261	2.473	3.021	2.606	5.646	0.788	4.708	0.641	2.624	0.905	3.016	5.900	6.030	5.497	1.959	5.
1	1	4	3	3	3	2	3	4	2	3	2	2	1	3	3	3	2	3	3	2	4	4	4	1	4	3	3	5	3

419	420	421	422	423	424	425	426	427	428	429	430	431	432	433	434	435	436	437	438	439	440	441	442	443	444	445	446	447	44
463.126	387.781	64.559	368.712	346.364	388.052	37.057	690.035	194.571	289.600	689.553	116.679	64.013	23.364	400.311	125.784	597.691	247.798	337.614	129.994	189.352	742.669	122.455	487.092	48.617	291.545	492.957	540.256	77.846	70
926.737	332.552	259.389	28.519	239.556	12.212	205.780	541.815	347.777	925.328	405.527	715.963	719.211	658.669	372.638	927.268	591.687	659.746	169.590	232.448	902.423	97.272	262.552	531.721	192.037	181.566	620.934	796.234	624.930	39
29.988	30.012	30.036	30.060	30.083	30.107	30.131	30.155	30.179	30.203	30.226	30.250	30.274	30.298	30.322	30.346	30.369	30.393	30.417	30.441	30.465	30.489	30.513	30.536	30.560	30.584	30.608	30.632	30.656	30
3.402	4.319	3.665	3.404	0.918	3.663	0.528	0.137	2.100	-0.000	2.493	0.665	3.409	3.918	3.933	4.717	4.829	2.891	3.283	2.217	2.241	5.867	1.330	4.459	2.896	2.375	5.600	1.856	3.515	0.
3	3	1	3	2	2	2	5	2	4	1	1	2	0	4	5	4	3	5	3	4	1	4	3	4	3	2	1	1	4

Process Compendium
2004 – 2010

The most important element of Process <NUMBER> is the text. The text is the Process described in English, written with the intent to translate its content into software. The Elements, Forms, and Behaviors referenced within the Process text are defined in the Library.

The software interpretation is secondary to the text. The text leaves many decisions open to the programmer, decisions that must be made using personal judgment. The act of translating the Process from English into a machine language interprets the text. Process <NUMBER> was implemented by <NAME> into the <LANGUAGE> language in <YEAR>.

The hardware is inconsequential and in time it will fail. It was selected to be robust, but electronic devices are fragile. If a component of the hardware fails, it may be replaced without diminishing the work. Eventually, compatible components won't be available. When this happens, a new hardware system must be acquired and the software modified for the new platform.

Forms
F1: Circle
F2: Line

Behaviors
B1: Move in a straight line
B2: Constrain to surface
B3: Change direction while touching another Element
B4: Move away from an overlapping Element
B5: Enter from the opposite edge after moving off the surface
B6: Orient toward the direction of an Element that is touching
B7: Deviate from the current direction

Elements
E1: F1 + B1 + B2 + B3 + B4
E2: F1 + B1 + B5
E3: F2 + B1 + B3 + B5
E4: F1 + B1 + B2 + B3
E5: F2 + B1 + B5 + B6 + B7

Process 18

A rectangular surface filled with instances of Element 5, each with a different size and gray value. Draw a quadrilateral connecting the endpoints of each pair of Elements that are touching. Increase the opacity of the quadrilateral while the Elements are touching and decrease while they are not.

Implemented by C.E.B. Reas
Summer 2007, Winter 2008
Processing 125 / 135

Process 17

A rectangular surface filled with instances of Element 5, each with a different size and gray value. Draw a transparent circle at the midpoint of each Element. Increase a circle's size and opacity while its Element is touching another Element and decrease while it is not.

Implemented by C.E.B. Reas
Summer 2010
Processing 1.1

Process 16

A rectangular surface filled with instances of Element 3, each with a different size and gray value. Draw a tiny, transparent circle at the midpoint of each Element. Increase a circle's size and opacity while its Element is touching another Element and decrease while it is not.

Implemented by C.E.B. Reas
Fall 2006
Processing 121

Process 15

A rectangular surface filled with instances of Element 3, each with a different size and gray value. Draw a small, transparent circle at the midpoint of each Element. Increase the circle's opacity while its Element is touching another Element and decrease while it is not.

Implemented by C.E.B. Reas
Fall 2006
Processing 121

Process 14

A rectangular surface filled with instances of Element 4, each with a different size and direction. Display the intersections by drawing a circle at each point of contact. Set the size of each circle relative to the distance between the centers of the overlapping Elements. Draw the smallest possible circle as white and the largest as black, with varying grays representing sizes in between.

Implemented by C.E.B. Reas
Fall 2006, Winter 2008
Processing 122, 135

Process 13

Bisect a rectangular surface and define the dividing line as the origin for a large group of Element 1. When each Element moves beyond the surface, move its position back to the origin. Draw a line from the centers of Elements that are touching. Set the value of the shortest possible line to black and the longest to white, with varying grays representing values in between.

Implemented by C.E.B. Reas
Fall 2009, Summer 2010
Processing 1.0

Process 12

A rectangular surface filled with instances of Element 3, each with a different size and gray value. Draw a dot at the center of each line. Draw a quadrilateral connecting the endpoints of each pair of Elements that are touching. Increase the opacity of the dot and quadrilateral while the Elements are touching and decrease while they are not.

Implemented by C.E.B. Reas
Fall 2006
Processing 121

Process 11

A rectangular surface filled with instances of Element 2, each with a different size, speed, and direction. Display the intersections by drawing a circle at each point of contact. Set the size of one circle to be relative to the distance between the centers of the overlapping Elements and make the other circle tiny. Draw the smallest possible circle as white and largest as black, with varying grays representing sizes in between.

Implemented by C.E.B. Reas
Summer, Fall 2006
Processing 115

Process 10

Position a circle at the center of a rectangular surface. Set the center of the circle as the origin for a large group of Element 1. When an Element moves beyond the edge of its circle, return to the origin. Draw a line from the centers of Elements that are touching. Set the value of the shortest possible line to black and the longest to white, with varying grays representing values in between.

Implemented by C. E. B. Reas
Fall 2005
C++/OpenGL, Processing 115

Process 9

Position three large circles on a rectangular surface. Set the center of each circle as the origin for a large group of Element 2. When an Element moves beyond the edge of its circle, return to the origin. Display the intersections by drawing a circle at each point of contact. Set the size of each circle relative to the distance between the centers of the overlapping Elements. Draw the smallest possible circle as white and largest as black, with varying grays representing sizes in between.

Implemented by C. E. B. Reas
Fall 2005
C++/OpenGL, Processing 115

Process 8

A rectangular surface densely filled with instances of Element 2, each with a different size, speed, and direction. Display the intersections by drawing a circle at each point of contact. Set the size of each circle relative to the distance between the centers of the overlapping Elements. Draw the smallest possible circle as black and largest as white, with varying grays representing sizes in between.

Implemented by C. E. B. Reas
Summer 2005
C++/OpenGL, Processing 115

Process 7

A rectangular surface filled with varying sizes of Element 1. Draw a line from the centers of Elements that are touching. Set the value of the shortest possible line to white and the longest to black, with varying grays representing values in between. Draw the perimeter of each Element as a black line and the center as a white dot.

Implemented by C. E. B. Reas
Summer 2005
C++/OpenGL, Processing 115

Process 6

Position three large circles on a rectangular surface. Set the center of each circle as the origin for a large group of Element 1. When an Element moves beyond the edge of its circle, return to the origin. Draw a line from the centers of Elements that are touching. Set the value of the shortest possible line to black and the longest to white, with varying grays representing values in between.

Implemented by C. E. B. Reas
Winter 2005
C++/OpenGL, Processing 115

Process 5

A rectangular surface filled with varying sizes of Element 1. Draw the perimeter of each Element as a black line and the center as a white dot. Draw a gray line from the centers of Elements that are touching.

Implemented by C. E. B. Reas
Winter 2005
C++/OpenGL, Processing 115

Process 4

A rectangular surface filled with varying sizes of Element 1. Draw a line from the centers of Elements that are touching. Set the value of the shortest possible line to black and the longest to white, with varying grays representing values in between.

Implemented by C. E. B. Reas
Winter 2005
C++/OpenGL, Processing 115

Process 3, 2, 1

The first three Process works are named Structure 1, 2, and 3. They were created for the *{Software} Structures* project, commissioned by the Whitney Museum of American Art's ARTPORT in 2004. Although the Process works originated from the Structure works, they are separate projects. There is more information at the URL: *http://artport.whitney.org*

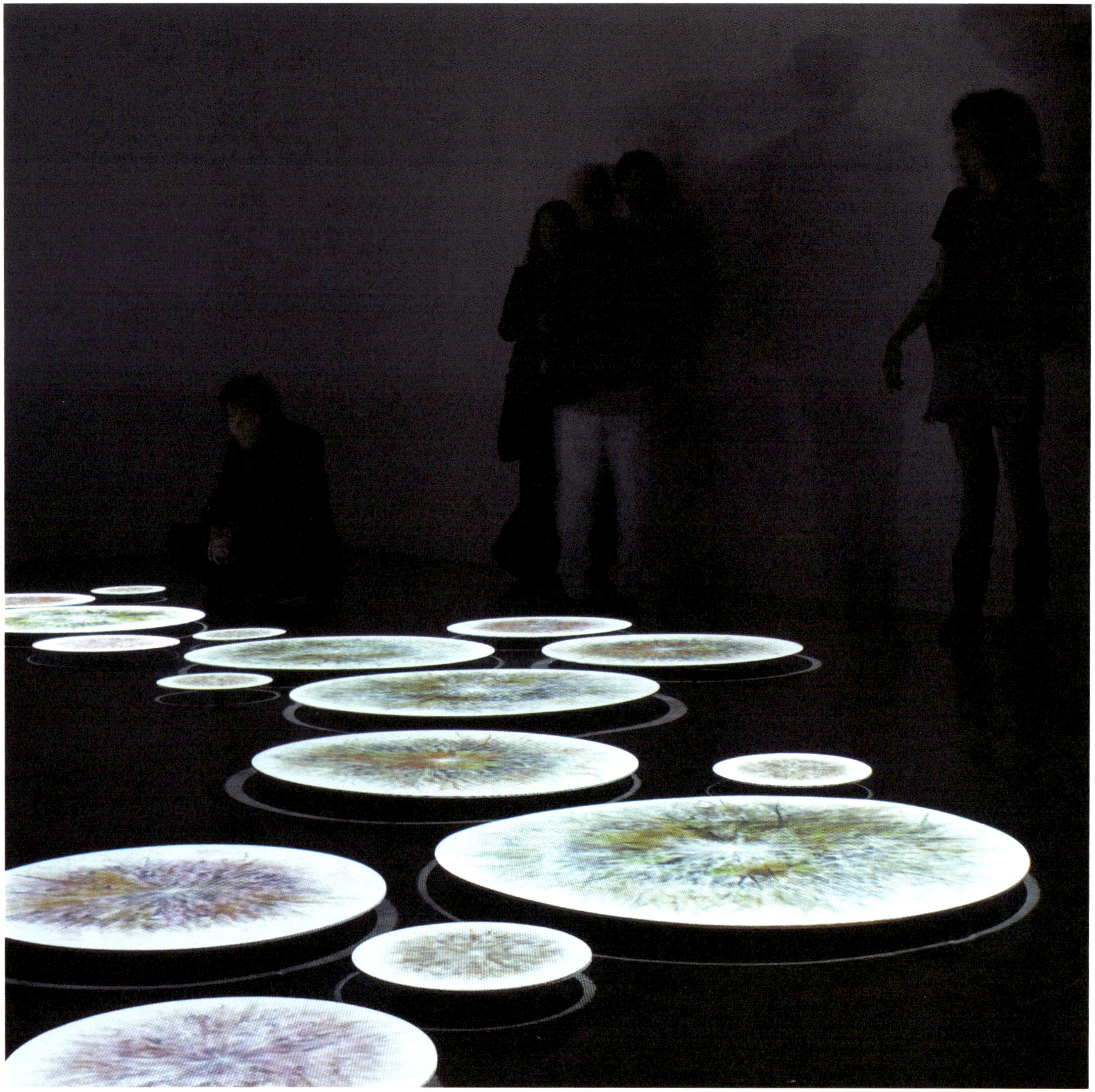

TI at the Natural exhibition, BANK gallery, Los Angeles, CA

Process Exhibitions
2004 – 2010

One- and Two-Person Exhibitions

Compendium 2004–2010. Gallery [DAM] Berlin. Berlin, Germany. 10 Sep – 3 Nov 2010. *Process Compendum 2004 – 2010*

Transfers and Actions: C. E. B. Reas and Ellie Harrison. Mejan Labs, Royal Academy of Fine Arts. Stockholm, Sweden. 15 Apr – 7 Jun 2009. *Process 18*

CODE and FORM: C. E. B. Reas & Marius Watz. Pittsburgh Center for the Arts. Pittsburgh, PA. 7 Feb – 19 Apr 2009. *Process 16, Process 14, Process 18 (Object 1, 2), Process 14 (Image 4, 5), Process 8 (Image 2)*

Process / Form. bitforms gallery. New York, NY. 6 Mar – 12 Apr 2008. *Process 18, Process 14, Process 18 (Object 1, 2), Process 18 (Image 3, 4), Process 14 (Image 3, 4, 5), Network 2008*

The Protean Image. <>TAG. The Hague, Netherlands. 19 Sep – 3 Nov 2007. *The Protean Image Machine*

Microstates: C. E. B. Reas & Austin Heitzman. James Edward Carlos Gallery, University of the South. Sewanee, TN. 16 Nov 2007 – 9 Jan 2008. *Process 14, Process 18*

C. E. B. Reas & Suzung Kim. bitforms gallery. Seoul, Korea. 15 Dec 2006 – 27 Jan 2007. *Process 12, Process 12 (Image 1, 2, 3), Process 11 (Installation 1), Process 11 (Image 1), Process 9 (Interaction 1), Process 9 (Image 1, 2, 3, 4, 5), Process 8 (Image 1, 2)*

Natural. BANK. Los Angeles, CA. 10 Sep – 15 Oct 2005. *TI*

Process / Drawing. Gallery [DAM] Berlin. Berlin, Germany. 2 Oct – 23 Nov 2005. *Process 8 (Software 2), Process 7, Process 6, Process 6 (Image 1, 2, 3, 4), Process 4 (Image 1, 2)*

Process / Drawing. bitforms gallery. New York, NY. 4 Mar – 3 Apr 2005. *Process 6, Process 6 (Image 1, 2, 3, 4), Process 5, Process 4 (Image 1, 2), Process 4 (Form 1, 2), Process 4 (Data 1, 2), Process 4, Pre-process, Pre-process Hex, Pre-process Execution*

TI. Telic Arts Exchange. Los Angeles, CA. 15 May 2004. *TI*

Selected Group Exhibitions

Quotidian Architectures. Venice Biennale 12th International Architecture Exhibition. Venice, Italy. 29 Aug – 21 Nov 2010. *Clad*

Immuring. SCI-Arc Gallery. Los Angeles, CA. 4 Jun – 18 Jul 2010. *Clad*

E-Volve. Gallery [DAM]Cologne. Cologne, Germany. 24 Apr – 24 Jun 2010. *Network A*

Process Becomes Paradigm. Laboral Centro de Arte y Creatión Industrial. Gijon, Spain. 23 Apr – 27 Sep 2010. *Process 18, Process 18 (Object 1, 2), Process 18 (Image 5, 6)*

Code:Craft. Millennium Gallery. Sheffield, UK. 27 Jan – 16 Jun 2010. *Network A*

Decode. Victoria & Albert Museum, Porter Gallery. London, UK. 8 Dec 2009 – 11 April 2010. *TI*

Vida Origen. Museu del Montsià. Amposta, Spain. 7 Nov – 8 Dec 2009. *Network B*

OPEN. Gray Area Foundation for the Arts. San Francisco, CA. 1 Oct – 18 Nov 2009. *Surface, Network A, Network B, Process 18 (Image 5, 6), Process 18 (Object 1, 2), Process 14 (Image 4, 5), Process 11 (Image 1), Process 8 (Image 1), Process 4 (Image 1, 2)*

Collider: Interactivity and New Media. Emily Davis Gallery, Myers School of Art. Akron, OH. 21 Sep – 31 Oct 2009. *The Protean Image Machine 2*

HelloWorld.show();. CreateHere. Chattanooga, TN. 31 Jul – 12 Sep 2009. *Pre-process Execution, Pre-process Hex*

Art and Electronic Media. bitforms gallery. New York, NY. 16 Jun – 10 Jul 2009. *Process 8 (Image 2)*

Incognito 2009. Santa Monica Museum of Art. Santa Monica, CA. 2 May 2009. *Network 2008 (Drawing 1)*

Abstract Cinema. Museum of Contemporary Art, North Miami. North Miami, FL. 26 Mar – 10 May 2009. *Process 16*

I'll Be Your Mirror. BANK. Los Angeles, CA. 21 Feb – 28 Mar 2009. *Fissure*

Scalable Relations. Beall Center for Art + Technology. Irvine, CA. 9 Jan – 14 Mar 2009. *Process 16*

Processing Light. TodaysArt 2008. The Hague, Netherlands. 26 – 27 Sep 2008. *Process 8 (Image 3)*

Matters of Sensation. Artists Space. New York, NY. 24 Sep – 15 Nov 2008. *07 Masses*

Alt_Cph: Platform for Nordic Non-profit Art Spaces. Copenhagen, Denmark. 19 – 21 Sep 2008. *Network 2008*

5th Seoul International Media Art Biennale. Seoul, Korea. 12 Sep – 5 Nov 2008. *TI*

Media Cabaret at the Philadelphia Live Arts Festival. Philadelphia, PA. 29 Aug – 13 Sep 2008. *Process 14, Process 16*

Holy Fire. iMAL Center. Brussels, Belgium. 18 – 30 Apr 2008. *Process 5*

Impermanent Markings. Pratt Manhattan Gallery. New York, NY. 6 Mar – 17 Apr 2008. *TI*

At Random? Netwerken en Kruisbestuivingen. Museum De Paviljoens. Almere, Netherlands. 5 Mar – 6 Apr 2008. *The Protean Image Machine*

Expanded Box. ARCO 2008. Madrid, Spain. 13 – 18 Feb 2008. *TI*

Project(or) Art Fair, Art Rotterdam. Rotterdam, Netherlands. 6 – 10 Feb 2008. *The Protean Image Machine*

Imaging by Numbers: A Historical View of the Computer Print. Block Museum of Art at Northwestern University. Evanston, IL. 18 Jan – 6 Apr 2008. *Process 6 (Image 3)*

Space, Color, and Motion. Block Museum of Art at Northwestern University. Evanston, IL. 18 Jan – 6 Apr 2008. *TI*

Ephemeral: Explorations in Light. Claremont Museum of Art. Claremont, CA. 16 Sep – 30 Dec 2007. *TI*

Scriptedbypurpose. FUEL Collection. Philadelphia, PA. 7 – 20 Sep 2007. *Process 14, Process 8 (Image 2)*

Summer Group Exhibition. bitforms gallery. New York, NY. 25 May – 20 Jun 2007. *Process 11*

Taste, 28th Annual Benefit Auction. LACE. Los Angeles, CA. 19 May 2007. *Process 6 (Puff 5)*

FEEDBACK. Laboral Centro de Arte y Creatión Industrial. Gijon, Spain. 30 Mar – 30 Jun 2007. *Process 4 (Installation 1)*

Design Life Now: National Design Triennial. Cooper-Hewitt, National Design Museum. New York, NY (8 Dec 2006 – 29 Jul 2007); Institute of Contemporary Art, Boston (28 Sep 2007 – 6 Jan 2008); Contemporary Arts Museum Houston (26 Jan – 20 Apr 2008). *Process 6 (Image 4), Pre-process Execution*

Cybernetic Sensibility. Daelim Contemporary Art Museum. Seoul, Korea. 26 Oct 2006 – 21 Jan 2007. *Process 6 (Image 3), Process 9*

Texelectronica. UNT Fort Worth ArtSpace. Fort Worth, TX. 26 – 28 Oct 2006. *Process 9 (Installation 1)*

Further Processing. Kunstverein MEDIENTURM. Graz, Austria. 23 Sep – 11 Nov 2006. *Process 9*

La Noche en Blanco. Madrid, Spain. 23 Sep 2006. *Process 7*

Interferenze New Arts Festival. Naturalis Electronica. San Martino Valle Caudina, Italy. 3 – 5 Aug 2006. *Process 6, Process 7, Process 8*

Second Natures. UCLA. Los Angeles, CA. 14 Sep – 26 Oct 2006. *Process 4, Process 4 (Image 2), Seoul B*

Drawing / Painting / Sketching. CCCB. Barcelona, Spain. 11 – 12 May 2006. *Process 6, Process 7, Process 8*

Drawing Conclusions on the Wall. Chapman University. Orange, CA. Spring 2006. *Process 6 (Puff)* prints

Software Art. DeCordova Museum. Lincoln, MA. 28 Jan – 16 Apr 2006. *Articulate*

SWARM. Fabric Workshop and Museum. Philadelphia, PA. 3 Dec 2005 – 18 Mar 2006. *Process 4, Process 6 (Image 1, 2, 3, 4)*

Moving Pictures: Digital Paintings. The Dallas Center for Contemporary Art. Dallas, TX. 4 Nov – 23 Dec 2005. *Process 4*

Generator.x. The National Museum of Art, Architecture and Design. Oslo, Norway. 24 Sep – 16 Oct 2005. *Process 8 (Software 2)*

Bioart. Gallery António Prates. Lisbon, Portugal. 23 Sep – 18 Oct 2005. *Process 6 (Image 3, 4), Process 6, Process 4 (Image 1, 2)*

White Noise. Australian Centre for the Moving Image. Melbourne, Australia. 18 Aug – 23 Oct 2005. *Articulate*

ThickDesign05. Betty Rymer Gallery, The School of the Art Institute of Chicago. Chicago, IL. 16 Aug – 28 Sep 2005. *Process 5*

Rhizome ArtBase 101. New Museum of Contemporary Art. New York, NY. 23 Jun – 10 Sep 2005. *{Software} Structures*

8 Abstractions, Now. Sónar. Barcelona, Spain. 16 – 18 Jun 2005. *Articulate*

Fresh. Museum of Contemporary Art Auction 2005. Los Angeles, CA. 4 Jun 2005. *Process 5*

Generative X. onedotzero09. Institute of Contemporary Arts. London, UK. 27 May – 6 Jun 2005. *Articulate*

The Algorithmic Revolution. Zentrum für Kunst und Medientechnologie (ZKM). Karlsruhe, Germany. 31 Oct 2004. *Seoul A, Seoul B*

Microwave International Media Art Festival. Hong Kong, China. 28 Oct – 20 Nov 2004. *Seoul A, Seoul B*

Sonic Acts X. Paradiso. Amsterdam, Netherlands. 23 – 25 Sep 2004. *Seoul A*

ARTPORT. Whitney Museum of American Art. New York, NY. Jun 2004 – present. *{Software} Structures*

Softwarekunst. Gallery [DAM]Berlin and Transmediale 04. Berlin, Germany. 30 Jan – 4 Feb 2004. *Articulate*

Abstraction Now. Künstlerhaus. Vienna, Austria. 29 Aug – 28 Sep 2003. *Articulate*

Selected Performances

Persee: Orchestrated Perception. Regent Theater. Los Angeles, CA. 10 May 2007. *Process 11 (Performance 1)*

Sónar Club. Barcelona, Spain. 17 Jun 2005. *Meta-Process (Performance 1)*

L'Espace Temporel. Ars Electronica Festival 2004. Linz, Austria. 6 Sep 2004. *Images for 18 Musicians*

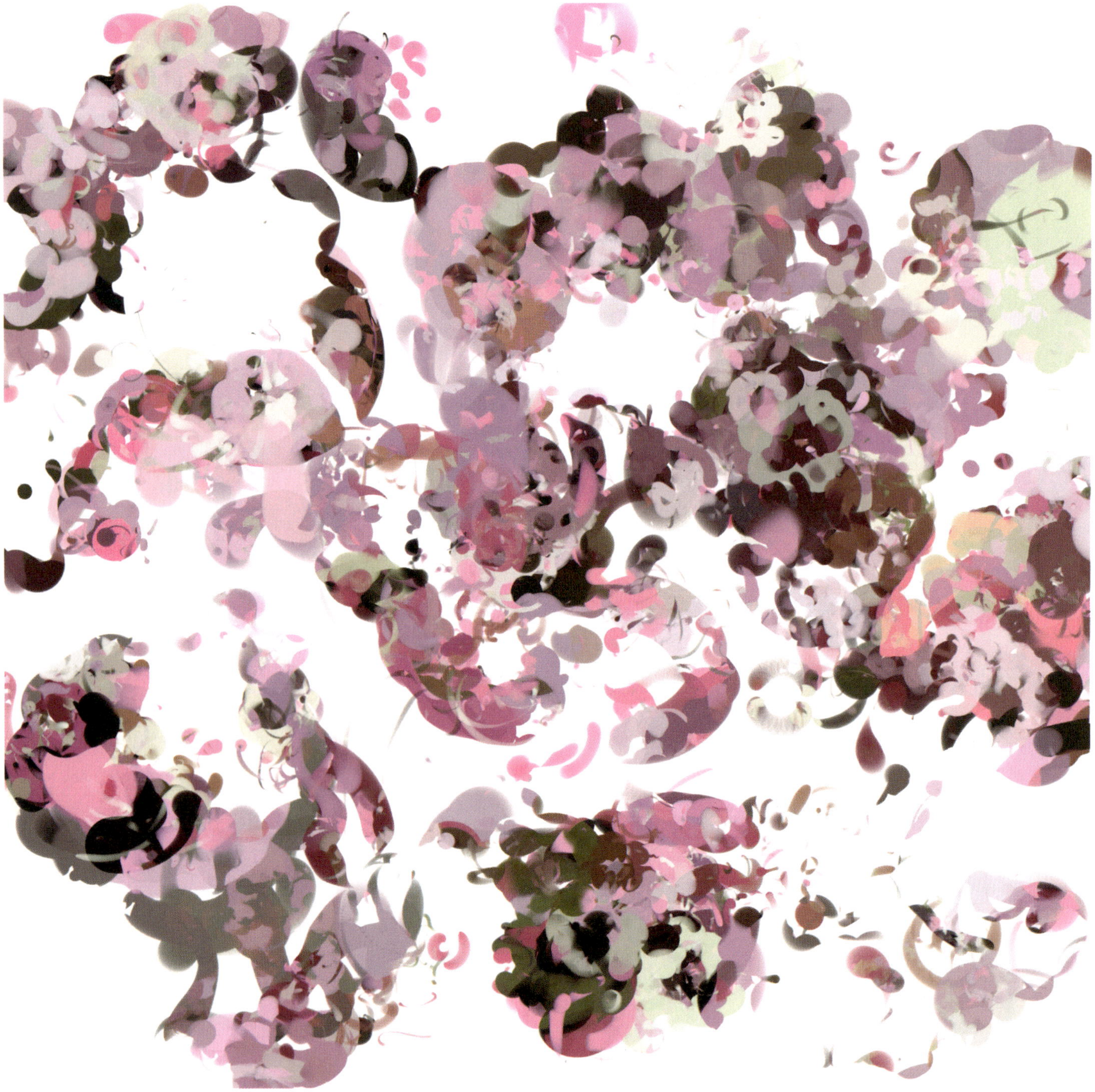

Process 14 (Image 5), 2008
Unique C prints on Fuji
Flex SuperGloss
27 x 27 in / 68.6 x 68.6 cm

Process Catalog
2004 – 2010

Process Compendium 2004–2010 (B), 2010
15 C prints on Fuji Crystal Archive
Pearl, metal box
Edition of 8 + 2 AP
19.7 x 19.7 in / 50 x 50 cm

Process Compendium 2004–2010 (A), 2010
15 C prints on Fuji Crystal Archive
Pearl, metal box
Edition of 8 + 2 AP
19.7 x 19.7 in / 50 x 50 cm

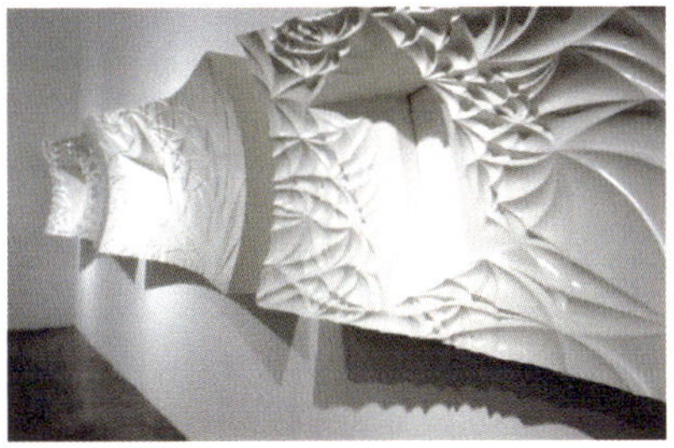

Clad, 2010
a.k.a. *Process 4 (Object 1, 2, 3)*
Triptych of glass fiber reinforced
concrete (GFRC) objects
59 x 78.7 x 19.7 in /
150 x 200 x 50 cm
Collaboration with davidclovers

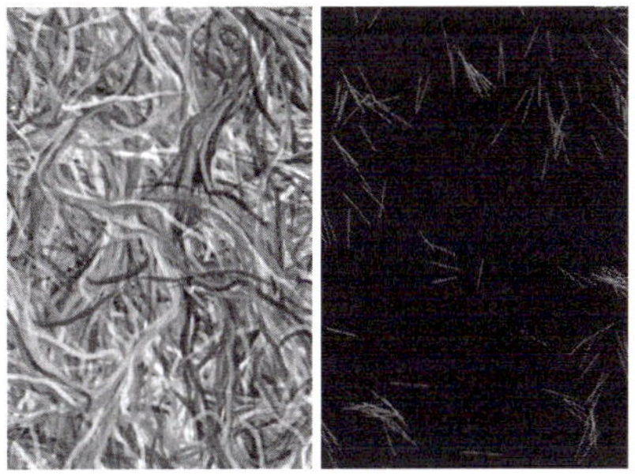

Process 17, 2010
Text, unique custom software,
computer, documentation prints
Dimensions variable

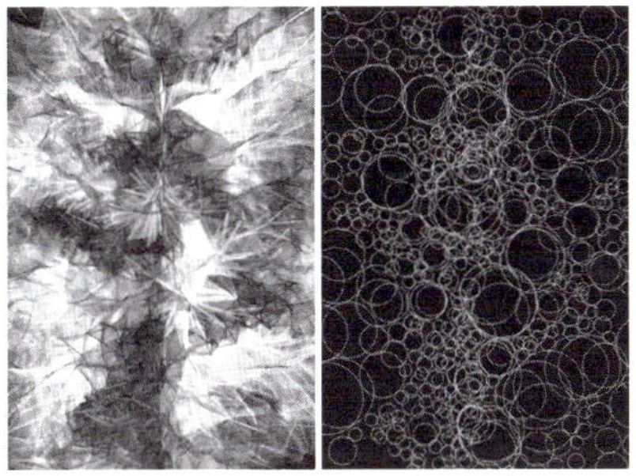

Process 13, 2010
Text, unique custom software,
computer, documentation prints
Dimensions variable

Network B, 2009
a.k.a. *Process 4 (Installation 3)*
Unique custom software, computer
Dimensions variable

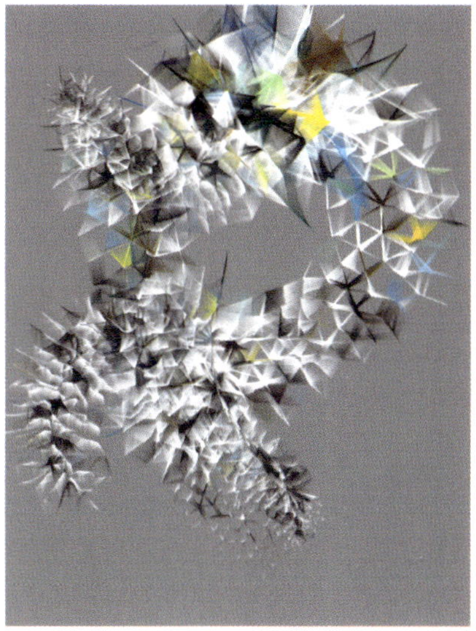

Network A, 2009
a.k.a. *Process 4 (Installation 2)*
Unique custom software, computer
Dimensions variable

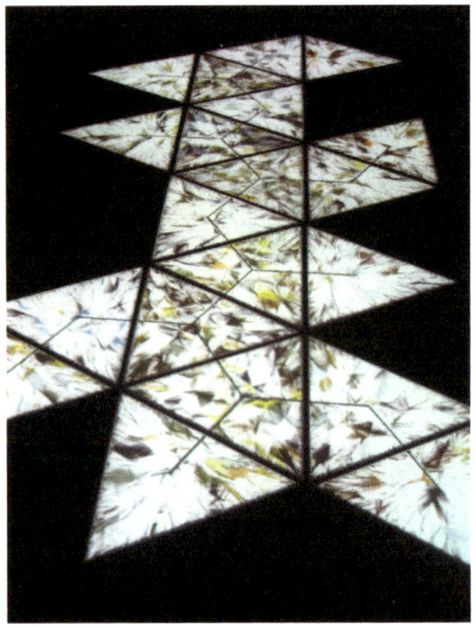

Surface, 2009
a.k.a. *Process 13 (Installation 1)*
Unique custom software, computer,
projector, 20 triangles
Dimensions variable

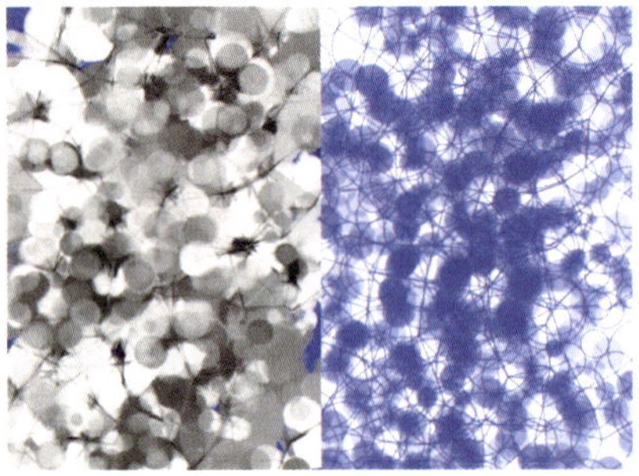

The Protean Image Machine 2, 2009
a.k.a. *Meta-Process (Installation 2)*
Unique custom software, computer,
projector, custom electronics,
cards, custom enclosure
Dimensions variable

Fissure, 2009
a.k.a. *Process 13 (Installation 1)*
Unique custom software, computer
Dimensions variable

Network 2008 (Drawing 1), 2009
Pencil drawing on board
10 x 8 in / 25.4 x 20.3 cm

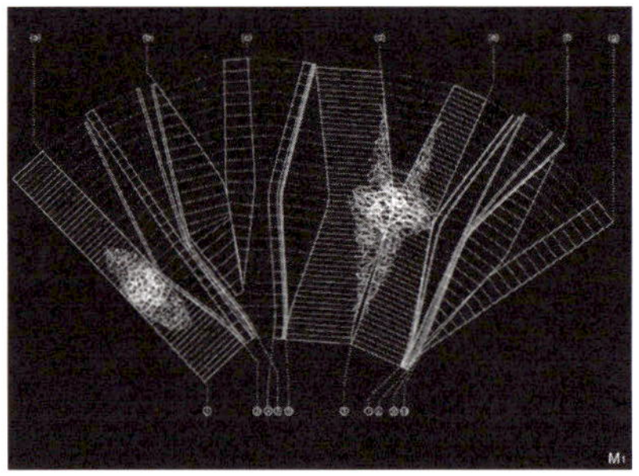

07 Masses, 2008
Drawings, Corian, custom
electronics, wood
Collaboration with davidclovers

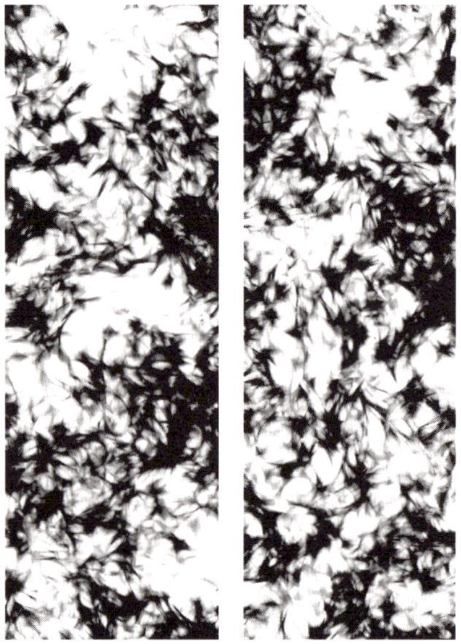

Process 18 (Image 5, 6), 2008
Unique C prints on Fuji Crystal
Archive Pearl
36 x 12 in / 91.4 x 30.5 cm

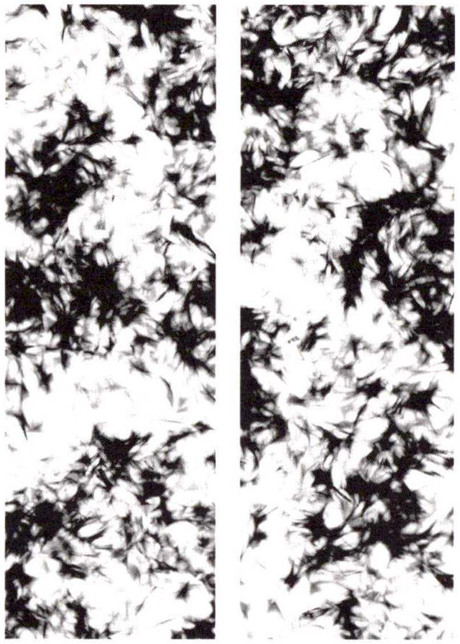

Process 18 (Image 3, 4), 2008
Unique C prints on Fuji Crystal
Archive Pearl
36 x 12 in / 91.4 x 30.5 cm

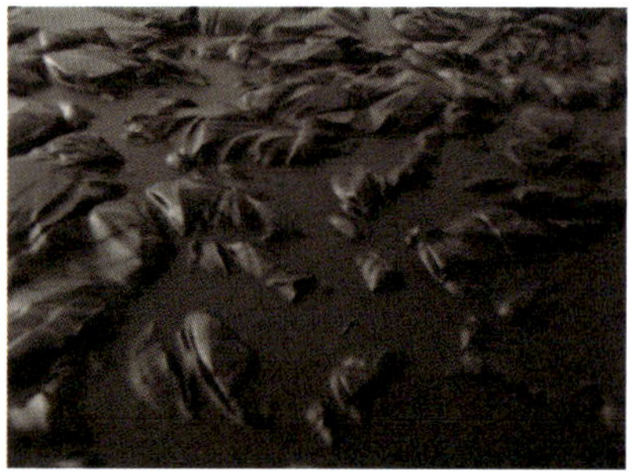

Process 18 (Object 2), 2008
Process 18 (Object 1), 2008
Unique milled fiber composite
18 x 18 x 1.25 in /
45.7 x 45.7 x 3.2 cm

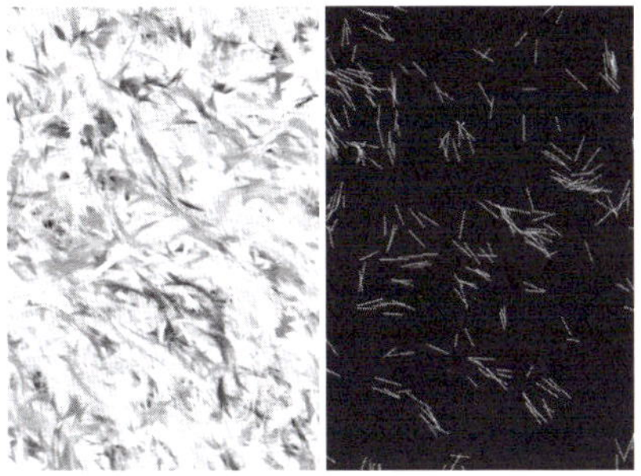

Process 18, 2008
Text, unique custom software,
computer, documentation prints
Dimensions variable

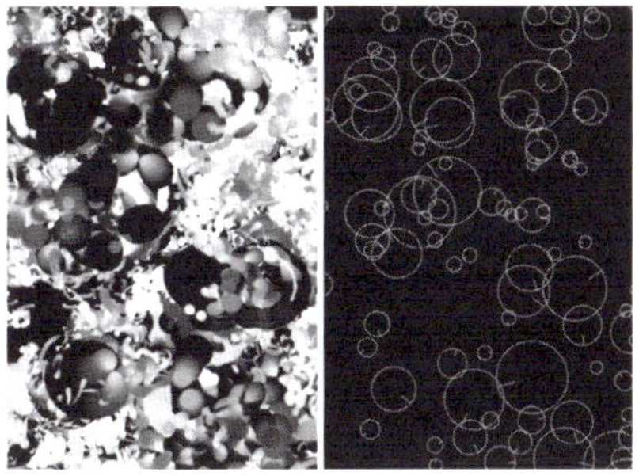

Process 14, 2008
Text, unique custom software,
computer, documentation prints
Dimensions variable

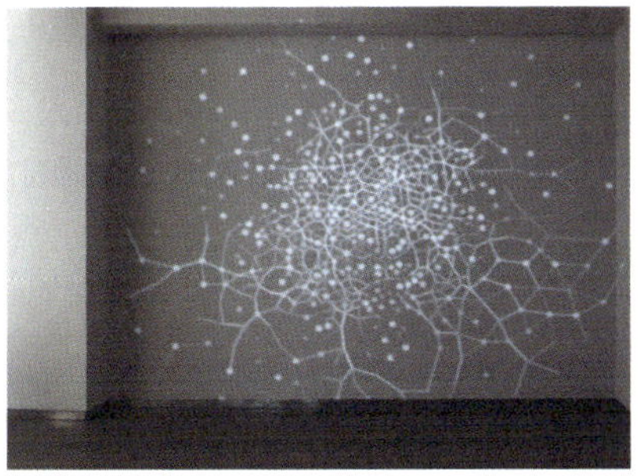

Network 2008, 2008
Unique custom software, computer,
projector
Dimensions variable

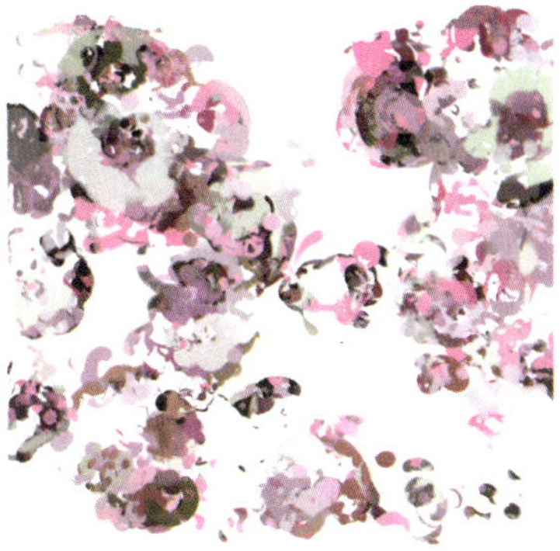

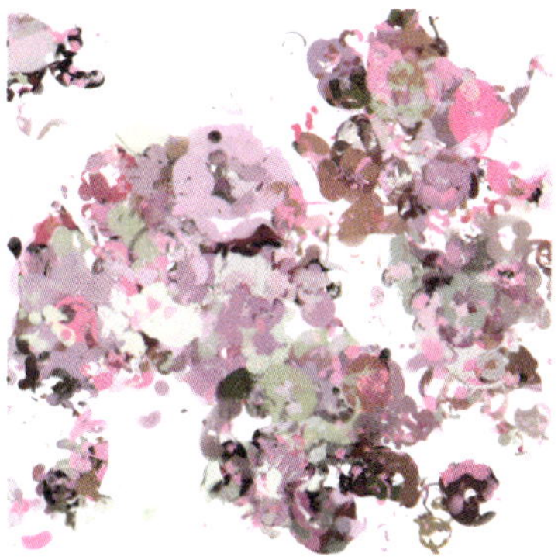

Process 14 (Image 5), 2008
Process 14 (Image 4), 2008
Process 14 (Image 3), 2008
Unique C prints on Fuji
Flex SuperGloss
27 x 27 in / 68.6 x 68.6 cm

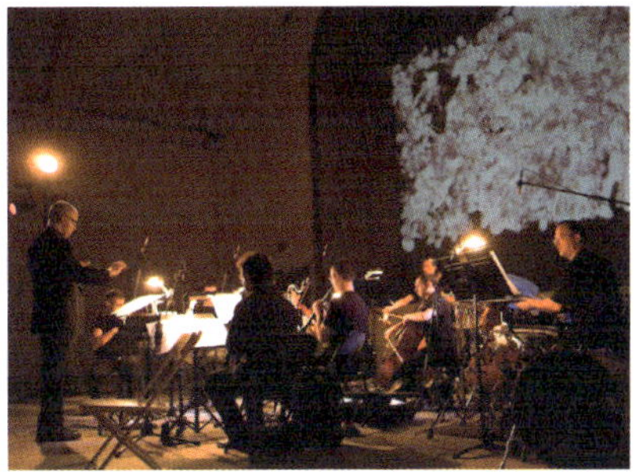

Process 11 (Performance 1), 2007
Unique custom software
Collaboration with Drew Schnurr

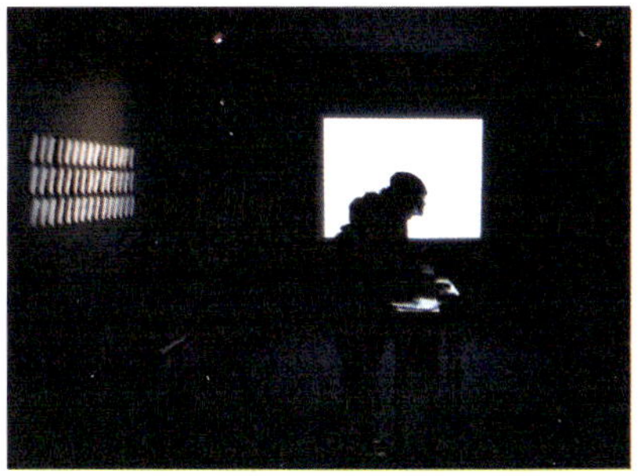

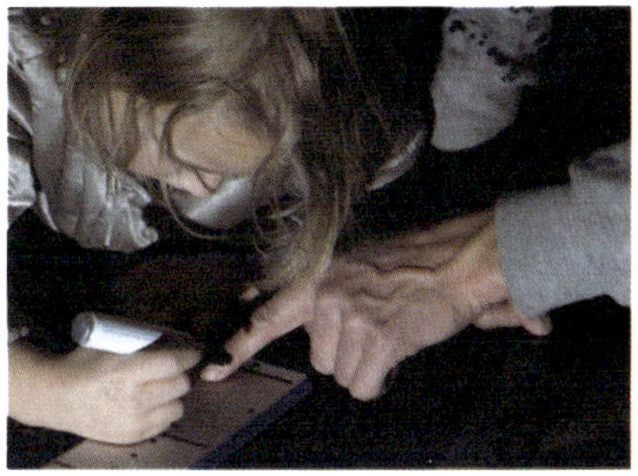

The Protean Image Machine, 2008
a.k.a. *Meta-Process (Installation 1)*
Unique custom software, computer,
projector, custom electronics,
cards, custom enclosure
Dimensions variable

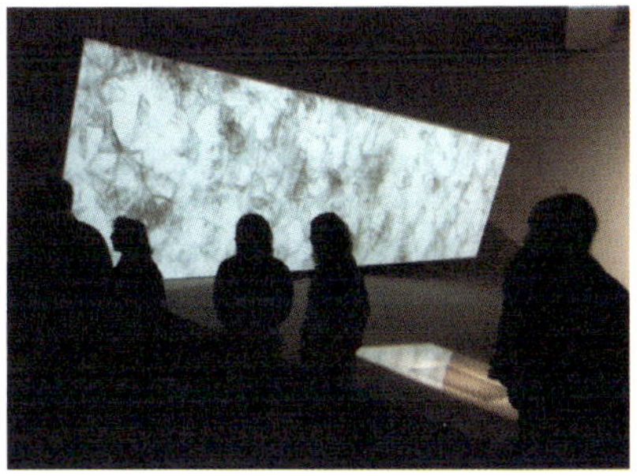

Process 4 (Installation 1), 2007
Custom software, computer
Dimensions variable

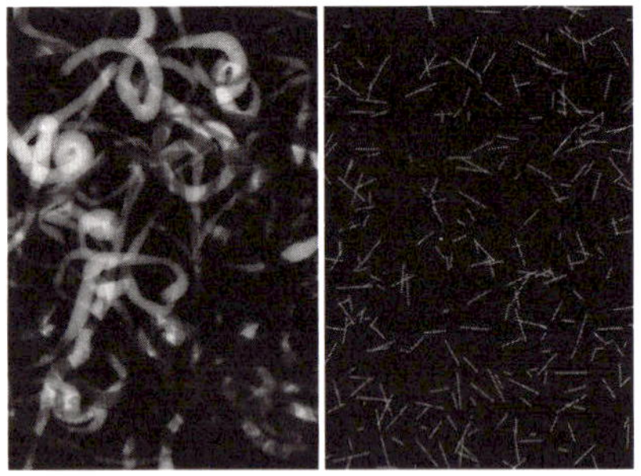

Process 16, 2006
Text, unique custom software,
computer, documentation prints
Dimensions variable

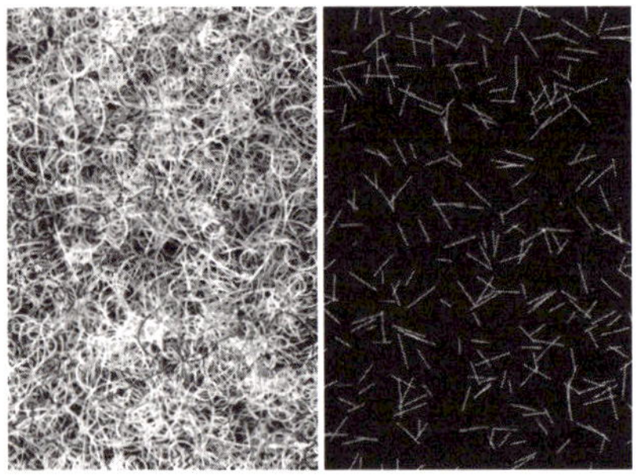

Process 15, 2006
Text, unique custom software,
computer, documentation prints
Dimensions variable

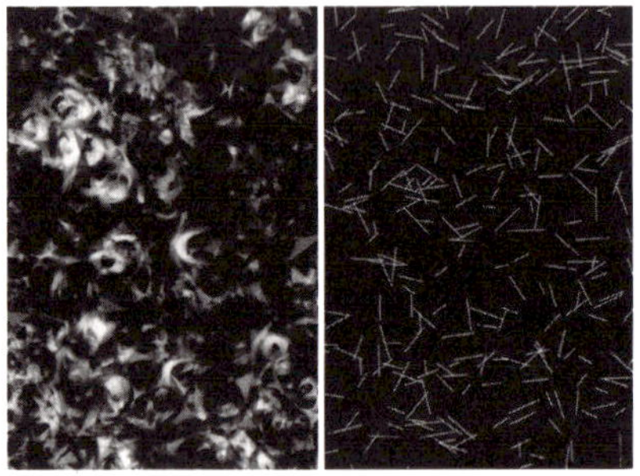

Process 12, 2006
Text, unique custom software,
computer, documentation prints
Dimensions variable

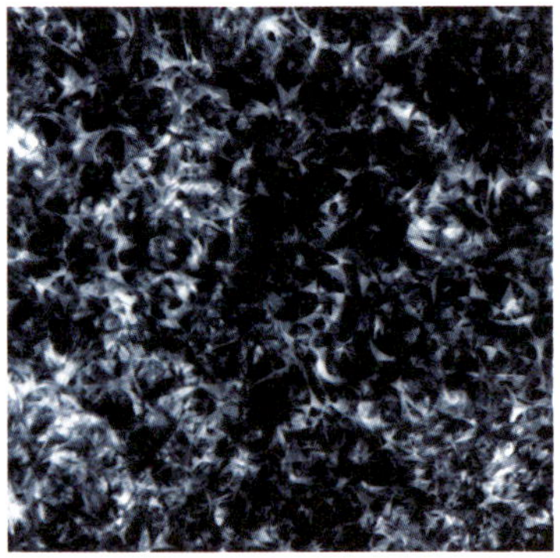

Process 12 (Image 3), 2006
Process 12 (Image 2), 2006
Process 12 (Image 1), 2006
Unique inkjet prints on
Museo Silver Rag
12 x 12 in / 30.5 x 30.5 cm

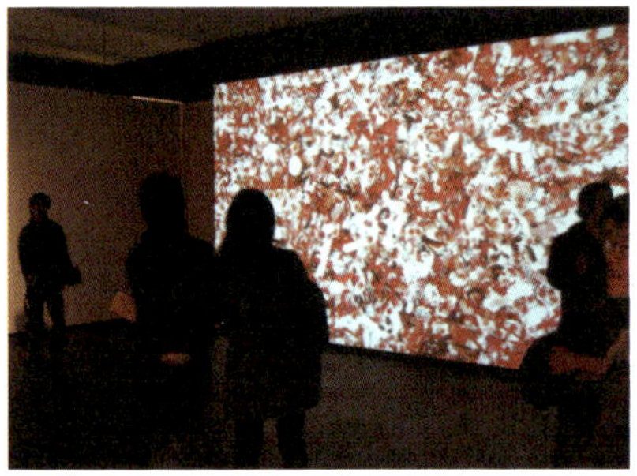

Process 11 (Installation 1), 2006
Unique custom software, computer
Dimensions variable

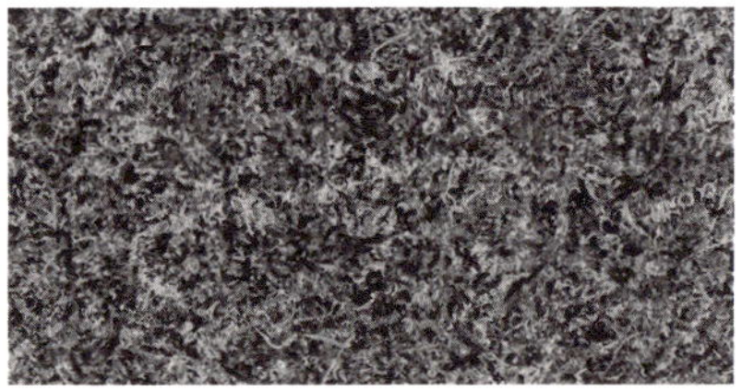

Process 11 (Image 1), 2006
Unique C print on Fuji Crystal
Archive Gloss
56 x 28 in / 142.2 x 71.1 cm

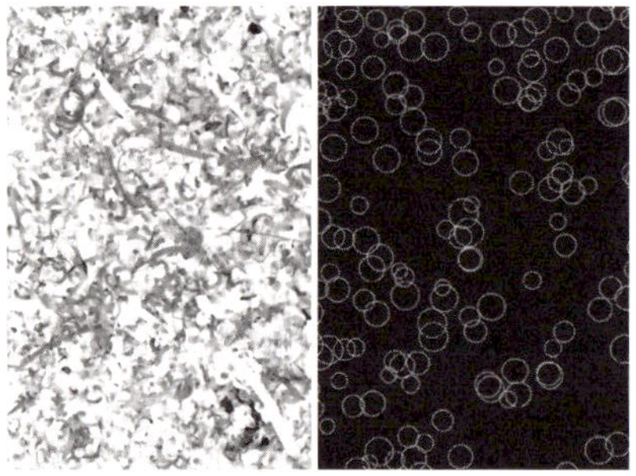

Process 11, 2006
Text, unique custom software,
computer, documentation prints
Dimensions variable

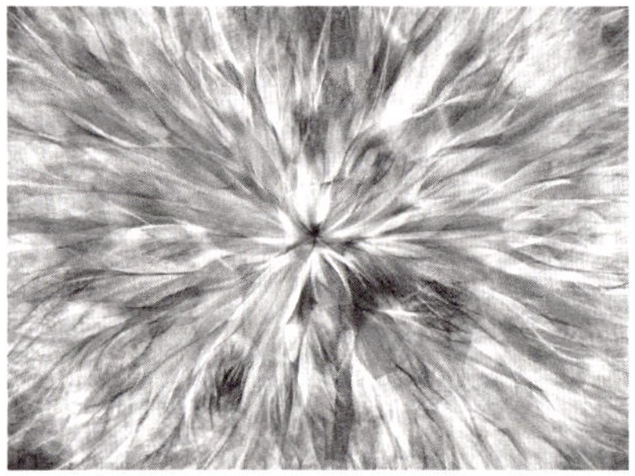

Process 10, 2005
Text, unique custom software,
computer, documentation prints
Dimensions variable

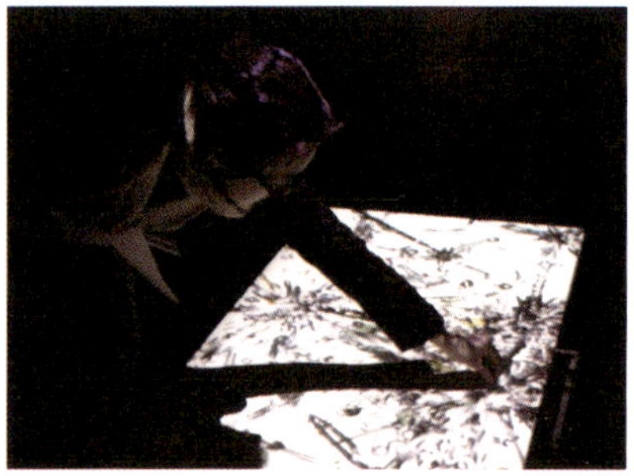

Process 9 (Interaction 1), 2006
Unique custom software, computer,
projector, camera, custom electronics
Dimensions variable

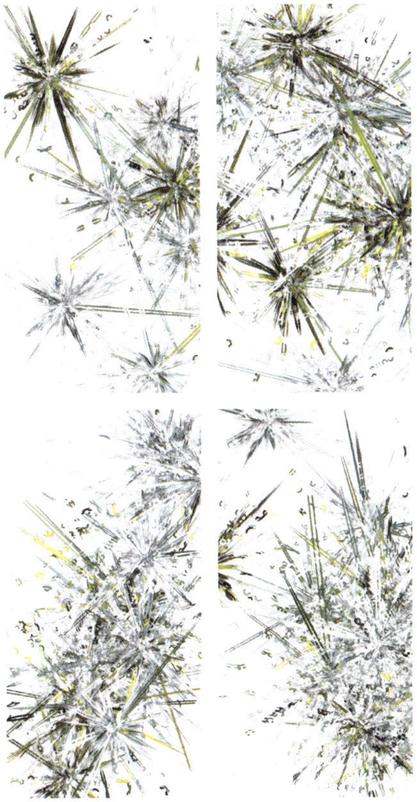

Process 9 (Image 1), 2006
Process 9 (Image 2), 2006
Process 9 (Image 3), 2006
Process 9 (Image 4), 2006
Process 9 (Image 5), 2006
Unique inkjet prints on Museo Silver Rag
8 x 16 in / 20.3 x 40.6 cm

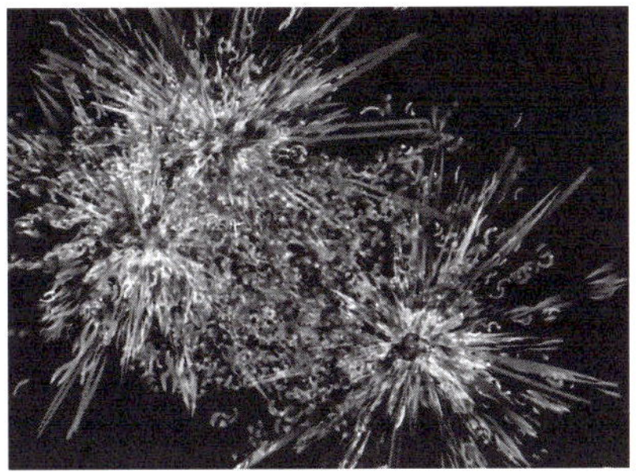

Process 9, 2005
Text, unique custom software, computer, documentation prints
Dimensions variable

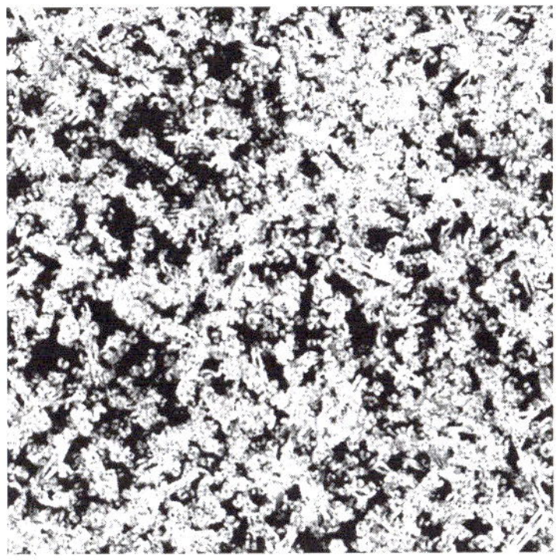

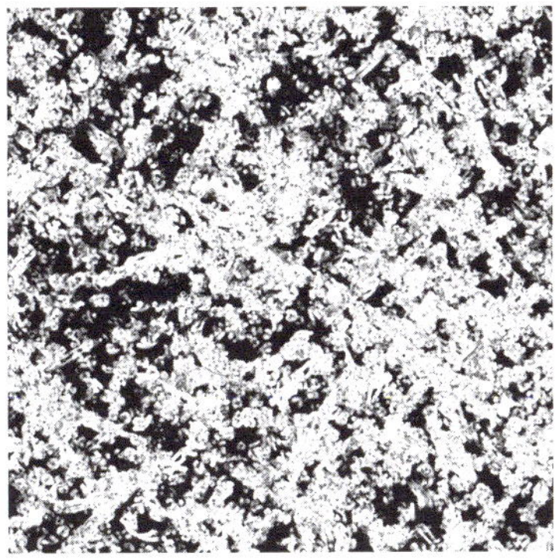

Process 8 (Image 2), 2006
Process 8 (Image 1), 2006
Unique C prints on Fuji Crystal Archive Gloss
28 x 28 in / 71.1 x 71.1 cm

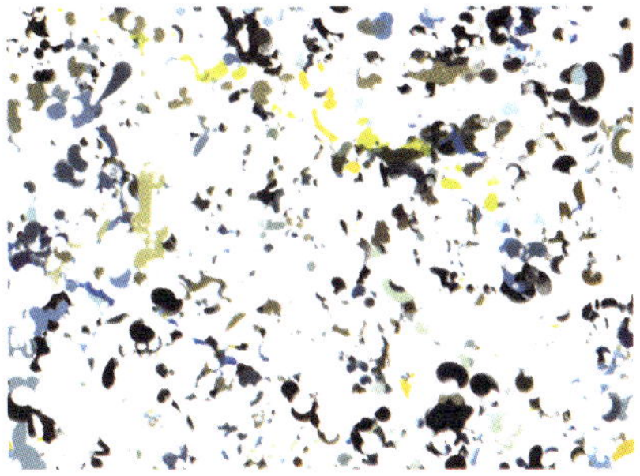

Process 8 (Software 2), 2005
Custom software
Edition of 50
Dimensions variable

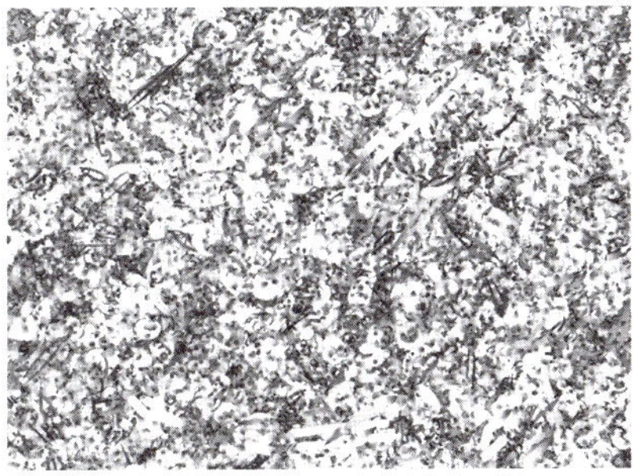

Process 8, 2005
Text, unique custom software, computer, documentation prints
Dimensions variable

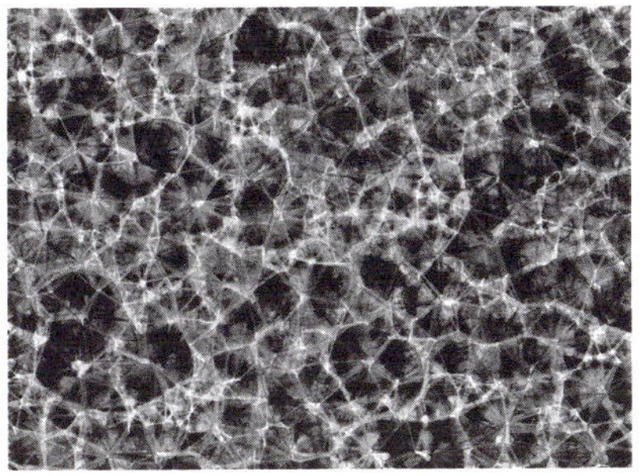

Process 7, 2005
Text, unique custom software, computer, documentation prints
Dimensions variable

Meta-Process (Performance 1), 2005
Unique custom software, computer
Dimensions variable

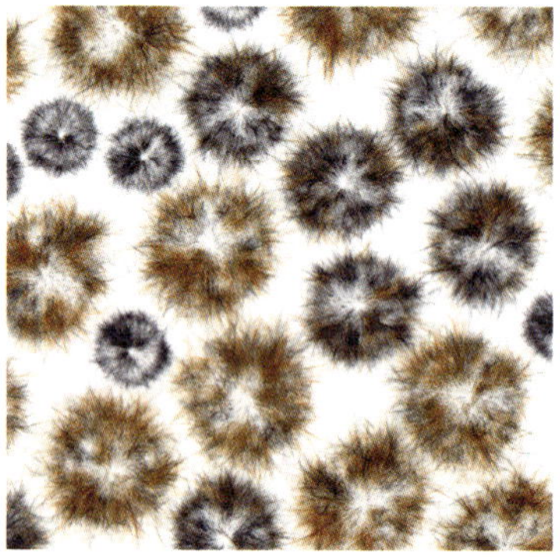

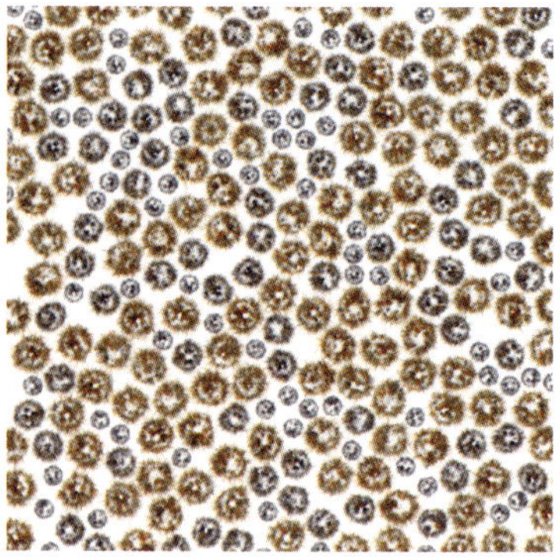

Process 6 (Image 4), 2005
Process 6 (Image 3), 2005
Inkjet prints on
Hahnemühle Photo Rag
28.6 x 28.6 in / 72.6 x 72.6 cm
Edition of 5 + 1 AP

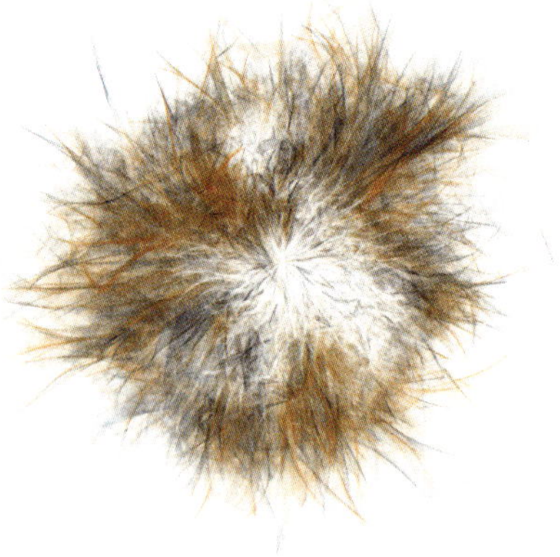

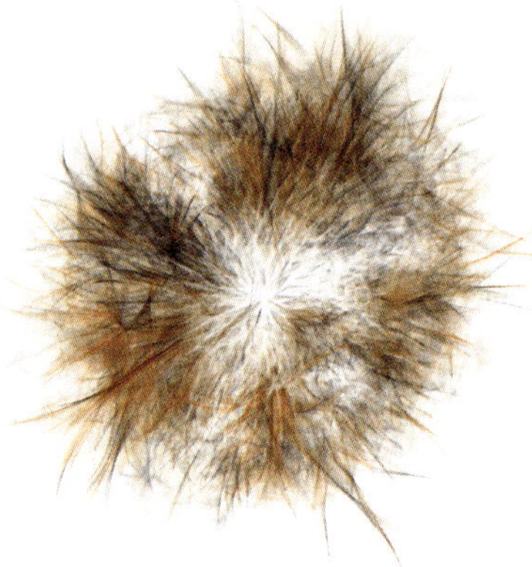

Process 6 (Puff 12), 2005
Process 6 (Puff 11), 2005
Process 6 (Puff 10), 2005
Process 6 (Puff 09), 2005
Process 6 (Puff 08), 2005
Process 6 (Puff 07), 2005
Process 6 (Puff 06), 2005
Process 6 (Puff 05), 2005
Process 6 (Puff 04), 2005
Process 6 (Puff 03), 2005
Process 6 (Puff 02), 2005
Process 6 (Puff 01), 2005
Unique inkjet prints on
Hahnemühle Photo Rag
12 in diameter / 30.5 cm

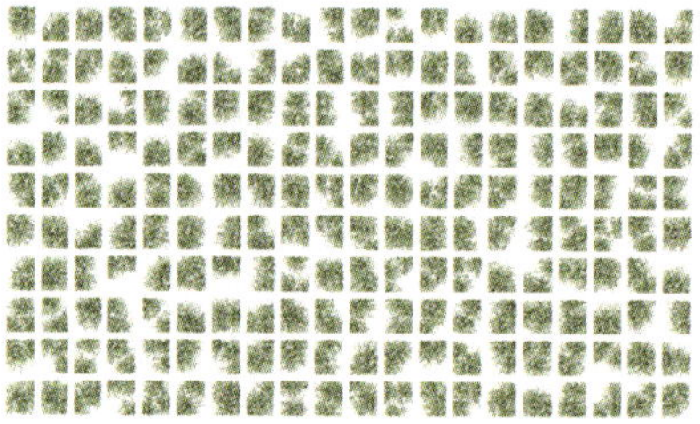

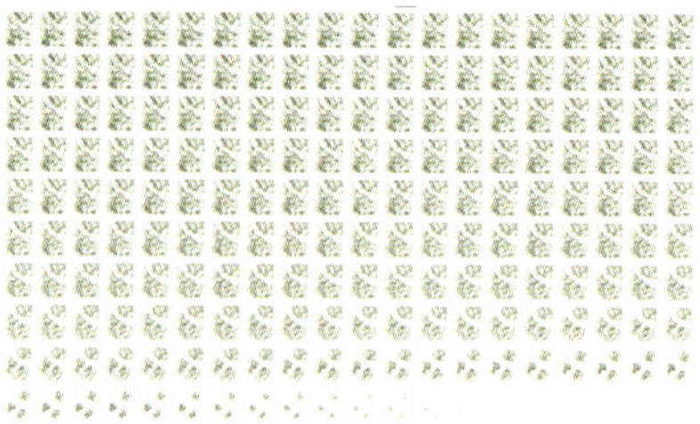

Process 6 (Image 2), 2005
Process 6 (Image 1), 2005
Inkjet prints on
Hahnemühle Photo Rag
36 x 22 in / 91.4 x 91.4 cm
Edition of 5 + 1 AP

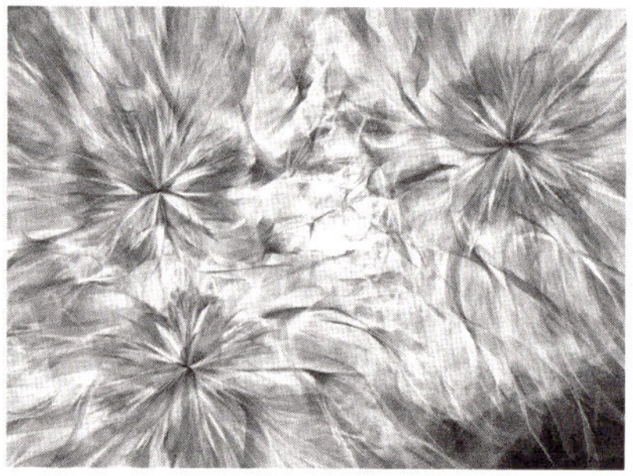

Process 6, 2005
Text, unique custom software,
computer, documentation prints
Dimensions variable

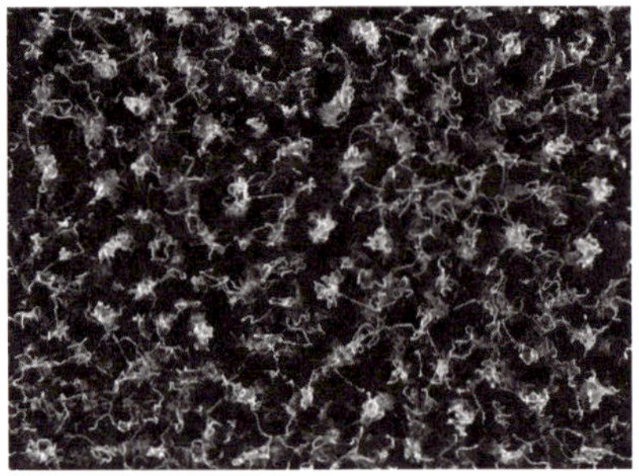

Process 5, 2005
Text, unique custom software,
computer, documentation prints
Dimensions variable

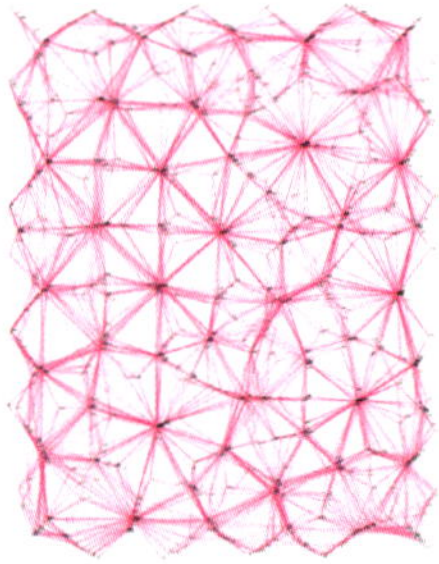

Process 4 (Form 2), 2005
Process 4 (Form 1), 2005
Process 4 (Data 2), 2005
Process 4 (Data 1), 2005
Inkjet prints on
Epson Fine Art Paper
Edition of 5 + 1 AP
11 x 14 in / 27.9 x 35.6 cm

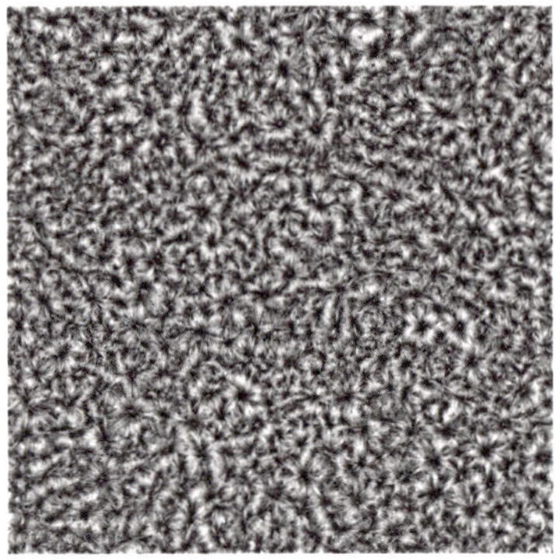

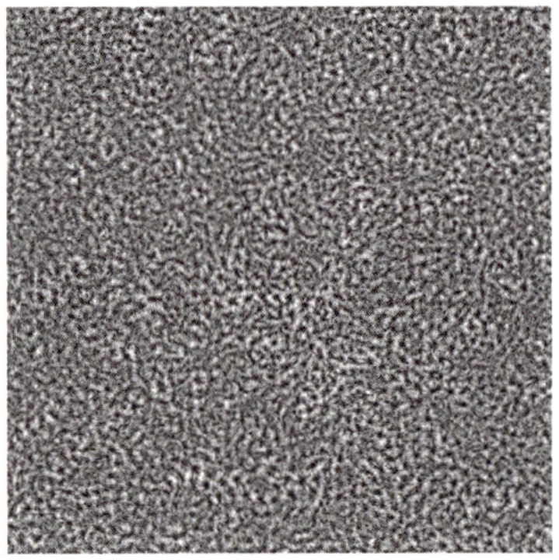

Process 4 (Image 2), 2005
Process 4 (Image 1), 2005
Inkjet prints on Hahnemühle Photo Rag
28.6 x 28.6 in / 72.6 x 72.6 cm
Edition of 5 + 1 AP

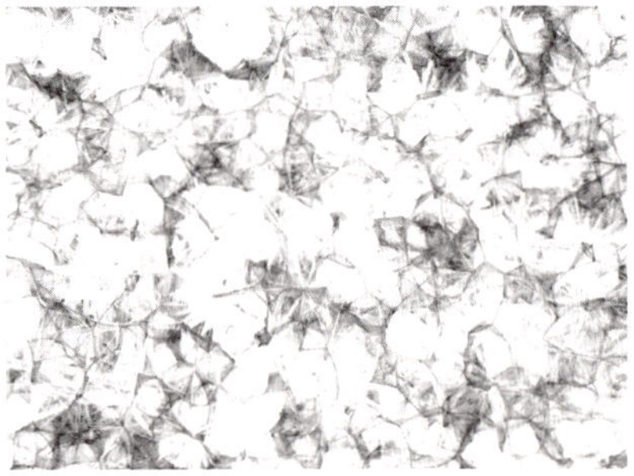

Process 4, 2005
Unique custom software, computer,
documentation prints
Dimensions variable

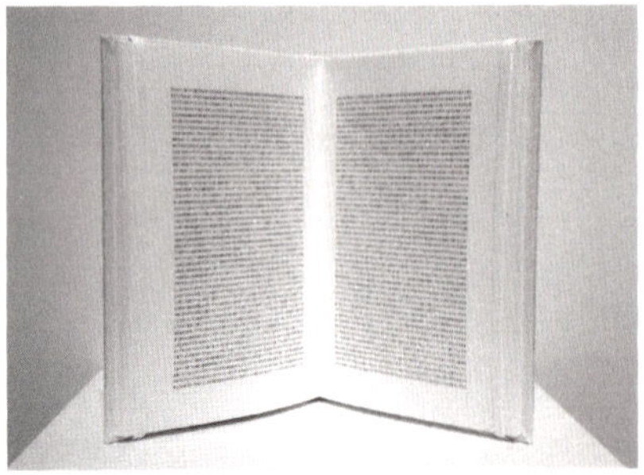

Pre-process Hex, 2005
Unique hand-bound book, 60 pages
Inkjet on Hahnemühle Photo Rag
6 x 8.5 x 1 in / 15.2 x 21.6 x 2.5

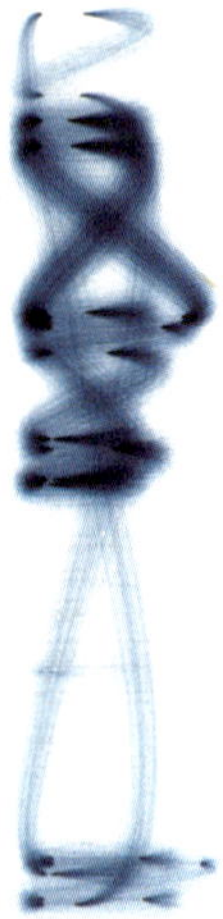

Pre-process Execution, 2005
Inkjet print on
Hahnemühle Photo Rag
Edition of 5 + 1 AP
12 x 36 in / 30.5 x 91.4 cm
Collaboration with Ben Fry

Pre-Process, 2005
Unique custom software
Dimensions variable

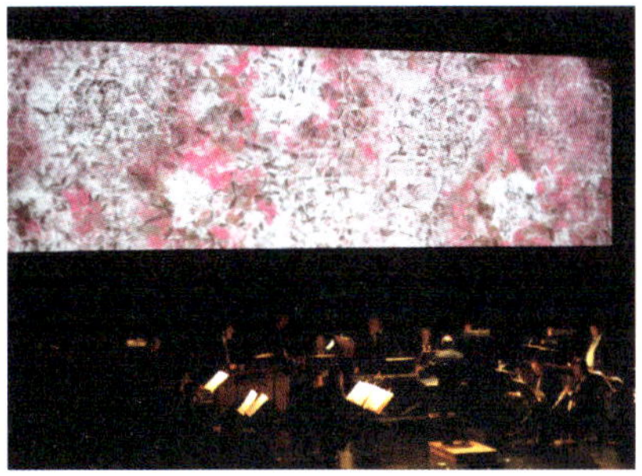

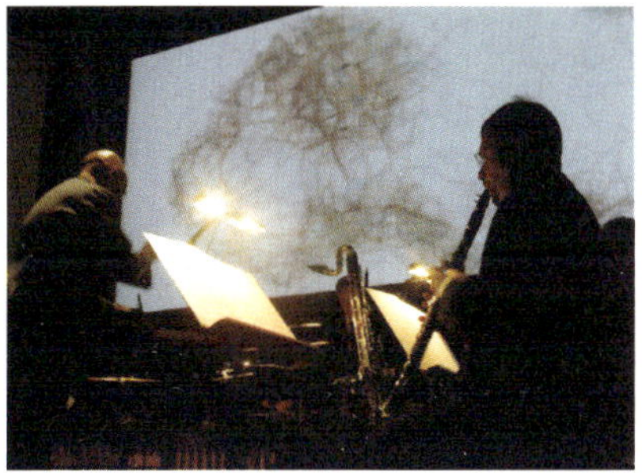

Images for 18 Musicians, 2004
a.k.a. *Process 4 (Performance 1)*
Unique custom software
Dimensions variable

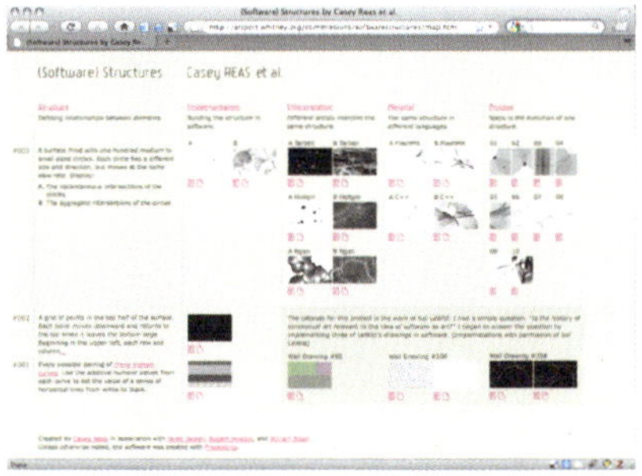

{Software} Structures, 2004
Text, Software
Collaboration with William Ngan,
Robert Hodgin, Jared Tarbell
http://artport.whitney.org

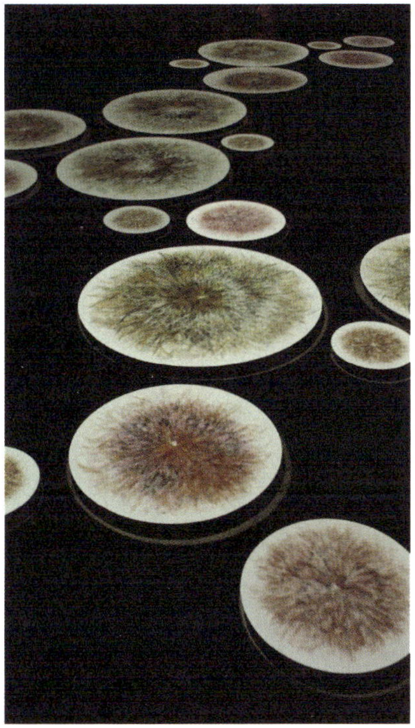

TI, 2004
a.k.a. *Process 10 (Installation 1)*
Custom software, computers,
projector, disks
Dimensions variable

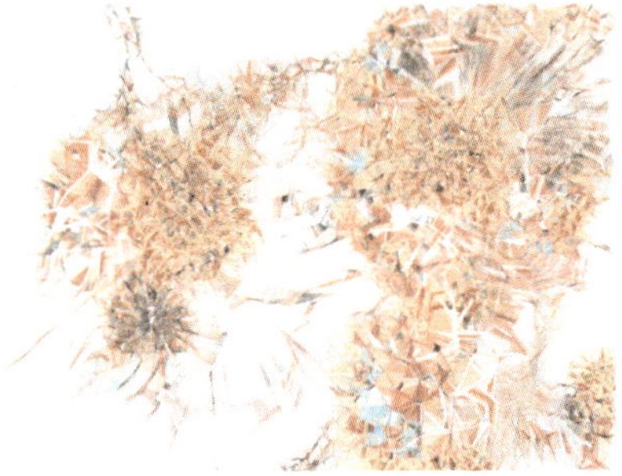

Seoul B, 2004
a.k.a. *Pre-process 4*
Unique custom software, computer,
touch screen, optional projector
Dimensions variable

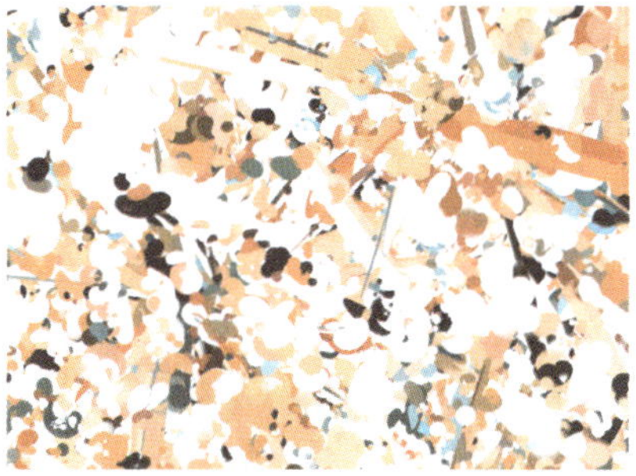

Seoul A, 2004
a.k.a. *Pre-process 8*
Unique custom software, computer,
touch screen, optional projector
Dimensions variable

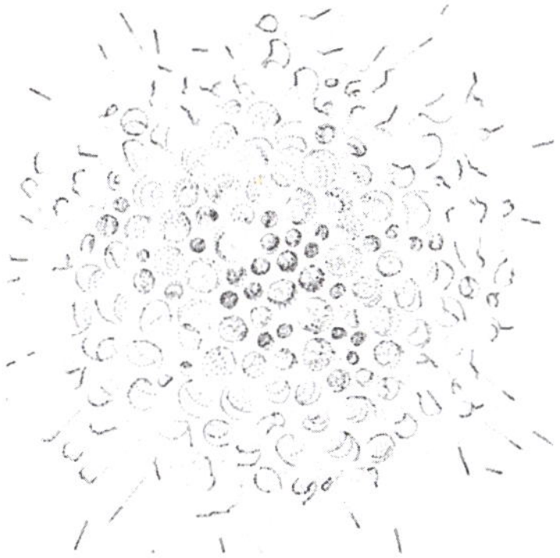

Articulate, 2003
a.k.a. *Network 2003*
Custom software, computer
Dimensions variable